Edge of Mercy - Up On Roan Mountain

Edge of Mercy - Up On Roan Mountain

MARTHA ARROWOOD PELC

ISBN 13: 9781533069429
ISBN-10: 1533069425
Library of Congress Control Number: 2016913055
CreateSpace Independent Publishing Platform
North Charleston, South Carolina

Dedication

This work is lovingly dedicated to my late father, Steve Arrowood,
my amazing husband, Russ,
and also to my wonderful Aunts,
Hilda and Ann.

Your love and support, means everything to me.

1

Come, ye disconsolate, where'er you languish,
Come at the shrine of God fervently kneel;
Here bring your wounded hearts; here tell your anguish-
Earth has no sorrow that Heaven cannot heal.

~ Thomas Moore, c.1813

COLD WINTERTIME STILL held its tight grasp on the mountain that lay just outside her window. It seemed to Ollie that its icy hold would never let go. The snow had begun to fall softly, once again, after a clear, cold morning of brilliant sunshine. The thick clouds had rolled in and soon the sun was nearly gone. Even the beautiful but brief sunshine had seemed to be just another cruel taunt to Ollie. She sat looking out, feeling heavy-hearted.

Winter was especially hard on Ollie, and it always had been. She dreaded its coming with a passion. *She tried real hard not to dwell on it. But each year, it would roll right back around, without fail, just as pretty as you please.* Winter's relentless blast of cold had always seemed to worm its way deep inside of her. *Slowly, it slipped its icy fingers in and soon wrapped them around her very soul.* Cold and dreary wintertime rain was the worst of all, for Ollie.

The snow was bad enough, but the rain that came before and after was nearly unbearable. The darkened, overcast skies combined with the dismal rainfall slowly drove Ollie ever deeper into the darkness.

Years ago, people suffered just as they do now from depression. The only difference was that they suffered from a malady with no name. *But those that suffered; why those poor tortured souls sure had plenty words to describe it.* Ollie's heart simply ached deep within her, and her bouts with it would last anywhere from just a few days to many long months. Tolbert simply called them her 'dark days'.

There was no easy way for Ollie to convey her feelings adequately to anyone, so she just tried her best to bury the hurt deep within. She had learned not to speak too much about it; she simply saw no need to share the misery. It was just better that way, and it always had been. Ollie had seen more than enough pain in her lifetime to understand that. Not even those closest to Ollie knew the true depth of her hurt. Ollie had learned early on, that sadness of the heart can easily cause a body real physical pain, as well. It doesn't just settle in your soul; sadness settles down deep into your very bones. It is like a dark shadow that lingers inside you.

Ollie took one last look out the window. Sighing softly, she stood up, straightening slowly. *My joints are just achin' me something fierce today.* Ollie reached up and rubbed her left shoulder, absently. She stepped gingerly over to the window and peered out. Suddenly, there wasn't a single flake of snow to be seen falling from the brooding sky. It was almost as if the snow had suddenly taken itself a notion of quitting, and it had simply stopped.

Ollie thought she'd better go see about her father. *He'll be looking for his breakfast, soon enough. He never did much cotton to the idea of it bein' late; not even one little bit.* Her father was a creature of habit, and as the years had rolled on past, he had become even more fixated on keeping everything routine. With all the upsets in his lifetime, she figured he had a right to want things to stay the same. *Poppa, I'm heading that'a way right now,* Ollie thought to herself with a slight nod. She quickly bundled up and made her way out the back door.

As Ollie walked down the steps at the back of the house, she raised her hand and waved toward Tolbert. Tolbert was standing down by the barn door with his axe in his hand. Tolbert hollered out, "You be extra careful, now. Stay up along the road, if you can. You'd best hurry up and get yourself on over there." Tolbert looked up and squinted at the sky for a few seconds and then spoke, "This weather looks to be a'changin' soon."

Ollie studied him momentarily and then she offered up a thin smile. With a quick studying glance at the sky, she nodded her head in agreement. Ollie pulled the collar of her coat together and buttoned it. She turned toward the well-worn path that started at the edge of the yard. It wasn't very far until the path opened out onto the dirt road that led the way to her father's house.

Ollie followed that path at least three times a day, some days, even more, to check on him. Tolbert stood and watched Ollie as she made her way along the path. He stood motionless, watching until he couldn't see her at all through the dense trees. Then, he turned back toward the chopping block out in the yard. He stood for a moment, looking down at the block of wood that sat on the ground before him. He held the large axe head in one hand and the handle in the other.

His brow furrowed deeply in response to his troubling thoughts. Tolbert knew that Ollie was struggling. *Things always just seem to be gettin' worse. Every passin' year, things are worse with that woman. There surely ain't a solitary thing a body can do about the weather. I can't do a dang thing to change it. No matter how much I want things to be different, I just can't make it so,* Tolbert lamented.

He knew that somehow or other, the weather adversely affected Ollie. He had no idea how, or even why. But, it was something that anyone that paid any attention at all could have figured out. Tolbert had also endured his very own private torture and heartache for a long time. He had been forced to watch the woman that he loved suffer through all their years together. *A sad-hearted woman is a powerfully hard thing for any man to have to deal with, all alone. Ollie being so downhearted all the time, why it just ain't never been right. It just ain't fair at all.*

It had always seemed to Tolbert that her sadness was something that he should've been able to fix. *If'n I rightly knew how. There just has to be somethin' that I could be a'doin' for her. Maybe I ain't been doing what's right by Ollie, and I ain't never have been.* Tolbert worried about that, nearly all the time in recent days. Tolbert was a good and decent man. He loved Ollie with all his heart, and had loved her right from the very moment that he had first laid eyes on her. He had fallen quick and hard. *She was just a pretty young'un back then. Just a mere slip of a girl, she was.* Somehow, she had needed him just as badly as he had needed her. He had never understood it completely, but he knew that they were surely meant for one another. *God had it all planned out for them to be together, right from the very start.*

They had gone ahead and gotten themselves married, not much more than a month after they had buried Ollie's two little sisters and her poor mother.

It was surely bad enough that those two little gals got drowned that'a way, and then her poor momma had just up and died as well. It was a terribly sad thing, that's what it was, her just up and a'dyin' and leaving that tiny baby boy in this world, without a mother. Why that baby was just the tiniest little thing. It was just about too small to begin life anyway, let alone without its momma to look after it. It just didn't seem fair a'tall. Not a bit of it was fair.

The wedding hadn't turned out to be the happy affair that they had both wanted. It had been a small somber ceremony that day, with just a few close friends surrounding them. Ollie hadn't complained about it. Ollie had just quietly accepted it, the way she always did when she was disappointed.

There wasn't much of the family left to come to the wedding. *Honestly, there just wasn't any way that her daddy could have stood up for her. He was beside himself with grief. That poor man's heart was broken, pure and simple. It sure was sad knowin' that Ollie didn't even have her father there to walk her down the aisle. Wasn't the right thing to do at all - us having ourselves a big 'to-do' wedding. Surely, it just weren't right to go and do that, not with all the sadness and grievin' a'goin' on. But marrying up, is marrying up, and it don't really matter whether you do it up plain or fancy,* Tolbert figured. So, they'd become man and wife. *That's all what really mattered. We was married up.*

The years had quietly slipped past the both of them. *Life just has a certain way of passing right along, when you ain't payin' attention to it, not close-like, you know.* Ollie waited patiently to have her own babies, but the babies just never came. *It's been nigh on to seventeen years now, and it ain't like we didn't try.*

As Tolbert chopped the wood, his axe delivered expertly placed precise blows each time. It was almost as if the axe knew where it wanted to go, on its own. *After so many years of choppin' wood, a man is pert near able to do it without having to give it too much thought.*

Tolbert's mind wandered back to when his pa first taught him how to hold an axe. He heard his father's words echo deep in his memory, "That same firewood will warm you up four times over, now boy. Once when you cut it down, once when you split it, once a'gin, when you stack it, an' one last time when ya' burn it." Tolbert smiled as he recalled how his Pa had always grinned down at him with delight dancing in his eyes after saying that. Then he would reach down and tousle Tolbert's hair lovingly with his large calloused hand. His father's hands were rough and worn from a lifetime of hard work, but somehow, there always remained an innate gentleness in them.

Reckon it was me? Was it me that couldn't have no baby? Was it me instead'a her, all along? He stopped for a moment, leaning with the axe tip resting heavily on the log. He pulled up the collar of his worn jacket to try and ward off the cold, blustery wind. He paused a few seconds to try and catch his breath, and his thoughts drifted back in time. He sure had wanted a son, and Ollie had wanted so badly to give him one. *But, sometimes the Good Lord just has a different plan from the one that you see for your own self, down this a'twistin' and a'windin' road of life. Sometimes it ain't at all like you, well, like you sort 'a have it planned out, and all, right from the git-go*, thought Tolbert. He lowered his head and sighed wistfully in an exhale of breath. The exhaled breath plumed upward in a white cloud before a blast of cold wind scattered it quickly away from him.

He knew for sure that he loved Ollie with everything that he had. She was his whole world. She always had been, right from the very start. No finer a woman could be found in all of Happy Valley, and he was certain of that. *Yes-sir, now that there's a fact. My Ollie's one of the finest women you ever did meet.* He had wanted to take her away to someplace else, just about any place else, after all the deaths had come. But, she had told him plainly that she couldn't leave. Ollie told him that it would be left up to her to tend to the graves and look after her father. Tolbert thought she was probably right, after all. Even still, it was hard for him to agree to it. He saw the lingering pain in her dark eyes just about every day. He knew that she would do what was expected of her, no matter how badly it tore her up on the inside.

Ollie had tried to be a mother to that tiny baby brother of hers, born the very day its poor momma died, but the child just wouldn't have a thing to do with her. Ollie had tried her level best, and no one in the valley could've said that she hadn't. She had held him, sang to him, whispered lovingly, and rocked that baby for days on end. *But, Lord'a mercy, that baby, why he just cried something fierce and wouldn't stop for nothin'. He wasn't soothed for nary even a minute out of the day. Ollie fretted herself sick over that little bitty child. It wasn't much bigger than a skint rat and t'was might near as ugly. But Ollie sure loved that little fella, ugly and all. She sat and rocked him in a chair and cried her poor self out a river, one pitiful drop at a time.*

Sometimes, even little bitty babies know when things just ain't right. Even babies have a way of knowing things, too. Why, that little one just wasn't gonna have any of it, right from the start. Wonder why in the world it is that some folks are given such a hard row to hoe in this life? Tolbert mulled it over, just as he had all through the years, as he sadly shook his head. *Ollie needed that child just as much as that child needed a mother, but it just weren't meant to be.*

Tolbert reached down and gathered up an armful of the newly split kindling, turned, and headed back up the path to the house. Just then, the snow began again. Silently, the snow fell quickly in huge fluffy flakes that swirled their way down to the ground. The large flakes stuck together mid-air and occasionally floated down in white clumps, covering the frozen ground. Tolbert's hat and shoulders were thickly dusted white by the time he had made it back up to the house. Tolbert's head was bent low, still deep in thought, as he started up the snow covered steps carrying the kindling.

A sudden piercing screech shattered the silence, and Tolbert's head jerked up toward the sound. An owl sat staring down at him from the branch of the old sycamore tree that stood over beside the steps. The owl made no movement at all; it simply sat there. It stared down at Tolbert with intense, piercing eyes. Suddenly it screamed out once again before unfurling its wings and taking flight. Startled, Tolbert grabbed a piece of the firewood that he was carrying and flung it up at the owl. He yelled, *Now, git on up outta here!* Seemingly undeterred, the owl landed in a tree close by and screeched out once again. The owl didn't show any interest in leaving. It simply sat and stared down intently at Tolbert.

Screech owls have long been believed to be harbingers of death by the people that lived on the mountain. It was thought to be an especially foreboding omen whenever it was heard right outside the window of the house and even more sinister when it was heard while it sat on the branch of a sycamore tree. The Indians believed that the sycamore tree connected the world of the living to the world of the dead. Tolbert had known this all of his life. The very thought of it terrified him. Instantly, Tolbert's anger boiled over to full-blown fury. He hurled yet another chunk of firewood up at the owl, hoping to force it to flee, but it only sat there. The owl perched stoically, silently conveying its message to Tolbert. It stared down at him, scarcely blinking with seemingly knowing eyes.

Ollie hadn't made it back home from her father's house yet, and despite the snowstorm that was coming on fast, Tolbert was terribly glad that she hadn't. He sure didn't want her to hear that owl screeching like a banshee, right outside the window. It would be yet another torment for his poor Ollie.

I sure hope that blasted ol' owl's long gone by the time Ollie gets herself on back up to the house. I reckon the best thing to do, would be for me to go ahead and hitch the mule up to the wagon, directly. Best get myself over there and fetch her on back.

When snow is moving in fast, it can brew into a full-blown blizzard in these mountains without much warning, at all. Tolbert had seen the weather on the mountain act like this many times before, and he knew that conditions could turn deadly in the blink of an eye. A storm on the mountain was surely nothing to take lightly. *You just can't take nothing for granted up here*, Tolbert reasoned to himself uneasily. His brow furrowed deeply. He turned and made his way to the barn to hitch up the mule.

2

There's a river somewhere that's called Jordan,
And they say that it's deep and it's wide;
And they say that the king and the beggar
On that shore will stand side by side.
At the crossing of the Jordan,
Why should I be afraid?
There'll be someone there who loves me
To guide me 'cross the river to endless joys above.
Though the river is dark and stormy,
It will pass like a dream in the night;
And my soul will awake in the morning
In regions of endless delight.

~ MOSIE LISTER

WILLIAM WAS JUST a fragile shell of the man that he once had been. Once tall and quite handsome, he was often tottering and shuffling, now. Time's passage had not been kind. It broke Ollie's heart to see her father this way. *How could the passing years have been so cruel to a man that was already so broken?* He had rambled around and around in that empty house until he had slowly lost what little was left of his mind. Ollie had, over time, begun to realize that he was constantly moving from room to room for a reason. She had come to the conclusion that he had to be searching for Calla and the girls. That seemed to be the only plausible explanation for it. It broke her heart to know that he wouldn't ever find them, at least not here in this world.

Some days he seemed more lucid than others, and on those days, he seemed to remember that they were gone. But, on his bad days he spent his time endlessly searching. Room after room, he would ramble on an endlessly futile circuit, muttering and murmuring to himself. Sometimes he would say, "Hold onto to that little baby, now, Calla."

Ollie didn't fully understand why he would say that, but she assumed that he was referring to little Billy. It always made her cry to hear her father talk about him. Ollie knew for sure that the 'old timers' had truly set in when he nearly burnt the house down trying to cook a bite of breakfast one morning, back last fall. He had put too much wood in the stove and had lit it.

Ollie had dutifully tended to him ever since then, doing his washing and cooking his meals. She wanted to make certain that he ate regularly. With his mind failing, she was afraid he wouldn't remember to eat at all. She had asked him to move in with her and Tolbert, but her father just wouldn't hear of it.

If William was anything at all, he was a man that was set in his ways. *Getting him to change his mind now, would prove to be just about as easy as milking an ol' ornery bull*, Ollie thought to herself with a sad smile. So, Ollie had quietly accepted his decision of staying alone. But, it surely wasn't easy, having to split her time between his house and her own.

She worried something fierce about him, the whole time she was away from him. *My Tolbert's such a blessing.* Tolbert helped with the bathing of her father, and Ollie appreciated it greatly. Her father was more receptive to Tolbert helping him bathe than he ever had been with her. It wasn't much trouble for either one of them, it seemed. *It's high time for him to have a good soaking bath*, Ollie thought.

Ollie called out for her father as she first entered the house, but he didn't answer her. She wasn't overly concerned. She knew full well that on his 'not-so-good' days, he didn't always answer her immediately. On his bad days, he might not even say one single word to her, or to anyone else, for that matter. How he answered her, depended on a number of different things, Ollie had come to realize.

She quickly noticed that the house was quite cold. She saw that the fire had dwindled down, and was nearly out in the fireplace. Ollie went from room to room, with her steps becoming progressively faster paced. Her steps hastened even further, as they kept up with the pace of her rising panic level. Eventually, she was nearly at a full run. As she passed through the empty rooms, she began to fear the worst.

Then, suddenly, she saw him. He was lying on the bed in the extra bedroom, perfectly still. She wondered why he wasn't in his own bed. He looked quite peaceful. She stepped into the room and her breath caught in her throat at the sight of him lying there. He was perfectly still, lying there in the shadowy dimness of early morning. She stood over him, staring down at him for a few seconds. He was too still. His face looked somewhat ashen. She was suddenly terrified. She could scarcely breathe.

My chest is too tight. The air is too thick. Can't breathe, Ollie's thoughts tumble out in a panic. Ollie gulps air and steels herself. She reaches out her hand to feel for his breath. She feels nothing. She stares down at his chest looking for a rise and fall. *Do I see him breathing or is it just my mind playing tricks?* Ollie picks up his hand off the coverlet and takes it gently into her own. It is stiff and cold to the touch.

It was that moment when the realization sank in. Ollie hoarsely whispered to the empty room, *My Poppa's gone. He's finally at peace. Angels of mercy, gather 'round him.* There were no more words to say.

No last goodbyes to be said, only the roar of deafening silence. It seemed almost suffocating to Ollie. She was surrounded by the thick silence, marred only by the ticking of the clocks. The realization that he was finally with his beloved Calla and the girls, only comforted Ollie for a brief moment.

She knew that peace for her father had come at last. His endless searching was over and done with, and he was finally at rest. Her mind knew that she should be happy for him, but her heart ached. She was ashamed that she felt no joy for him. She knew that she should, as a Christian. But somehow, she felt only the consuming pain of her own loss.

Her fragile heart had no time to brace itself for the blow. The loss cut deeply into her, like a sharp knife. Her hands fell limply down from the shock. She moaned, again and again, unable to stop the wrenching sobs. Some time later, after the tears had subsided somewhat, she sat down beside him. The quiet stillness of the morning passed slowly. There was no need to try and go for help, now. Even in her state, she realized it. She knew that the nearest neighbors were much too far away for her to shout and have anyone hear her. Anyway, there was nothing that could have been done for him, at that point. There was nothing Tolbert could have done, either. Her father was finally at rest. If anyone deserved a peaceful rest after all of the torment that life had heaped onto him, he did.

All the years of remembering and endless heartache had worn him down, slowly. He was like a worn down millstone. And much like a millstone that has been used for grinding for well over a hundred years or more, the grief had ground him down to where he was just about useless. *My father's heart never did heal.* The truth was he'd been lost to Ollie for many years before he ever physically left her. The 'old timers' had seen to that. The dreadful disease robbed you of your loved one. *It robbed you, just as surely as any thief could have possibly done.* The relationship you had, as well as the person that you once knew, was stolen away. You suddenly didn't have the mother or father that you had always known and loved. It was a heartless disease that ate away the person from the inside. It took their memories and with it, their relationships and personality as well. You were left with the same face, the same body, but certainly not the same person.

Ollie had kept hope, that the gradual loss of his memories had wiped at least part of the pain away, for her father. It had given Ollie unspeakable sadness to look at him and not be able to see even a glimpse, of the father she remembered.

Gone was the father from her childhood, all that was left were his expressionless eyes. A misty glimmer of who he once was passed over his face like an apparition every once and awhile, and just as quickly as it had come, it would vanish like a wisp of smoke. Just like the elusive thin tendrils of mist that settle over the mountain ridges in the evening, and fade come first morning's light, it would quickly disappear. *The misty glimmers always burn away in the light of day, almost as if they had never really been there at all.*

Ollie sat there, looking down at her hands but not really seeing them. She laid her head down on the bed, beside her father's cold body and wept. She cried for him, and she also cried for little Ruby and Minnie. Then she cried once again, for her poor Momma. Ollie shed tears for all of her Daddy's years of tormenting loss, as well. For the both of them, life had been turned upside down in an instant.

Life was always hard, up in these old mountains. *It just is, what it is,* thought Ollie. *Nothin' we can do will change it.* It was the way that it had always been. Ollie knew that even as bad as life had been for her family, some poor folks on the mountain had it even worse. *Life never promised anyone an easy run of it. None of us are free from pain and suffering.* But Ollie's deep faith in her Lord and heavenly Father sustained her. She never once wavered in her belief that God was watching over them all with his tender love and mercy.

Her mother had made sure that her faith was strong, even from an early age. Faith was one of the many priceless gifts that her precious mother had given her, and she was sure that it was the only thing that had seen her through this far. *Thank goodness for my sweet mother's guidance. If God leads you to it, he will surely see you through it,* Ollie thought.

Her mother's words remained etched deeply on her heart. Now those same words once again echoed through her mind. She had held fast to her mother's teachings all these years, especially during her darkest bouts of depression. Sometimes they would loom in her thoughts so clearly; it was almost as if they were being spoken aloud. *Faith will hold you up, daughter, even when you can't stand up by your own power. God's love will sustain us; that's something that you need never forget. Without faith in the dear Lord above, you won't ever be able to stand under the crushing weight that this ol' life can heap on you. Thank the precious Lord in heaven, for helping us through it all, no matter what life throws at us. God's sweet love and mercy will sustain us, sweet child. He's with us every step of the way.*

Ollie bowed her head and prayed earnestly for her father's soul to be granted safe passage as it crossed over into heaven. She prayed for angels of mercy and light, to guide him safely along his way. A fragile smile danced tentatively across her face, as her lips trembled slightly. Tears welled in her eyes, as she lifted her head. Her prayers had been heard, and she knew that as well as she knew anything at all.

Go quickly to God, Poppa. Ollie stood up and gently folded her father's arms across his chest. She tried to close his eyes by lightly brushing her fingertips down over his eyelids, but they simply wouldn't close completely. Ollie opened the bedside dresser, pulled out the drawer, and reached for the small leather coin purse that had once belonged to her dear mother. Smiling slightly, she took it out and admired it. She opened the clasp on the delicate purse and took out two silver coins. Ollie looked at the coins as they lay in the palm of her hand. Her grandfather's words echoed in her mind as she looked down at them, *Two coins are to pay your way. They pay your passage, as you cross on over the river Jordan. You can't make it on over the river, without a'payin' your way.* She smiled remembering the words of her grandfather. A barely visible mist had settled over his sky blue eyes as he had spoken. He had an innate way of conveying his innermost thoughts without uttering a word, and he had undoubtedly passed this ability on to his son.

Ollie hesitated for a few seconds. And then she gingerly took the coins and placed them on her father's eyelids. It was the common practice, up on the mountain. *There, Daddy, now you can pay your passage and cross on over, safely.* She placed the small coin purse back into its spot in the drawer, right where her father had always kept it all of these years. He hadn't allowed anything that had belonged to Calla to be moved from where she had always kept it. He always said it somehow made him feel better, knowing that her things were where they were supposed to be. Ollie supposed that it did.

Ollie let her mind drift, and she was instantly transported back through the mists of time. She remembered back to when she had closed that drawer as a small child, on a warm summer's day, many years ago. From the shadowy recesses of her mind, the long-forgotten memory came flooding back to the foreground. The scene played out crisp and clear in her mind.

Her mother had sent her into the bedroom to get a coin from this very same purse, from exactly where it lay in the drawer today. She had asked Ollie to go over to Mrs. Schnitzler's house to buy a few eggs from her. The chickens in their own coop had just about quit laying any eggs.

They hadn't gotten more than a couple of eggs since that mountain lion had torn up the chicken house real good. *The mountain lion hadn't actually gotten all the way inside the chicken house, but the fright of it all had certainly caused the chickens to quit layin'*, Ollie thought, as she remembered back. *It had to have been somethin' else to witness, with that big ol' mountain lion just a'pawing and a'scratching like forty at that coop; all the while, screaming and a'hollering, at the top of its lungs.* Ollie had heard the ruckus and had ran outside to see what was going on, and just as she had turned the corner of the barn, she had nearly run smack-dab into that old cat.

She'd surely never forget the fright that mountain lion had given her. Her daddy had told her time and time again, not to just up and run out whenever she heard a noise out there. She hadn't listened, once again. He hadn't scolded her when she had run back to the house like a streak of lightning. At least, that time he hadn't, anyway. She remembered that she ran straight to him and buried her head into his midsection as he had been standing there, right in the doorway. There hadn't been any need to scold his daughter that time. Her lesson had been learned that day, and he could plainly see it.

It was a good thing the mountain lion had just up and decided to turn and run away on its own. Ollie and the mountain lion had run off in opposite directions of each other, with neither one looking back, not even once.

Ollie was lost in thought again, thinking about the young Miss Schnitzler. She had been the middle daughter of Old Lady Schnitzler, she recalled. The last that Ollie had heard, the family had stayed right in the area near the Roan, all these years.

Ollie wondered, *How old would've the younger Mrs. Schnitzler had to have been, back when I was just a kid, eight or nine years old?* Old Lady Schnitzler had been a lady in that small community that had the strange ability of 'knowing'. Some folks called it the 'gift of sight'. *She was one different lady, and that was for certain.* Ollie had heard most of the ladies around town talk about her, from time to time. She knew that Welzia had known the elder Mrs. Schnitzler back when he was just a boy.

She knew that the town's resident 'hens' all had a penchant for clucking a bit too much and a bit too loudly, from time to time. She often wondered if some of the clucking done by the ladies was nothing more than just good-natured banter. Their clucking often served a useful purpose by making life in the secluded mountains and hollows just a mite more tolerable. Sometimes storytelling was just about all the entertainment a body could find for themselves here.

Isolation made for some mighty lively stories. Ollie knew herself that a good story always helped make the work go by faster while you were shelling peas or snapping beans. *It works better than just about anything else I know. If all those outlandish tales about Ol' Lady Schnitzler were the truth, well now, Lordy help, she was something else. Her daughter didn't set much store in such bally-hoo as telling folks that you somehow or other already knew things, way a'fore they even happened. Well, at least she didn't claim for herself, right out, to have the same gifts that her mother possessed.*

God rest her soul, thought Ollie with a slight shake of her head. "Well, land's sake, I haven't thought about the Schnitzler family in years," said Ollie aloud to the room. She wondered how old the little granddaughter would be, about now. The granddaughter's name had been 'Lorna', or 'Loretta' or something like that. She couldn't remember exactly, but for certain it had started with an 'L'. Ollie bowed her head slightly as she searched her memory, trying to recall the little girl's name. Tapping her fingers on her cheek, she stopped mid-motion. Her hand fell to her lap. Quietly, Ollie whispered it to the silent room where her father lay, cold in death. The name had just come to her, seemingly straight out of nowhere. *Lorena.*

Ollie's stomach suddenly lurched deep down in her belly, and she wrapped her arms around her waist and practically doubled over in pain. She cried out, and reached out with an unsteady hand, toward the bed. She steadied herself and slowly, after taking her time, she carefully stood upright again.

What in tarnation brought on hurt like that, and so terribly sudden-like? Ollie wondered with widened eyes. *Mercy, what had that been about?* Ollie slowly began to feel normal again as the wave of pain subsided. She whispered to herself that it was most likely just a case of the nerves. *Nerves can cause you to up and do just about anythin', just right straight out of the blue. Why, they can do just about anythin' at all, to a body. They can make you think that you were just about nigh on to the point of dying. They honestly can. It sure wouldn't be something to go and get yourself all worked up over; not something as silly as all that.* Given the shock she had just been through, finding her father laying stone cold in his bed, it would stand to reason that a strange passing pain was nothing to worry yourself over. *Surely a shock like that could do just about anythin' in the world to a body,* Ollie surmised. *It was nothing to get all worked up into a lather over.* She took in a slow and ragged breath, and her heart began to slow its rapid pounding in her chest. *Surely that pain didn't have anything to do with me just saying her name, out loud? Things like that just don't happen, now. Surely they don't.* She shook her head to try and clear it of the crazy thoughts that were racing through it. *I'm just plain tuckered out;*

that's what this is about. I'm a bundle of nerves, and I need some rest, and in the worst way.

Ollie tried to calmly gather her thoughts, and she began to focus on what would happen next. The custom of how death was handled up in the mountains hadn't changed that much at all, down through the passing generations. There were countless time-honored traditions that were still closely adhered to, up in those hills. To deviate from any of those ways, even slightly, would be seen as unseemly, by most in the community. Ollie sat and pondered, trying to sort it all out carefully. She wanted her father's funeral to be fitting for the man and respectful of just who he was in life. She was thankful that he had been allowed to pass gently, in the old-timey 'mountain way' of death. He had died right here, at home. Certainly, he was right where he had always wanted to be.

She had heard tell that in the cities, folks were going to the county homes to live out the remainder of their days. The older people were either going on their own accord or being packed up and sent there by their family that simply didn't want the responsibility of watching over them in their feeble old age. It just didn't seem right, to Ollie. *It's a dadgum shame and an honest-to-goodness travesty; that's what that is. Why, just imagine it. Doing your own folks that'a way. It's shameful, and there ain't no two ways about it. That's what it is now, shameful. The same folks that faithfully took good and tender loving care of their own young'un's, and now that the tide has turned, the young'un's can't be so much as bothered. Why, they just up and shed themselves of the responsibility, plain and outright. They just up and walk away as if it wasn't anything that concerned them in the least.*

Ollie shook her head in dismay. Her father had dearly loved this mountain just as his father had, before him. *He had died right here on his own land, where he belonged. It happened just the way that it ought 'a.*

Ollie sat down in the rocking chair once again and slowly rocked back and forth. The floorboards of the old house softly creaked beneath her. She took a long breath and gazed out the window at the falling snow as she rocked. She absently wiped the steady stream of tears that rolled down her cheeks with the back of her hand.

The rocking of the chair was soothing to Ollie, and it always had been. She had wanted a rocking chair badly when she had first married up with her Tolbert. She had thought that she needed one, so she could rock the babies that would soon be coming. She finally got the chair that she had wanted. But sadly, the chair sat motionless for many years. Ollie got to where she just couldn't bear to sit in it, even after Tolbert had so painstakingly and lovingly made it for her. It was a beautiful chair. It was quite ornate and beautifully crafted. Tolbert had always had a way with his hands and had carved beautiful designs onto the rocker. Even the handles were intricately carved. The designs had taken him quite a while to complete. He had carved the red lilies that grew up on Roan Mountain from Ollie's detailed descriptions. She had heard her mother describe the lilies so lovingly, and in such exacting detail that she felt she had actually seen them herself. Her mother had even sketched them herself, from time to time.

So, the years passed and that beautiful rocking chair just sat there motionless, over in the corner of the bedroom. It served as a constant heart-breaking reminder to Ollie of the babies that just never came. As the years passed, it became increasingly hard for Ollie to look at it. Finally, Tolbert toted it on over to her father's house and left it there, for him to use. At least her father had found its soothing motion comforting in his later years. She had found him rocking quietly in the chair on many mornings when she had come to check on him.

Ollie rocked as the tears continued to course down her face and she thought about all the years that had somehow moved right on past her. *You honestly do think that you'll never really grow old. It's just natural to think that'a way when you're young and full of life. You think of your dreams and all of your hopes that are yet to come. You just hang on to the silly old notion that the passage of time just ain't goin' to affect you the same way that it has your elders and all those around you. You grow up, and as you do, you can plainly watch your parents as they age. You see the changes slowly take place in them, but you still won't accept that it is also happening to you. The lines form around their eyes and the gray slowly appears in their hair. You still keep on thinking you are somehow immune to it all. But the real truth is that you ain't immune either; not a bit. One day you will wind down slowly, just like an eight-day clock. All of a sudden-like, you blink and turn around twice, and without much warning at all, your clock mechanism down inside of you will fall silent, as well. We all will just wind down one day when our time comes. It's as simple as that. It's just how life is. The hands on the big clock of time keep on a'turning, Lordy, but they surely do,* Ollie thought. The sorrow in her dark eyes darkly mirrored the sadness that she felt deep within the recesses of her broken heart.

3

There is in every true woman's heart a spark of heavenly fire, which lies dormant in the broad daylight of prosperity; but which kindles up, and beams and blazes in the dark hour of adversity.

~ *Washington Irving*

To live in this world, you must be able to do three things: to love what is mortal; to hold it against your bones knowing your own life depends on it; and, when the time comes to let it go, to let it go.

~ *Mary Oliver*

A s if on cue, the clocks hanging on the wall beside her clanged and chirped out in various melodious chimes. In the seconds shortly after that, all the clocks along the hallway wall, clanged out as well. *Daddy sure loved all of these ol' clocks*, thought Ollie with a sigh. Strangely enough, the same clocks that were so annoying to her, during her growing years, were now oddly comforting. She could remember lying on her bed in her old bedroom just down the hall, with the 'tick-tocks' clicking out into the darkened quietness of the house. The clocks were just about the only disturbance in the deep hours of the night, high up on the still mountain. Any sound at all seemed deafeningly loud when you were so used to the quiet of the mountain. *Should I go around and stop all the clocks, or is that just plumb silly?* Ollie thought to herself. *I'll just leave the clocks a tickin', where's the harm in it?* Stopping the clocks until the next day was considered the thing to do when death came to the house. Ollie sighed softly as she remembered back to her childhood years.

The nighttime noise of the clocks was the worst for Ollie. The minutes slipped by one by one, with her eyes wide, staring out into the darkness. The ticking clocks seemed to take on a life of their own. Some nights, sleep was next to impossible. *Apparently, I was the only one in the house that the clocks kept awake. It seemed as if they'd never bothered Momma or Poppa, now that I think about it. Not even one little bit,* thought Ollie with a wry smile and a shake of her head. Each one of the clocks had a distinctive tick and chime. The whole house clanged as they each, in turn, rang out announcing the top of the hour. Small cuckoo clocks hanging in a row on the parlor wall 'cuckooed' out, repeatedly. Then tiny dancers emerged from within and pirouetted around the tiny wooden trees atop the clocks.

After they danced they would slip quickly back into the clock and the tiny door would snap shut with a resounding 'click' behind them. Ollie, as a little girl, often wondered what it was that the tiny dancers did in the tiny room after the door snapped shut. She would smile as she imagined them sitting down and having supper as soon as they were safely inside. Tandem ravens peeked out, and their heads nodded in unison from either side of the tree, and then they cawed out aimlessly into the night. To Ollie, they were positively the scariest looking fixtures on the clocks.

Ollie shuddered as she remembered them and how they had struck fear in her young heart. The black bird's beady eyes glittered in the light of the moon that streamed in through the window of her bedroom. Those same eyes often seemed to follow her menacingly around the room. The chimes of the cuckoo clocks played a lilting tune that was very familiar to Ollie. She had heard those chimes play repeatedly all through the years.

Her father's clocks were all meticulously timed, right down to the second. He busily went around winding them up with expert precision. The memory of how to wind up the clocks was somehow left intact, despite his illness. Each one was wound in a certain fashion, and always in the same order, at each and every winding. The eight-day clocks were his favorites. He had proudly taken Ollie around and told her the history of each one with a beaming smile on his face. The man had certainly loved them. Some, he had acquired during the early years of his marriage to Calla, but most had been handed down from his father, and his father before him. The familiar ticking and chiming had taken Ollie instantly back to the sweet memories of the happy days of her early childhood. The ticking and chiming had served as a sort of music to many events of her young life.

Ollie enjoyed stepping back into her memories; back to the days when life was good and she was truly happy. Her eyes misted over and she drifted back, once again. Her mother was in the kitchen, baking. The smell that wafted down the hall, and drifted into the open door to her bedroom, was heavenly. Her mother loved to cook and somehow Ollie never quite learned to share that love, completely. Her mother had tried to help her acquire it, but it had just never happened for Ollie. Ollie guessed it was something you are either born with or you're not.

But, Ollie had diligently helped out as best she could in the kitchen, and she had tried to learn everything that her mother had shown her. Ollie always thought that one day she would pass the same way of making Calla's pumpkin and black pepper pie on to her own daughters, but it never happened. She would never have that opportunity, and it made her sad to think about it.

Then, when little Minnie and Ruby had come along her mother hadn't even had the time to show them her recipes. That day sadly never came for them, either. The smell of her mother's pie slowly left her and her mind floated back into the moment, where she now sat, alongside her father. A single tear trailed slowly down her cheek, once again.

Suddenly, after a flurry of movement, there appeared a small silver and gray screech owl sitting on the tree branch right outside her window. Ollie had instantly noticed the flash of movement and had turned quickly toward it. Ollie flinched visibly, as the owl's screech suddenly shattered the silence. Her breath caught in her throat and just as suddenly as it had appeared, the owl lifted its wings and with yet another piercing scream, it flew off into the edge of the woods and disappeared. The sight of the owl terrified Ollie to the bone. The flesh on her arms crawled. She drew her arms up around her, and her body trembled. She reached down and gripped the arms of the rocking chair until her knuckles turned white.

Screech owls are almost always foretellers of death. They sound out the alarm. Death is a'coming, thought Ollie as a sudden sick dread washed over her midsection. *My daddy always told me that an owl screeching by the house nearly always brings the angel of death right along with it. Just like the dark clouds in the summertime sky bring on the rain.* Ollie's eyes flashed with a sudden revelation. Slowly, a sardonic smile formed on her face, still wet with her tears. *Well, don't that there just take the cake, now? Just as surely as I'm a'sitting here, that wise old owl's runnin' a bit late today. He's runnin' behind in spreading his own special brand of misery. Well, you ol' hateful owl, my poor ol' Poppa's already dead and gone. So, you just go on about your business and fly on away from here. Leave me with this chunk missin' out of what's left of my heart. You got no news to share with me; you blasted old owl. Go on and peddle your torment somewhere else, t'day. Death's already come here, I tell ya'. Death's already come.*

Ollie's head hung to her chest, and the tears fell again, in a torrent.

Back at the house, Tolbert was finally beginning to get somewhere with the wood chopping. *Before too long, I'm gonna have this 'ere spot of work licked, for sure. Then, I'll git right on over and bring Ollie home. Better try and finish getting the wagon loaded up with wood.* His mind soon wandered off as he bent to his task. *After little Billy had grow'd up just big enough to run off, well, that's exactly what he just up and done*, thought Tolbert with a derisive snort, as the sharp axe blade came down. He wanted to make at least enough kindling to see them through the snow storm that was surely coming. The axe made a resounding '*thwack*' in the still air as it made solid contact with the wood.

Most of the people in the valley didn't even rightly know what had happened to Billy. But, they all knew for sure that he was just about as wild and untamed as the old mountain itself. He was just another pitiful orphan of the mountain. There always seems to be a slew of them around, up in these parts, 'specially these days. Poor thing didn't have himself any momma right from the very start, and not a daddy that he could rightly speak of, either. Billy knew he was pretty much an orphan, and that he didn't seem to belong to anybody. So, the boy just roamed wild and free, living right out under the stars. That's where he felt like he belonged, I'd imagine, Tolbert reckoned to himself. *T'was the way of life he chose for himself early on, and he sure seemed to take straight to it. That young'un just took to it right away, like a duck takes t' the water. It was almost as if'n he was born to it, and maybe he was, at that. He was living out in the wilderness like a wildcat, roamin' wild and free.*

They did see him, on occasion. He'd stop by the house from time to time, but certainly not as much as he used to. Billy would bring them a ham and some rabbits, and sometimes, an occasional chicken or pig. Tolbert never asked questions about what he brought to them, and Billy sure didn't offer up any explanations. Tolbert knew that it wasn't right to take ill-gotten food, but times were tough for just about everybody. They all had to make do, as best they could.

Starving was just a week or two away, up here on the mountain, just as it was down in the valley below, and Tolbert knew that just about as well as anybody else. *Yep, I rightly figure that I do.*

Poor Ollie had held tightly through all those passing years to the silly notion that one day 'Wild Bill' would settle down and act just like regular folks did. But, Tolbert knew that it wouldn't ever happen. *Some folks are just 'that-a-way' and there just wasn't nothin' a'tall that anyone could do to make it be any different. Not a single, solitary thing could'a been done to make him see what was right. There weren't no use a'tryin' to make Billy be any different, and that was for sure. Some folks just hear a different drum beatin' deep inside of 'em, and there just ain't anythin' that any ol' body can do about that. Not nothing at all,* Tolbert sadly reasoned with a slow shake of his head. *Things just are the way they are. There's no sure-fire way to force a body to change, lessen they want to, themselves. They were just beatin' themselves a plain ol' dead horse hopin' for 'Wild Bill' to change, even one iota.*

Tolbert lifted his head and raised his squinted eyes to inspect the darkening clouds, once again. Turning, he studied the sky in every direction. He clutched his worn coat tighter around his chest. *Better git this 'ere wood a'chopped and git Ollie on back up towards the house before this snow comes a'pourin' down on us with a vengeance,* Tolbert thinks quickly. He peers once again, up at the darkening sky. He wonders if it's going to be a full-on blizzard that's coming. *The sky sure looks like it this time.* Tolbert knew that when the clouds look like a blanket made out of raised tufts of cotton balls rolling in, you can nearly count on snow to come down by the bucketfuls. *We may just be 'in for it', directly.*

Lordy, we may just be.

4

Heaven knows we need never be ashamed of our tears, for they are rain upon the blinding dust of earth, overlying our hard hearts.

~ CHARLES DICKENS, GREAT EXPECTATIONS

Lord, as I walk through this world, let your grace light my path, your mercy shelter my soul, and your love heal my heart.

~ UNKNOWN

OLLIE DABBED HER tears as she quietly sat and studied on the owl that appeared just outside the window.

Sometimes things just happen, for reasons that you just can't figure out, for the life of you. Sometimes you just have to accept it, no matter how hard it is, and let it go. You can't go and get yourself all worked up over something that don't even make a lick of sense. More than likely, it ain't never gonna make any sense, Ollie thought in the quiet of the house.

Ollie rocked slowly and tried to calm herself by taking slow, even breaths. Ollie began to pray. She offered up a prayer that sweet angels would gather around her father, take him by the arms, and gently guide him home. She prayed that his transition into heaven would go easily. William was notoriously resistant to change, and when she thought of how obstinate he could be, Ollie managed to chuckle softly through her tears. She asked that God would allow her father's strong will to soften, maybe just a bit. Hopefully, God would soften him just enough, that he would allow the angels to guide him gently homeward. She envisioned him gruffly pulling back his arms in protest as the angels reached out their angelic hands toward him. She couldn't help herself from laughing out loud for a second or two. *Poor old stubborn, Poppa. Stubborn as a dad-gum mule, I do declare, he is.*

When the sound of her own laughter filled the still room, she clapped her hand quickly over her mouth, fearful that someone may hear her. *Folks just wouldn't understand that, at all. Not even hardly.* No one laughed at anything when the poor departed soul hadn't even been dead long enough for the body to properly cool. It was unseemly, to say the least. No one would quite understand that, especially since Ollie hardly ever laughed at anything much at all. Ollie's head fell as she silently began to weep, once again. The grief caused her emotions to ebb and flow quickly. Her chest heaved, but she made very little sound. She had learned long ago to keep her grief silenced and to always carry it hidden, deep within her heart. Silence was always better, especially when those around you whisper. She had carried her grief like a stone hanging heavy from her heart for many years, now. Sometimes, she felt like the rope that fastened that stone around her neck would tighten up all by itself, growing slightly tighter, inch by inch. She could almost feel it cinch tighter and tighter, and she felt sure that one day it would completely cut off her air, and she would suffocate from it.

Grief had always seemed to lay heavy in Ollie's chest. The elders in the church had tried to console her many times. They had told her that given time, her burden would lighten. But, Ollie knew better than that. Some grief just runs too deep and too heavy. It never gets any lighter for some. It just keeps on grinding away at your insides until it works its way down into your soul. Then it sends down roots, and it stays. Ollie knew about these things, just as well as anyone ever could. Her thoughts drifted once again, back to an earlier time when she was still just a girl.

She went back in her mind to another time when she had heard the owl's terrifying screech. The horrific scene played out once again, vividly, in Ollie's memory. For many years, it had replayed like a broken moving picture reel, rewinding itself and playing again, over and over.

As Ollie slowly drifted back, a leaf appeared in the mist. It was the pale leaf that had lost its vibrant fall color, that same leaf floating along on the swiftly moving current of the creek that she had seen that day. It was floating along in the creek that flowed and meandered alongside her childhood home. The cold water was moving the leaf quickly along, twisting and turning it this way and that. The leaf moved steadily on the water, just as time has its way of carrying us all along down the path of life. It takes us where it will. *You eventually find that you are truly at the mercy of whatever flow that has you caught up within its grasp. It's the same flow that's carrying us all along in this life,* thought Ollie. *We are blessed to have God's grace and mercy as he watches over us and, of course, we have our prayers. We pray that God will gently guide the waters that direct which way we go in this life. We may get tossed this way and that, but surely it's God's plan that keeps us ever moving forward toward the right destination. It's the same destination that we all seek and hope to find, one day. If we walk closely with the Lord, seeking his guidance, the waters will eventually carry us to where we are truly meant to be.*

Back in present day, Jane wandered through the rambling old house up on the mountain, admiring the polished, gleaming woodwork with a happy heart. Her house was finally complete. She surely had her doubts when she had first inherited the rambling old place, but it had somehow all came together. Her tie to the house went deeper than just loving the house itself; her family had built this house, stone by stone and bit by bit. They had carved the first cabin out of the forest that once stood here. That cabin was still here, and the old stones in the fireplace were the same ones her ancestors had placed. Jane's history was here and the voices from the past echoed in these old walls. *I have a definite blood-tie to this house and to the land on which it sits*, she thought.

Jane did love it here, even though she occasionally had that same odd prickly feeling that she wasn't exactly alone. That eerie feeling, as if there were someone peering directly over her shoulder, came from time to time. But even still, the house had begun to honestly feel like 'home' to her. She had accepted that the old house had other 'guests' from time to time. These guests were from another day and another time. She had come to the realization that they just weren't planning on going anywhere, not anytime soon, anyway. These angels of hers were going stay.

Dad would be so proud and happy for me. Jane just knew it. *He'd approve of my using the inheritance he left me for the house. It was probably what he intended for me to do, all along. He would have wanted me to put it to good use, and I surely did.* The house was restored back to the condition that Jane had always hoped it would be. Jane smiled brightly and then sighed. *Home, home at last, Dad.*

She had winterized all the piping under the house, and Jake had finally gotten the backup generator installed. Jane felt confident that winter weather would not cause her any major problems this year, for sure. *Let the snow blow however hard it wants to*, she thought with a grin. *Bring it right on; I'm ready! Jake will be coming home soon, now, and I can't wait*, thought a smiling Jane. *He's been gone for nearly four weeks now, and that's just way too long to be apart from your fellow.*

But, the job he had been offered up in Nashville was just too good to pass up. They had both agreed that it was a great opportunity for his new full-fledged construction company, especially just starting out, so he had jumped at the chance. His crew was finally established and working well, so Jake was going to get to come home for a few days, and she was thrilled about it. At first, he had two guys that just up and quit, saying they weren't keen on being away from home so much, but the ones that remained were carrying the workload without any glitches. Progress on the project was proceeding almost seamlessly.

Everything seems to be working out so well, Jane smiled with the thought. Jane had decided to spend these last few days doing something that she had managed to put off for quite some time. She was going to clean out the 'cobweb city' attic finally, despite all those pesky spiders that she felt sure were still lurking up there. She knew it was going to have to happen sooner or later, and lately 'later' just sounded better to her. She just didn't want to have to deal with the spider webs. She decided that this would be a great time to tackle it, and to finally get it finished and behind her.

Besides, the days remaining until Jake would be home would pass a lot faster, if she was deep in the attic removing old boxes and stuff. Working and staying busy would help, she was sure of it. So, she donned a pair of Jake's coveralls, rolled up the legs and sleeves, tied a scarf over her hair, put on her goggles and gloves, and climbed the stairs. She caught sight of her reflection in the hall mirror, and she stopped and laughed out loud. *Why, you look like you're prepared for deadly scorpion removal or a lethal ecoli virus outbreak, girlie! It's just a few spiders or maybe even just a few harmless, abandoned spider webs,* she laughed at herself. But deep down, she shuddered at the very thought of crawling through the webs. Just the thought of a spider crawling on her skin or even worse, in her hair, caused her to cringe. The hairs on the back of her neck prickled up with just the thought of it. *You sure talk a good game, now girlie-girl, but can you walk the walk?* She heard her dad's words echo once again in her mind. "Don't know if I'm gonna make it through this, or not Dad." "This is going to be some pretty rough stuff." Jane wrinkled her nose and smiled.

Carefully, she climbed the narrow ladder that led up to the small opening of the attic space. She had opened the hatch door a few days earlier and left it propped open on purpose. She did this thinking that maybe any big spiders could escape without anything to hinder their speedy exit. Plausible or not, she remained hopeful that they had all left the premises with haste. *Some things are just better not seen,* Jane thought with conviction. But, she did have three flashlights hanging from her coveralls, just to be safe. *Overkill perhaps? Well, you just never know,* she thought, *I could lose one or one could even have weak batteries. Be prepared, and all that, y'know. It's the just the Girl Scout in me,* she chuckled out loud. There was a loud cracking sound when she put her hand out to steady herself as she peered over the top rung of the ladder. The wood of the ladder was old but appeared to be sound. She sure hoped that it was. *That cracking sound just means that the wood is dry,* she thought hopefully. Faint outlines of torso forms came into sight. She sucked in a breath and recoiled instantly. *What in the world is that?* After she caught her breath she leaned in slightly to get a closer look at the shapes, while illuminating the area with the beam of her flashlight. She quickly determined that they were just old dress maker's forms. Jane pursed her lips and blew out a heavy sigh of relief.

The scant light of the early morning coming in through the murky window panes lit the area dimly, and everything was washed in a dusty shade of gray. Judging by the thick layers of dust, it appeared that nothing had been disturbed up here for many years. Old boxes were stacked up three or four high in rows. Antique furniture was just waiting to be discovered and maybe even happily repurposed. She was excited about looking at everything. Jane truly loved old things, just as her father had. *Oh my, the stories that this old furniture and stuff could tell me if it only could. It's just amazing, every bit of it.*

Jane used a small bungee type cord that she had attached to her coveralls and secured a small flashlight to the beam over her head. She wound the cord tightly and clicked the switch on the flashlight. Light filled the space instantly. There was way more stuff up here than she had originally thought and it appeared that the spider webs were mostly abandoned, after all. A smile of relief flashed across her face. *Thank goodness.* Jane let out her breath in a large exhale. As she looked around, she saw the amazing view from the small window. She could see more of the mountain ridges from this higher vantage point than she could see from the yard. She was instantly enthralled. *Oh, my goodness,* Jane thought. The window gave her a totally different view of her beloved mountain, allowing her to see a much wider expanse.

Jane thought that she might use the old rocking chair sitting over by the window as a nice and quiet reading nook. *A wonderful little private reading nook with the most awesome view ever,* Jane thought with a broad smile. *Surely Jake wouldn't mind too much, if I asked him to put in a permanent staircase. It would sure make getting up here a whole lot easier,* she thought to herself. *Jake.* Jane sighed softly. She knew that she couldn't postpone the wedding for very much longer. She was convinced that she was beginning to feel less apprehensive, than she did at first. *Sometimes you just need to give yourself a little time to let an idea settle itself in down deep,* she thought plausibly. *I have every right in the world to be skittish about it. After this many times of being dumped at the last minute, anyone would feel skittish. Even plain ol' scared stiff, would be understandable. Hey, now, I've got a right to feel this way.* She bounced her head quickly up and down as if to confirm her own thoughts.

Jane bent over a box to peer behind the stacks, and held lightly onto the nearby rafter for support. There was plenty of headroom to walk comfortably, and there appeared to be ample flooring already installed. Behind the boxes, she could just make out some shelving. Intrigued, she worked quickly, hauling the boxes down the ladder, one by one. Soon the walls outside the bedrooms below were lined with crates and boxes. Some of the heavier items would have to wait until Jake came home, but she cleaned out the bulk of the stuff that was on one side of the attic, and a portion of the other, all in just a few hours' time.

Tired and dirty, she decided to call it a day and hauled the last crate down the steps. After a quick bite of supper and a nice hot shower in her brand new shower that she had helped Jake install, she slipped into some pajama's and settled in front of the roaring fire to read. She had started re-reading Isabelle's journals awhile back, just in case there was something that she had maybe missed in the excitement of the first reading. She felt so close to her great-grandmother now. She felt that she had her own guardian angel, to watch over her and the house. She smiled as she thought of the beautiful old apron left on the chair. She had hung Isabelle's apron on a special hook in the kitchen. She loved seeing it there every morning, it was comforting to her as she made her morning coffee. Jane knew in her heart that Isabelle was there still, in spirit, watching over her. It seemed only right that her apron still hung in the house that she loved. *It will always remain just where it is,* Jane thought with conviction.

With a cup of hot chocolate in her hand, she read the journals intently for about an hour and a half, before she began to feel drowsy and her eyelids grew heavy. Stifling a yawn, she reached over and turned off the lamp leaving the journals lying on the chair, and padded on off to bed. Lingering for a moment she admired the family pictures that lined the hallway. She had recently restored and re-framed them all. She felt surrounded by Arrowood love. She knew her Dad would have just loved it. She paused and smiled at his picture, as it hung beside her mother's beautiful portrait in the center of the grouping. They made such a beautiful couple, each smiling happily out from the frames. *Good night, all*, she whispered to the quiet, darkened house.

Jane turned, went into the bedroom, and pulled down the quilt on the poster bed. She climbed in and snuggled down deep. Exhausted, Jane was asleep almost as soon as her head hit the pillow.

The sky was studded with stars that winked and sparkled like diamonds, scattered about on a thick indigo blanket. A light September breeze stirred lazily down from the high peaks along the rolling ridges of the Roan. The glittering stars peeked out from behind small passing puffs of clouds. The sweet smell of fall was heady in the night time air. The pine scented forest was alive with the sound of nocturnal wildlife. Small animals scurried about, as they left their nests to forage for food in the stillness. The mountain seemed to sigh contentedly, under her blanket of deep blue.

The Roan had begun its settling down in earnest, for the quickly coming fall and the long winter's nap that would soon follow. The mountain slumbers deep in wintertime, and beginning in early fall, you can almost feel the drowsiness beginning to take its hold over her. The whispering in the wind continued down into the deep valleys below, from high up on the Roan just as it has done for centuries before. The Roan remembers.

She never forgets, Jane murmured lightly, deep in sleep, as she heard the faint strains of fiddle music as it floated down into the valley from high atop the Roan.

The music was comforting, and Jane sighed softly in her sleep. *Band's playing again*, Jane murmured with a smile. She saw the couples dancing on the magnificent dance floor of the Cloudland as the fire roared in the massive fireplace. Their shadows cast long silhouettes on the wall behind them, as they swirled about in unison to the lilting strains of music from days gone by.

5

Your feet will bring you to where your heart is.

~ IRISH PROVERB

*There is a quiet light that shines in every heart. It draws
no attention to itself, though it is always secretly there. It
is what illuminates our minds to see beauty, our desire to
seek possibility, and our hearts to love life. Without this
subtle quickening our days would be empty and wearisome,
and no horizon would ever awaken our longing. Our
passion for life is quietly sustained from somewhere in us
that is wedded to the energy and excitement of life. This
shy inner light is what enables us to recognize and receive
our very presence here as blessing. We enter the world
as strangers who all at once become heirs to a harvest of
memory, spirit, and dream that has long preceded us and
will now enfold, nourish and sustain us. The gift of the
world is our first blessing.*

~ JOHN O'DONOHUE

E ARLY THE NEXT morning, Jane had dressed in her coveralls once again. She was fully prepared to battle the rest of the attic clutter. Today, she decided to add a mask to keep out the dust that swirled thickly in the attic air. She sipped a second cup of coffee as she intentionally lingered, reveling in the magnificent sunrise over her beloved mountain. Radiating rays of peach laced with wine framed the mountains beneath the clear blue of the endless sky. The complete view that rose in the sweeping distance before her was breathtakingly beautiful. The mist of the morning slowly burned away as the bright sun rose steadily in the sky.

Realizing that she couldn't put it off any longer, she gazed out over the mountain ridge one last time and headed back into the house. *My goodness, but these steps somehow seem quite a bit steeper than they were just yesterday,* she thought with a sarcastic grin. She was certainly feeling every sore muscle that she had. Surely it was from all the trips up and down the steps yesterday. *Girlie, today will be yet another adventure, so buckle on up,* she smiled to herself. *This old house keeps offering up her old dusty secrets, and I'm thrilled with the gift of discovering each one. I'll never get tired of this, not ever. I'll never quit seeking her secrets, either.*

She took a deep breath and climbed the rest of the way up the ladder. *Okay, girlie, enough woolgathering and belly-achin' for one day,* Jane admonished herself as she determinedly focused on the task at hand. Once she had climbed back up into the attic, she hung the light from the rafter with a drop cord attached. It lit the whole area up a far cry better than the beam of the small flashlight ever had. She began working. She moved a tall stack of boxes and saw that a bookcase had been built into the wall beside the window. It had been mostly hidden from view, before. Someone had already built themselves a quite beautiful reading nook here, sometime in years past. *How neat is that?* Jane asked herself, smiling. She worked on, going through each box, discovering its contents with delight. There were stacks of delicate old linens, finely hand-sewn quilts, and even several trunks and boxes full of vintage clothing.

Jane kept rummaging until she found a quaint pair of old lace up shoes that were quite tiny. It was hard to believe that anyone had ever worn them, but the bottom of the shoes told the story. She held them up closer to the light, so that she could see them better. They were scuffed and worn smooth, indicating many steps had been taken in the shoes by very small feet. The buttons that laced the side of the shoes were also petite. The leather of the shoe was surprisingly supple, but the pieces that fastened them on the sides were curled and cracked with age. Since the arid condition in the attic hadn't dried the leather out completely, Jane surmised that they had been expertly tanned. Jane guessed the strips of cloth had protected them as well. Someone had taken small strips of what looked like cotton and had wound them tightly around them. *Who placed these shoes here, and when?* Everything had been packed away very carefully, and every effort had been made to protect the contents of the boxes, Jane felt sure. *Someone had loved these things.*

Attics had always held a special place in Jane's heart. She had always been fascinated by them. The attics of old houses were places that people put the story of their lives, carefully and lovingly tucked away in tissue. They store the items that they cannot bear to part with and hope that one day, they will be loved again. *What wonderful time capsules from days long ago, are just waiting under these layers of dust, beckoning me to come and find them?* She rolled her eyes with amusement at that thought. *Boy howdy.* Jane laughed lightly. *Beckoning from under layers of dust? Really, girlie? Well now, it seems as if the thick dust has clouded your brain, just as badly as it has coated your nasal passages. Whew. Don't you think that's being just a tad dramatic?* She giggled merrily to herself and suddenly crinkled up her nose and sniffed while shaking her head. She felt a huge sneeze coming and it soon did. *How's that for rattling the rafters, Dad?* Jane giggled. She could almost imagine his reply to that. Her 'Daddy thoughts' always came to her when she least expected them.

But, she knew that digging through a dusty attic would have been every bit as magical to him, as it was to her. She smiled wistfully at the thought. *Dusty old attics would certainly have topped the list of my Dad's all-time favorite places. Guess I am my Daddy's daughter, after all.* "Hey, I can't help how I am. It's just the Arrowood in me." She could almost hear her Dad chuckle as she spoke aloud to the swirling dust and boxes. She worked on for quite some time. Still smiling, she gathered up an old lace crinoline and the tiny pair of shoes that she had found, and made her way back over to the ladder. *Enough dirt, dust, and adventure for one day,* she thought as she clutched the shoes to her chest and mounted the ladder. It was Jake's voice she heard this time. She thought, *Okay, you need to maintain a healthy three point contact on that ladder, now missy.* So, she shifted the items she had in her arms and held onto the ladder securely with both hands. She made her way down and shucked off her shoes, and left her dusty coveralls in a heap on the floor, by the bedroom. *One more day or so of steady work and I will have that attic licked.*

She was tired and happy, at the same time. She showered and blew her nose repeatedly. *There's just way too much dust up there for me. Especially when you keep taking off your dust mask, silly,* she thought. *You've also been spending too much time alone, again. Surely you know that giving your imagination full rein, unsupervised, is never a good idea, girlie,* Jane pursed her lips comically to her reflection in the mirror, as she passed by. Still laughing, she made her way down the hall and thought, *Yep, girlie, you are slightly nuts. Let's just face it. But, you know, that's okay. I guess I fit right into this family, and quite nicely, I might add.*

After a hot shower, Jane slipped quickly into her night shirt and stepped into her fuzzy slippers. She thought maybe she'd just have herself a bowl of soup, watch a little TV, and call it an early night. She was nearly wiped out from the countless trips up and down the attic ladder. She stifled a big yawn with the back of her hand as she padded softly back down the hall toward the kitchen. Suddenly, the definite sound of footsteps falling heavily behind her in the hall caused her to stop in her tracks. Jane took a quick breath and turned around to peer into the darkened hall. She stared into the darkness, trying hard to see. She was half-hoping that she would see Minnie and little Ruby come skipping past her, but they had never made the sound of actual heavy footsteps before. *Those steps sounded all for the world as if they were being made by heavy men's shoes,* Jane shuddered. Nothing could be seen in the shadowy hall. She slowly turned and started back down the hall, but the sound of footsteps began again, and they sounded as if they were following closely behind her, still. She shuddered again, involuntarily, and said a silent prayer. Her lips quivered as she spoke the 'Amen' aloud. This time, she didn't feel the soothing warmth of protection that she normally felt. This time, the eerie feeling was quite unnerving.

There was a different sort of 'darkness' attached to the feeling she had with this experience, and Jane didn't like it, at all. Suddenly, she had no appetite and decided that leaving the kitchen alone tonight, was for the best. Spending just one more minute at the end of the long darkened hall was not something she wanted to do, so instead she turned quickly on her heel and went on to bed. She practically ran the last few steps and jumped right into the bed. Once safe and under the covers, Jane laughed at her silliness and said, *What in the world, did you do that for, you silly girl? Surely, there ain't nothing in here, except one big ol' chicken.* Even the conscious attempt she made to kid herself didn't quell the strange feeling that she felt. She was afraid; truly afraid for the first time in quite awhile, and she very well knew it.

Jane lay in the darkened room listening intently for any strange sound for well over an hour. Then, Jane's exhaustion finally allowed a fitful sleep to overtake her. Unsettled dreams interrupted her sleep cycle frequently during the long night. Jane's dreams were far worse than she had ever experienced before, but come the first light of morning, Jane remembered nearly nothing.

When she was back up in the attic and wearing all of her protective gear, Jane made her way over to the reading nook and rocking chair. The chair was ornate and beautifully handcrafted. There were rosettes and flowers carved into the woodwork. The carved flowers closely resembled the Gray's Lilies that Jane had found blooming in clusters along the balds just last summer. They are rare and beautiful flowers. On a portion of the Appalachian Trail just along the balds, they bloom with abandon when the conditions are just right. Jane had taken her camera on her last hike up to Jane's Bald and when she saw the lilies she was so glad that she had. Now, she never hiked anywhere without her camera. There was always something beautiful to see up on the Roan. It didn't matter what season, beauty can always be found there.

Jane sat down in the chair and rocked, totally absorbing the moment. She ran her hands over the smooth wood of the polished curved handles. She leaned back in the chair and closed her eyes. She let her mind wander back to that day in June when she had first encountered the lilies. The chair's movement soothed her as she quietly rocked back and forth. Something about the gentle rocking motion of that old chair was intensely calming and relaxing. The wood on the hand rest was exceptionally smooth and velvety under her fingertips. Her fingers fit perfectly into the grooves. Jane could almost feel the love and care that had gone into the making of the chair. *This chair was undoubtedly made for someone that was loved with a passion.* Jane smiled as she ran her fingertips over the ornate armrest and enjoyed the rhythmic motion. The sunlight illuminated the attic gradually. It became more brightly lit with each passing moment.

A shaft of light eventually beamed through a small dimpled pane of the wavy glass in the high arched window. The sunlight flooded the corner of the attic over beside the bookcase. In the corner, the light bounced off of a small shiny latch. It caught Jane's eye and she stood up and peered over at it. The latch was attached to what appeared to be a small wallpapered door. The latch itself was quite small and tucked deep into the dark corner, so Jane hadn't even noticed it before.

Intrigued, Jane couldn't take her eyes off of it. As she made her way closer to the bookcase, Jane could tell by the faint outline that there had to be some sort of small cabinet hidden within the wall. The latch was ornate but almost hidden completely in the pattern of the old wallpaper. *Exceptionally crafty camouflage*, thought Jane as her eyes narrowed. The latch was very effectively hidden, almost as if it were on purpose. It slowly dawned on Jane. *This was not meant to be found so easily. Why?* Jane took a deep breath as she reached out and slid the latch open. The wooden door swung open easily enough, revealing its contents instantly in a streaming shaft of sunlight. A puff of dust and the smell of old wood wafted out at Jane. She waved a hand in front of her face to clear the dust and peered closer, still.

A stack of what appeared to be old thick journals had been placed on the shelf. Alongside them, were smaller bound notebooks that had been neatly stacked. There had to be at least a dozen of them, all total. Jane squealed out in delight and clapped her hands together. Her mind quickly calculated what those journals must surely contain, and utter joy of the moment overcame her and she let out even a higher pitched squeal. *Oh, my! This wonderful old house has truly, only just begun to reveal its secrets to me. The past has been carefully and lovingly written down and preserved. And it has stayed here all this time, and simply waited for me to come and find it. I am so honored to have been given such an amazing gift. This gift of love, from so many generations, has been handed down to me. This just gets better and better. Oh, Daddy,* Jane thought, as a tear left a trail on her dusty cheek, *there is nothing that I wouldn't give, to be able to share this adventure with you, too.*

Jane's smile slowly faded, and her expression grew somber. Then, her brows knit together as she formed the thought, *Is there something more that I need to know, Isabelle?* She carefully reached in and took out the stacked journals. She realized that these didn't look as old as the ones that were written by Isabelle. The paper was in much better condition, even though it was yellowing and beginning to crumble on the edges. It was still certainly old. There were two large journals with clasps. One was bound in leather and the other was covered with plush but faded green velvet. The green journal had an ornate mirror set into the cover. Jane estimated that they both probably date to somewhere around the late 1880's. Under the journals, there was a small stack of old letters. Everything looked to be more recent than the first papers she had found, but these paper were still pretty old. The corners of the envelopes and the pages were also yellowed with age, but the writing was still clearly legible. *There is page after page, documenting the lives of my family, right here, hidden away in a place of safe keeping. Surely, this was placed here for me. Someone put it here, knowing that someday the next 'Keeper of the Legends' would come and find it. What a treasure.* Jane thought, *This must be another Arrowood tradition. Maybe, writing everything down into a journal is something that I need to be doing. Maybe this is why I was led here and feel such a deep connection with this old mountain and this old house. Maybe, this is just exactly where I'm supposed to be.*

Without wasting a moment, Jane turned and made her way over to the chair by the window, where she'd have better light for reading. Jane sat in the beautiful old rocker that had once belonged to Ollie. She crossed her arms and held the journals close to her heart as tears slid down her smiling face. She bowed her head and said a silent prayer of thanks. *Oh, thank you so much.* She put the journals down on her lap and laid her hand lightly on the stack.

Jane wondered whose hand had touched these journals last, before they had been secreted away in the small niche hidden in the wall. Jane laughed lightly as she thought, *Ol' Sentimental Sallie, that's me for sure.* She quickly opened the latch on the side that held the old worn leather journal's pages closed. Jane opened to the first page and she began to read.

Ollie had been silently weeping for hours. Ever since they had brought her sister's tiny limp bodies back from the creek, her tears had fallen. The neighbor men had waded into the icy creek water after the violent flow had slowed down somewhat. The men had gently taken the girl's bodies down from the tree branches where they had been found. Minnie and Ruby had been caught up and entangled in the branches and their clothing hung in tatters where the branches had snagged them. It was a ghastly sight to see them both hanging there like broken rag dolls. The able-bodied men of the town didn't wait to be asked to attend to the gruesome task; they just did it. It was something that simply had to be done.

This was just the natural way of the mountain people, as it had been, through the years. People simply did whatever task that needed to be completed, and they treated each other the way they would want to be treated themselves. No one stopped to think about such things; it was just the way life was, up in the hills. You helped your neighbor out as best you could.

Soaked to the skin, Ollie had been picked up and toted right on up out of that cold creek. Her hair hung heavily about her pitiful face in frozen strands. Her blank eyes stared out of her stark white face, glazed and unseeing. Her screams had echoed down the gorge and beyond while she kicked and flailed her arms about wildly. *That poor girl couldn't have been held accountable for her actions, given the circumstances. The girl clearly didn't know what she was doing. Anyone could have seen that for themselves. She just couldn't let her mind accept that sweet little Minnie and Ruby were gone.* She was caught up in a whirlwind of torment, deep within herself. There was just no way of reaching her.

Minnie and Ruby had been right by her side in the house right before she had left that morning. They had both been chattering away, laughing and playing, just as little ones do. Then, just a short time later their laughter was silenced forever. For Ollie, innocence was gone forever, as well. She had a heartache that cut so deep, that she would never fully heal. For quite some time to come, she wished with everything in her being that she had drowned in that swollen creek right alongside her two little sisters.

6

Death leaves a heartache no one can heal, love leaves a memory no one can steal.

~ From a headstone in Ireland

We must embrace pain and burn it as fuel for our journey.

~ Kenji Miyazawa

THE HOUSE WAS full of family and neighbors, but, the lively banter and laughter that was usually heard with a crowd was keenly absent. Everyone walked quietly and respectfully around the young pale-faced Ollie. It was the custom when death came to the valley. There was a reverent respect paid to death. Everyone talked in hushed tones and whispers. There were chairs brought in and placed around the perimeter of the room. The pain in Ollie's dark eyes was heartbreaking. It was hard for anyone to bring themselves to make eye contact with the girl. Even the minister, who could just about preach up a storm while up in the pulpit, was suddenly at a loss for words after looking closely at Ollie.

Untimely death was sadly commonplace; it was almost the usual way of life for those up in the mountains. People died, and more were born, and the cycle continued. Sometimes it was easily accepted and sometimes it was hard. Tragedy had struck once again, and this time, nearly everyone in the tiny community felt the bitter sting.

Little Minnie and Ruby were just the sweetest little girls. Always kind and thoughtful children, they had quickly endeared themselves to the community in the few short years of their lives, and many were heartsick over their untimely deaths. The two sisters had always re-membered to take an extra basket when they went down the meadow to pick wild strawberries or over to the next hollow to pick blackberries. They had always happily shared their bounty with Marjorie Finger and Grace Blanks. Miss Grace and Miss Marjorie were two sweet women that lived together in a small house up on the mountain. They spent a lot of time watching out their window on sunny summer days, hoping to see the girls running through the tall grass on the footpath heading up to their door, with a basket of berries to share. They would try to always have the girl's favorite cookies made and waiting for them. They both loved those little girls dearly and looked forward to their visits.

Yes, many souls grieved the heartbreaking loss that stark cold morning in January. Many tears fell for little Minnie and Ruby, and their precious mother, Calla. Poor Ollie's tears mingled right in with the river of tears that was shed for those three lives, cut so short. Surely, Ollie's tears were the ones that stung the worst, but we will never know for sure.

Ollie sat by the fire with a thick wool blanket around her, but she still shivered visibly. She stared out, blankly, as the horrible scene kept replaying itself over and over, behind her dark eyes. It was im-printed on her memory, like an etching made on glass. It was a scene that she would see for the rest of her life. *She was such a pitiful sight, just sitting there staring off into the distance.*

Ollie thought back to the early morning hours of that horrible day when the sound of a screech owl's scream had woken her from a deep slumber. The elders in the community feared the screech owl and believed adamantly that it brought along with it, the ominous angel of death. At first, Ollie had refused to believe any such nonsense. Now, she didn't know exactly what to think. She didn't want to believe in old wives tales or any such notion, for that matter. Ollie shook from the sudden shock when she heard the first toll of the church bell. The bell rang out as notice to all that death had come once again to the tiny community.

The bell tolled slowly, seven times, once for each of Minnie's years, then, there was a pause of silence. Then it rang out five more times, for Ruby. The bell always tolled out the sad news of death. Ollie's breath caught in her throat. She held her hands over her ears, trying to block out the terrible sound. She tucked her head to her chest, and her body went rigid. She could scarcely breathe until the bell fell silent. Ollie wailed out in agony. She had never felt such pain and desperation.

Tolbert knew that Ollie had changed the very day that death had come. He knew even then, that she was most likely changed forever. But, he still loved her, through it all. He had rushed to her side that day, just as soon as he had heard the bell begin tolling. He had been in the barn, tending to his father's cows. He'd known instantly that it had to be the little ones. He had torn out of that barn at a dead run, knowing that he had to get to her, and try to help her, if he could. But, it seemed that he couldn't do even one thing right. Not anything at all. *It was terrible for Tolbert to see his Ollie as he saw her that day. It tore Tolbert's heart right out of his chest.*

He had tried his best, through the passing years, to make Ollie happy once again. Tolbert always kept hope that one day the bright sparkle would return to her eyes, and her sweet musical laugh would return, as well. But it was never going to be the same again with Ollie. He finally accepted it, because he had little choice. Somehow, the sorrow that had festered up in Ollie's heart had spilled right over into his, over time. He figured that they had been, for the most part anyway, pretty happy during all their years together. It wasn't what it could have been, but it could've always been worse.

Tolbert was mighty disappointed when they weren't able to bring children into the world. He had known right from the very start, how desperately Ollie had wanted children. A part of him knew that had they been able to have their own children, Ollie would have finally found some happiness. She maybe even would've been her old self, once again.

You just can't keep on a'wrestlin' with demons that won't show you their faces, Tolbert thought to himself. *You can't just keep on a'worryin' and frettin' yourself over somethin' you'll never even know for sure*, he thought with a sigh. *There's just no use a'tall in worrying your life away over what's already done and gone with. What would be the point in it, anyway?*

Oh, poor Ollie. Jane thought as she closed her eyes briefly. Jane laid the journal down on her lap and looked over at the stack of old letters. She found herself curiously drawn to them. Intrigued, she picked one up from the stack. She carefully took the paper out of the tattered envelope and unfolded it. The paper had worn thin and had torn slightly at the folds. She held the letter up gingerly, with just her fingertips and she began to read.

7

Give sorrow words; the grief that does not speak whispers
the o'er-fraught heart and bids it break.

~ WILLIAM SHAKESPEARE

POOR OL' OLLIE. Lordy, have mercy, that poor, pitiful girl. Ollie had tried her level best to get into that room. Oh my, but she surely did, now. She had tried to get in there to help her momma. Ollie had nearly fallen plumb to pieces when she heard those blood curdlin' screams. Oh Mercy, but how that sweet woman did suffer. Mary Calla suffered something awful. It was terrible to just stand by and not be able to do nary a' thing. Mary Calla went into labor straight away, after hearing the dreadful news of the girls' drowning. Ollie had screamed right out and cried something fierce when she realized how much pain her momma was a'havin'. Then she had tried to get to her momma, but she was pushed back out of the room by the midwife. That midwife was sure a stout woman and certainly no match for a slip of a girl like Ollie. Ollie was nearly out of her poor mind with grief, but the screams of her mother soon drove her past that, and she went into a state of pure panic. She honestly had the look of a wild animal in her eyes. She was just 'out of herself,' I tell you. No other way to describe it. She wasn't even able to realize, that she wouldn't have helped her mother a'tall *in the state she was in, on that very day. She couldn't have helped even one bit. But, she sure tried to, anyhow.*

When they finally told her that her mother hadn't made it through the delivery, the look on Ollie's face was plumb scary. Never saw the likes of it, not in all your live long days, I tell you. She just, all of a sudden-like, looked as if the light had just gone plumb out of her eyes. It was just as if a lantern burnin' in the dark had been blown clean out, I tell you. Never saw the light of somebody's soul dim straight out like that before and I sure don't want to, not ever again. But, I knew it for sure, when I saw it, that was exactly what had to be a'happenin'.

Then, when they had cleaned up the bed, washed everything up and put fresh linens on it, well, that's when they had let Ollie come back into the room. Well, they tried to get her calmed down some first, of course. Mary Calla was lying there looking mighty pale, but she was never so beautiful. So, at first, Ollie thought it was all just a horrible mistake and that she was just asleep. She was just as beautiful as she could be. Mary Calla honestly was, even in death. She looked like an angel just a'layin' there on that bed. Even after all that horrible suffering she had gone through, birthin' that little bitty baby. Ollie screamed out that it just wasn't so, that her mother wasn't dead, and that she was just asleep. But the looks on the faces of the folks that were standing around in the room soon convinced her otherwise.

She hadn't cried any more tears. I figured that it was because she simply didn't have any more left to cry. The pitiful little thing was hard to look at, she really was. Her whole world had plunged deep into a dark hole in one single day's time. It was the saddest thing a body could've ever seen; I tell you that for sure. It was just the saddest thing.

Jane recognized the writing that she was reading now, as very similar to her own. She somehow knew that this had to have been written by her great-grandmother, Isabelle. She read on, spellbound.

The men in the community had all gone straight to work, a'sawing up the logs to make those coffins. They didn't usually have a need to make three coffins, all up at once, mind you. They hadn't made that many at one time since the Hicks family all burnt up in that horrible house fire. That, of course, was back quite a few years ago, now. After the coffins had been all made, they had carefully rubbed them down with linseed oil. They rubbed them up real good. That oil puts a real nice shine on them, you know. They made 'em up extra fine and in fact, they were quite purty. If'n a casket can even be called purty, I suppose. Well, if'n they can, well, then these surely were. They were the purtiest boxes for the dead I ever did see, and understand me now, I saw myself a'plenty in my time. These were generally made up and given to the families of the deceased. Sometimes if they were outsiders, now, they would charge 'em for them. But, now, if they were folks of the community, they wasn't charged a single dime. It was just somethin' the townsfolk did for one another, out of respect, you know.

Many acts of kindness were shown when a family's loved one dies. People often had to travel many'a mile by wagon or horse to come and help. They'd come to help out with the buildin' of the coffins, the digging, and the fillin' up of the graves. Sometimes to even help wash and dress the bodies. They did whatever they could to try and help. They helped 'em do it all, didn't matter what it was that was a'needin' doin'. Why, now, it all just had to be done, did it not? Somebody or other had to do it. No one complained, not a bit. They didn't say nary a word they just pitched in and got what needed to get done, done. It was the old-timey mountain way a'doing things. And for certain, it was a good and honest way. People looked out for one another back then. We all had a genuine and honest love for one another. Weren't no other good way to explain it. The Good Book tells us that we are supposed to be kind to others as we walk along the path of this life, and we tried to be. The old timey ways were good ways.

All the church women and the local midwives that had been attending to Mary Calla had gotten poor Ollie to lie down, finally. Ollie had only just dozed off when she had heard the banging and the hammering start up. Her eyes flew wide open when she realized the hammering meant that they had to be making the coffins.

Ollie pushed back the covers on the bed and looked down at herself. She realized she was now wearing a different dress. Lying on the chair, right beside the bed, was the dress that she had been wearing the morning before. The hem was ripped and torn jaggedly in places. It was caked with dried mud from the creek bank. She stared at the dried mud and drew a small shaky breath. She suddenly remembered everything in clear, exacting detail. If the mud clinging to the hem was still there, then it had all been real. The mud was real. It *had* all happened. Tears welled up in Ollie's swollen eyes like prisms, catching the light and reflecting it back again.

Ollie pulled her shawl around her thin shoulders and quickly headed out toward the sound of the hammering. The ladies were talking low among themselves, off in the kitchen. She made her way down the hall as quietly as she could. No one seemed to have noticed her. She blew out a shaky sigh of relief. Her head felt hollowed out and strange. It ached down deep inside. She supposed it was from all the crying. She was slightly sick to her stomach as well. As she went around the house toward the outbuildings, the noise of activity grew louder. Ollie suddenly heard men's voices murmuring low, peppered amongst the sounds of hammering. She moved quickly away from the sound.

Ollie came around the side of the barn, and with caution, she approached the barn door from the side and peeked inside. There were several men in the barn. Two were bent over their work, intently. They were crafting together a tiny wooden coffin with a cross etched into the wood. The foot of the coffin was narrow, and it tapered out slightly wider, at the head. The two larger coffins were standing up on end, tilted up against the far wall of the barn. They had finished them, after working through the night, and now they were working on the last one, the smallest of all three.

Ollie realized that it had to be little Ruby's casket. Ollie couldn't bear to look at them standing there and she turned her eyes away quickly. The thought of her momma and her two little sisters closed up in those dreadful boxes was just too painful. She turned and fled, running straight toward the smokehouse.

The smokehouse was just about the only place that Ollie knew of, where she could find complete solitude. It had become her private refuge.

She ran around the building and quickly ducked inside. She made her way carefully around the hanging hams, deeper, toward the back. She plopped herself down dejectedly, sitting in the soft sawdust shavings that covered the floor.

My family is really gone. Her mother had been her best friend in the whole wide world, and now she lay dead in her bed. Her tiny baby brother was just barely hanging to life by a delicate thread, and her sweet little sisters were drowned. The baby that her mother was so happy about having was here, and now she wouldn't even get to see it. She would never know that it was the little boy that she had wanted so badly. Ollie sobbed and buried her face in her hands.

The women solemnly prepared Mary Calla's body for burial, washing her carefully and combing out her long auburn hair. Minnie's and Ruby's bodies had been washed the same way. Gently and respectfully bodies were prepared for burial. Following the custom of the time, the women clothed the two young girls in long white dresses. Mary Calla was dressed in her finest dress. The faces of the women were stoic as they focused on the grim task. They each were deep in their own thoughts, and only the few words necessary to complete the task were exchanged.

Sometimes, they simply sewed the deceased body up in clean sackcloth, but William adamantly refused and wouldn't allow it. He wanted them buried in their best clothes, with a branch of holly and a sprig of cedar in their hands, since there were no flowers to be had in the bitterly cold month of January. The women had taken it upon themselves to take small branches of holly and fragrant cedar and weave them into crowning wreaths. They placed them on the heads of the girls as they lay in the caskets. Sometimes if the deceased had no good clothes for burial, clothing was provided by neighbors or family. Generosity was plentiful in the mountains. When they had stripped the bed sheets off the bed where Mary Calla had died in a pool of her own blood, they had put them over to the side. Then, after they ripped the soaked straw mattress up, they carried it all out and burned it in the field. They burned it quite a distance away from the house so that William wouldn't have to see it. No discussion was made concerning this; it was just done.

After they had washed and carefully dressed the bodies, they placed each of them gently out on a plank, supported on each end with chairs. They were laid out in the front room. There they waited for the caskets to be finished and brought inside. All this was done in preparation for the funeral and the period of 'sitting up with the dead'. This was when the friends and family would sit all around the room, surrounding the caskets. They would often pray and sing all during the night while sitting up with the deceased, staying until the next morning's light. It was the mountain way of showing your respect. And it also served to make sure that the deceased was truly gone. Sometimes, they would be presumed dead when they actually weren't, so the tradition served two purposes. Deep-seated traditions were almost always upheld in the hollows and hidden coves deep in the mountains, and traditions tended to die hard. It was regarded unfitting to do things other than the way they had been taught.

The people of the mountain may not have had much in the way of worldly possessions, but they had a true respect for one another, and they had a deep and unshakable faith in the Lord above. This love of the Lord and their unwavering, resolute faith saw them through many troubled times.

Since they had heard the church bell toll so briefly, twice, everyone knew instantly that something terrible had happened to the young girls. All of the people that were in earshot of the church bell stopped whatever they were doing and immediately started making their way up to the house. *Somehow, people respected life more, back in the olden days. It was just somehow held more precious.* Maybe they understood that life was fleeting and perhaps it was because even a bad case of dysentery could prove fatal. Sickness came and inexplicably took loved ones away; it was just a part of everyday happenings then. It was a hard life up on the isolated mountains.

As soon as Ollie had emerged from her hiding place in the smokehouse, she saw the people walking up the road, past the barn, and toward the house. She stood in silence, watching them come. A sense of dread clawed its way up from the pit of her soured stomach. The stark reality of the moment washed back over her, and the painful tears began anew. She would remember the sight of the somber-faced townspeople filing silently past her, for the rest of her days. She stood unnoticed, off by the side the smokehouse, partially hidden from view. The faces of the mourners told the story, plainly. You could see the sorrow in all of their eyes, and the pain that was etched on each face.

Ollie wanted so badly to believe that it just wasn't real; that it just couldn't be. She prayed that it was all just a horrible dream and that she would wake to find that none of it had happened.

It's odd how certain moments in life, somehow mark themselves indelibly on our brains, while others, seemingly just as important, slip silently into the mist, lost forever. *Our rememberin' must work different at times*, Ollie thought. It seemed to Ollie that some memories are written in our minds with ink, and some memories are just sketched in lightly with pencil. *The ones written in pencil are likely to just fade away over time. I want these moments to be written in my heart with the blackest ink. I want to remember every single moment, so I can keep my memories of my sisters and my momma safe within me. I want to always remember them just as they really were. I can't allow them to slip away into the mist; I just can't. I will remember their sweet faces and hear their voices, and they will never leave me, entirely. I won't let them. I just can't. I have to remember everything. Please, dear Lord. Please, help me remember.*

Folks came in by wagons, on horseback, and some were even on foot, but nearly every able-bodied person in the community dutifully attended the funeral. It was such a pitiful sight to see, Lordy, it was. Those two tiny coffins were hoisted up on the wagon. There was one lying on either side of the larger one that held Mary Calla. It was just the way that Mary Calla had walked, hand in hand, with both of them when they made their way down to the creek to take a swim.

Ollie saw them once again in her memory, laughing and swinging their arms, as they walked along the sunny path just ahead of her. The tall grasses swayed in the breeze as they made their way down to the creek's edge. The hot summers were miserable at times, especially with all the humidity. Taking a cool dip in Abram's creek had been a welcome relief for them all.

Ollie's mind allowed itself a brief moment of reprieve from her grief, as she traveled back to the misty memories of those carefree summer days. She realized that all she had left of them was her memories. Taking a swim in the cool creek would happen no more. The ache washed over her once again, and Ollie felt the crushing weight in her chest, once again. Her grief dropped her to her knees.

8

There are things that we don't want to happen but have to accept, things we don't want to know but have to learn, and people we can't live without but have to let go.

~ AUTHOR UNKNOWN

The Lord is close to the brokenhearted and saves those who are crushed in spirit.

~ PSALM 34:18

*M*Y SWEET, PRECIOUS *little girls are gone. How can it be? Both of them gone, before they were barely even given a chance to live.* William's choked thoughts formed in his mind as the excruciating pain within his chest crested once again. *Buds blossomed on earth, to bloom in Heaven. Ours is not to question the way of the Lord,* William's random thoughts echoed repeatedly as he hung his head as he stood beside the open graves.

We are not supposed to question, but precious Lord, how can we keep from it? My beautiful family is gone. Gone, in the blink of an eye. My wife. My sweet, beautiful Calla. Torn from my arms, during the happiest years of our life. Dear Lord, how can this be?

William struggled to keep his composure during the funeral, but inside he was broken. The man had been broken like a glass bottle, scattered about the ground in jagged pieces. Just like that bottle, he'll never be the same again. *Some things can never be pieced back together, no matter how hard you try to do it. Oftentimes, there's just ain't nothing that will mend a shattered heart. Once it's broken, it'll never be the same again. Time's the only thing that will help, and sometimes even that, ain't no help.*

"Our Heavenly Father says 'Draw nigh; I will comfort thee'," drawled out the elderly Reverend Love Dixon. His wavy white hair is combed back off his high forehead. It's shiny with the thick pomade he has slicked it back with while trying to tame the unruly waves. The waves in his hair seemed to each have a mind of their own. Some had already sprung themselves loose and lift with the passing breeze. His well-worn suit fits slightly taut, across his ample belly. *Reverend's done went and et himself far too many chicken wings at a few too many church socials,* Ollie thought stoically. She had absolutely no forethought of malice. It was simply her beleaguered mind's attempt to take her away from the intense pain of the moment. Sometimes her mind just had a way of running away with itself. Ollie hung her head in shame for thinking such a mean spirited thought about such a decent man of God, as the Reverend. *Our lives are held in the very palm of God Almighty,* the sweet-tempered Reverend continued on in a drawl as slow as molasses in December.

A kind and good man, he looked over the crowd with soft, loving eyes. *God knows what's best for each of his children. God said, "Suffer the little children and let them come unto me, for theirs is the kingdom of God." The Good Lord tells us to keep the faith and keep our eyes on Heaven above. We must eternally keep our eyes lifted up, just like hopeful children. We must keep our eyes fixed on the prize, my dear brothers and sisters in Christ. We must keep our eyes on Jesus. We will all be gathered up together again, my dear people, in His glorious mansion on High. This life on earth is fleeting. Ours is not to question why, because only God in his Heaven above knows why.* A scattering of hearty 'Amen's,' were heard coming up from the crowd. Everyone stood silently around the open graves and waited. Ollie's father walked over to the side of the first grave, reached down, and grabbed up a handful of the cold, wet earth. Tears streamed down his face. He held the dirt tightly in his clenched fist for a few seconds and then he slowly opened his fist and let the dirt fall onto Mary Calla's casket, down below. The clump of earth made a thudding sound that echoed in his ears and on down into the hushed valley that stretched out below.

For William, it was that very moment that was forever etched in his memory; the instant that he felt the cold, damp earth in his hand. It haunted him. It was the sound, too, as it hit the casket below that burrowed its way deep into his memory. He could even vividly recall the distinct metallic smell of the wet earth. That very moment in time haunted William for the rest of his life. It possessed his every thought on many endless nights during those dark hours before the coming dawn. Not even the painful memory of seeing Mary Calla's pale death mask haunted him nearly as badly.

He was tormented by those memories, over and over, almost daily for the rest of his life. His precious Calla, gone, and little Minnie and Ruby drowned. It was unthinkable. *My baby girls, hanging from those branches like ragdolls that had been tossed from the bridge, above. Little ragdolls with their eyes staring out, unseeing, with their mouths open, still seeming to gasp for air.* It was all an unspeakable torment to William. His true love and darling daughters, all lost in the blink of an eye.

William's thoughts go back to the tiny bundle he placed gently into Mary Calla's arms just before the casket lid was nailed in place. The bundle was his twin baby son that never drew his first breath. He had asked the midwives to keep secret that little Billy's twin had died at birth. William had known that Ollie didn't need more heartache heaped on what she already had. He was afraid that she just couldn't bear it. Besides, she didn't need to ever know. There was nothing that anyone could have done. But as for poor William, his heart would never be able to forget.

Everyone, in turn, had then filed past the open graves and tossed in a handful of dirt. As Ollie reached down for each handful and her hand closed over the coldness, her mind instantly flashes back to the cold water of the creek. Her eyes stare straight ahead, as yet again, she relives that horrible moment second by second, frame by frame. At that moment, a dense fog crept in slowly over the mountain, slipping stealthily down into the valleys and low places. It quietly covered over the area, like a dense blanket made of gray wool. As Ollie came back into the moment, she raised her head and looked out over the ridge and saw the mist. *Death comes to the mountain just like a misty vapor,* thought Ollie. *A creeping, evil vapor that lies low, down close to the earth. Quickly and silently it slips in unnoticed, and it brings along with it, its own special kind of torment.* Every mist she saw, from that very moment forward, was a reminder to her of how death can come creeping in so quickly, without even so much as a whisper of warning.

Ollie knew, deep in her heart, that she should leave this place behind her, and soon. *This place holds nothing but pain for me.* But even as her thought forms, there's a whisper that comes up from somewhere deep inside her, and she knows she never will. Some roots plunge themselves deep into the soil of your being, permanently settling in their twisting roots, without ever being seen in the light of day. The mountain itself had seeped in, and it was inside her. It had become a part of her and a part of who she was. Just as Ollie had her mother's dark eyes and her same petite hands, she had the love of the land inside her, as well. How could she ever leave, with the family that she loved so much, resting now, here in that very same cold earth? Someday, her father would eventually join them, in their eternal quiet rest beneath the newly fallen snow.

Jane wipes a tear from her cheek as she lowers the notebook and lays it down in her lap. She raises her hand and holds her forehead with her palm. Her hand slips down over her eyes, *This has to be Ollie writing, now. This journal just has to be Ollie's*, Jane thinks to herself. *Oh, Ollie, the horror of having to watch your little sisters drown, all the while knowing that there was nothing in the world that you could do to save them. After enduring that living nightmare, then you had to go through the torment of watching your mother die in agony during childbirth? Now, your father's gone, too. Surely, there's only so much heartache that any one soul can bear.*

Jane shook her head dejectedly and sighed. She took the notebooks and placed them into a small wooden box that she had found earlier in the corner of the attic and carried the box down the ladder. She continued to bring down the remaining boxes, making trip after trip. She left the larger, bulky furniture items, for Jake to move after he returns home. Some things are far too heavy for her to ever manage them down the ladder by herself. She swept the attic floor and tidied up. The daylight is rapidly fading and lengthened shadows are beginning to form on the far wall of the attic. Jane closes and latches the opening behind her. Jane begins her descent down the ladder. She pauses for a moment and listens. Jane hears a strange sound that seems to be coming from up above her, in the attic. She recognizes the faint sound of the rocking chair squeaking as if someone was slowly rocking back and forth in front of the window overlooking the mountain.

The chair had made the exact same sound when she had rocked in it, just moments earlier. The hair on the back of her neck stands on end. Jane tries to breathe slowly as her mind races. She starts to go back up, but as she moves her hand toward the latch to open it, something tells her not to. She reaches out her hand, and it hovers above the latch, and it stays there for a moment. *Just leave it alone, Janie girl. Leave it alone for now, it's for the best*, Jane can almost hear her father's voice softly echo in her ears. *Maybe it is best*, Jane thinks, *best to just give myself some time to try and sort everything out.* So, Jane does just that. She pulls her hand back away from the latch and begins her descent back down the ladder, once again. Once she is down on the landing, she stands motionless, listening.

The squeaking of the chair, rocking back and forth continues for just a few moments more. Jane stands there, with her hands clasped in front of her, as if in prayer, with the tips of her forefingers resting lightly on her lips. She silently stares up at the latch, with her eyes fixed on the door to the attic above. *Ok, so what exactly am I supposed to do, now? What could all of this possibly mean?* Her thoughts race as she scarcely breathes. *Was I supposed to find the cache of journals this time, too? Or should I have just left it alone?* Jane feels uneasy and draws in an unsteady breath. *That infernal creaking is just plain scaring the mush right out of me. It's crazy, but I honestly think I can still hear it. Surely I'm not just imagining all of this.* Even with everything that had happened to Jane in the house so far, she wasn't, by any means, at ease with it. She knew that she had to keep her wits about her, despite being scared silly at times. The feeling of that same heavy rock in her midsection, instantly lets her know that something's just not quite right about any of it. *Can't put my finger on it*, she thinks with her mind reeling, *but something's just not right about this. Most definitely not right.*

Jane tossed and turned the whole night through. She would eventually succumb to elusive slumber, only to awaken seemingly without reason, just a few moments later. Even though she was bone tired from all the physical work of the hard day, she simply couldn't turn off her mind and allow sleep to come. She finally gave up, got up out of bed and put on her slippers. She took the wooden box of journals and letters into the great room and switched on the lamp. With the box sitting on the coffee table, Jane stood in the glow of the lamp and stared down at it. Somehow, this time, she was full of apprehension about reading these journals. *What have they held, silently, for all these years?* This time was going to be hard for Jane and somehow, instinctively, she knew it. She picked up the journal and traced her finger lightly across the heart shaped center medallion in the center of the faded green velvet that covered it. She opened the book and said a quick prayer. *I know this has to be read, even though it's going to be painful. Poor Ollie suffered through so much in her life, and it just doesn't seem fair. Just how much torment can one soul take in a lifetime?* Many years had passed since Ollie had painfully written down her thoughts and still it's as fresh as if it were only yesterday, to Jane. Ollie's pain was palpable. Jane could feel it coming straight off the pages, as she held them in her hand. *Had Daddy known that these letters and journals were here? Had he known I would want to know? Or have these journals only been revealed to me?* Jane could only wonder about it now. There was no one left to ask these things.

She curled up with a thick blanket wrapped around her for warmth and settled in for a long night of reading. As she turned the page to begin, a small folded paper packet fell out. Jane caught it just as it was sliding off her lap. She turned it over, inspecting it carefully. The edges had been meticulously folded in an intricate manner that she had never seen before. She felt the fragile–looking, almost transparent paper and realized there was something tucked inside. She carefully unfolded it, and she found two locks of hair tied up in faded ribbons. One lock was longer and darker than the other one, and it hung in a ringlet. Jane stroked the smooth locks with her fingertip. Tiny locks of beautiful hair. Then it suddenly occurred to Jane. *These locks of hair belonged to little Minnie and Ruby. Tied up lovingly in ribbons and kept, tucked away, all these years. Amazing.* Keeping hair for a memory locket had been very popular years ago, and Jane remembered seeing items like this among her grandmother's things.

Jane turned her thoughts back to the journal with rapt attention. She smoothed the hair with her fingers, and she laid the locks carefully down on the cushion beside her. After one more glance at the hair, Jane turned her attention back to the page before her and began reading again.

9

Our hearts where they rocked our cradle,
Our love where we spent our toil,
And our faith, and our hope, and our honor,
We pledge to our native soil.
God gave all men all earth to love,
But since our hearts are small,
Ordained for each one spot should prove
Beloved over all.

~ RUDYARD KIPLING

JOHN WAS QUITE a fiddle player. He'd displayed his innate musical abilities at a very young age and had mastered the fiddle
easily in his early years. This was due in part, to the fine instruc-
tion by his father, an excellent musician himself. John practiced in
the evenings when the light on the mountain was slowly beginning
to fade, and the gently rolling hills of North Carolina were slowly
awash in a rosy shade of pink. John loved it when the sun began its
slow descent on the horizon and dusk fell in earnest. The fiddle was
only brought out in the evening, after the chores were all finished,

of course. His father had always insisted on this, and John adhered to his father's wishes without questioning.

John's deep love of twilight may have been because the coming on of evening signaled that fiddle playing was about to commence. But, John's affinity to evening could just have easily been explained by the beautiful peach and rosy glow on the mountain at each day's end. From his earliest memories, John had loved the coming of evening.

Once the lamp was lit in the front room of the Arrowood house and the room was bathed in a warm glow, the playing began. The fiddle in John's gentle, coaxing hands produced a lilting tune that carried itself far over the mountain and up along the highest ridges. The music always evoked an unspoken longing for days gone by, in his father. But as he played, John only saw the faraway look that passed over his father's eyes. John never glimpsed the beloved scenes from the past that his father saw. Countless evenings were spent by the roaring fire, as the family all played together. These times were held dear in the hearts of this close family and many fond memories were made. John usually played more often than the rest and his father would listen intently while tapping his foot and nodding his head.

James Hensley Arrowood had a soft spot for his son, John, and regarded him as hands down, the finest musician in the family. But, he tried hard to not let his true feelings show to the others. John only knew that his father delighted in the music, and for John, that was more than enough reason to play. Seeing the joy in his father's eyes inspired him to learn to play even better over time. He became quite masterfully skilled, as the years wore on. The whole Arrowood clan that lived along Jack's Creek in Yancey County was known, far and wide, as a family of exceptionally fine musicians. The girls in the family were equally skilled musically and often joined in. The boys were growing fast, and they all were quite individual in their way of thinking and doing, but they had a true and close bond between each and every one of them. This bond continued for the duration of their lives.

There had always been a deep love bond within this family; more than enough love to see them each through whatever hard times that came. After John's uncle had passed, the family grew quite a bit. John's young cousins were taken into the home and soon they were all just like siblings, in the large Arrowood home place.

By the time 1812 had rolled around, England and France had been at war for many years. The Embargo Act of 1807 had just about ceased all coastal trading. This embargo had caused more harm to the United States than it had to any other country. The British were constantly trying to increase their efforts to prevent the passage of ships out on the high seas. The British searched passing vessels arbitrarily, rationalizing that their nationals could easily be stowed away beneath the decks of any of these ships. They searched for anyone that could be hiding to try and dodge serving in the British military. The British forces then forced thousands of American seamen into service with the British Royal Navy, against their will. This action did not set well at all, with young John Arrowood. He was only fifteen years old, but this action infuriated him and immediately, he was more than ready to join in the fight.

Many of their neighbors had also had enough of Britain's hostile acts, but some were still quite divided in their way of thinking. There was talk among some that America had been bullied for many years by Britain, so why in the world we should get so upset about it now? John knew that they would only continue bullying until they were confronted. John, for one, was more than ready to confront Britain. He knew that we had to protect our seas, no matter what.

President James Madison declared war on Britain in 1812. President Madison's wife, Dolley, was a native of North Carolina. Many North Carolinians were naturally quite proud of that fact. After awhile, the President had finally had more than enough of Britain's hostile acts toward the Americans. In 1813, the British troops made landfall for five consecutive days. They landed right on the banks of Ocracoke Island, North Carolina. The troops soon marched their way to the capital in Washington, D.C.

Shortly before the troops arrived, Dolley and the President had made their quick escape. The British wasted no time. They torched the President's residence just moments after their arrival in Washington. Dolley turned around in the fleeing carriage and looked back, frozen in horror. She watched helplessly as the flames lit up the nighttime sky. Eager to get to safety, the driver whipped the horses, as the carriage sped away. Dolley looked back one last time at the frightening scene, with tears streaming down her face. She watched in horror as her beloved home burned. She watched the red flames as they grew ever larger, filling the horizon off in the distance. Luckily, Dolley had kept a cool head in spite of the imminent danger. As soon as she had been alerted that the troops were close by, she had hurriedly grabbed up the presidential silver and various documents that she felt were important. She had taken a knife and cut the portrait of George Washington away from its frame, as it hung on the wall in the President's office.

America was at War. News of it spread quickly, and even those that lived in the isolated mountains knew about it before very long. John heard the call to arms loud and clear, as did many other young patriotic hearts. In the year of 1813, John Arrowood was still very young, but he was wiser than most his age. He was rather headstrong in his thinking, as well. So, in 1814, when his brother Jesse received his papers summoning him to serve in the military, John knew without a doubt just what it was he had to do. Drafted or not, Jesse was his brother and sometimes you just have to do what your heart leads you to do.

Jesse's physical health had continued to deteriorate as the years passed. John knew that Jesse's unwieldy gait alone could easily cause him to become entangled in just about any obstacle that he met up with along the path. Marching through the rough terrain into battle was just no place for him to be. Even as young as he was, John's mind was set, and there was no deterring him once his sight was set on a certain course. John was determined to fight. John soon enlisted in Jonesboro, in Washington County, Tennessee. He joined up as a substitute for his brother, Jesse. Then, he traveled nearly a hundred miles out to Knoxville, where on September 20, 1814, he was mustered into service as a Private in Captain Abner Pearce's Company of the 3rd Tennessee Militia. Representatives of Britain and the United States of America signed the peace treaty at Ghent, Belgium, officially ending the War of 1812, on Christmas Eve in 1814.

John served until that following spring and was then discharged at Fort Williams in central Alabama, on April 10, 1815. After he had sold his final pay voucher to a man in Western Tennessee, he returned once again to Jonesboro. He soon made his way back toward the rolling misty mountains that he called home. Jane thought, *The mountain called him back home, just as she does us all.*

John received a modest plot of land that had been set aside for him by his father, at an early age. As soon as he returned home from his military service, John took possession of the land and built his cabin on the most level section of the parcel, situated at the base of the mountain. Most of the land consisted of rolling hills and deep gorges, and John figured that the protected flat area would be the best location for his home. He quickly started to clear the land and fell the trees. His brothers, William, James, and of course, Jesse, came and helped him with the logging of the larger timber. Jesse did all that he could, despite his limited abilities, and came, for the most part, to support his brothers. With the brothers working together diligently, the work went quickly. As the siblings stood shoulder to shoulder; the laughter and conversation flowed freely, and the task at hand seemed much lighter.

Just as soon as the cabin was complete, John settled right into his cozy new home. Bright and early the next morning, after spending his first restful night in the cabin, John went out to gather some more kindling for the fire. He had awakened to find that the morning had dawned quite misty and wet. There had been a soaking overnight rain that had lasted for several hours.

John walked out and feeling quite content, he looked out over the meadow. There, in the clearing not very far away from the cabin, was a large bear wallowing in the thick mud. Young John stood still, mesmerized. He silently watched the large beast as it rolled and rocked in the muck. The large bear seemed to be totally oblivious to the fact that a human now lived in the small cabin nearby. John chuckled to himself, amused at the sight of the bear with its feet stuck up high in the air. The bear seemed to enjoy the wallowing thoroughly, and finally, it stood up, shaking itself free of the excess mud that flew off in clumps every which way. John smiled, and the thought came to him quickly. *I will call this land, Bear Wallow.* And from that very day forward, that was what it was called.

John planted apple trees down along the creek that flowed through his land and raised bees in hollow logs for their honey. He planted a large garden that very next spring, following the way of his family for many generations. Life was good in Bear Wallow, and John wanted for very little. He lived on for nearly a full year, with nothing lacking. Nothing, as John soon realized, except for female companionship. He had set his sights just a few months back on a pretty young girl by the name of Frances Barnett that lived over in Harrell's Township. He thought earnestly about making a call on Miss Frances. Now that he had his homestead ready, he figured the time was right to make a social call on the pretty little lady, sure enough.

The wild, untamed wilderness of the mountain lay right outside the door of the little cabin, and John couldn't have liked it any better. Living in a city had never been the sort of life that John would have chosen. It didn't seem to him to be a proper way of life, for anyone. There was no way he would have lasted even one full day in a city and John knew that to be a fact. John felt as if all the townsfolk were cooped up just like chickens, just as in all the cities through which he had marched. All the houses were set too close together along the streets bordered with white picket fences and such. *No fences were ever going to keep me penned up, no sir. No dang fences are ever goin' to corral John Arrowood. Not if I can help it, they sure ain't.* The land that had broad blue skies above and mountains with hidden coves and valleys beneath it, as well as clear cold streams, was where he wanted to live out his days. This untamed misty mountain was his home and would remain so, forever.

Wide open spaces and rolling mountains called out to the restless soul that dwelled deep within John. These mountains were in his blood, and he had always heard the call. Perhaps it was a deeply rooted blood memory, coursing deep in his veins, but John didn't know exactly why he felt the way he did. But, he knew that the deep bond with the land would remain in his heart forever. This old mountain beneath his feet was his home. John was young and free in the year of 1816, living on his own land in his little cabin, up in the misty highlands of what was then known as Yancey County, North Carolina.

Several months later, John rose hours before the sun and pulled on his patched and well-worn britches. Next, he laced on a pair of soft doeskin leather boots. He stretched and absently scratched the bristles on his unshaven chin and yawned loudly. He was still quite sore from pulling heavy logs and hoisting them up into place while helping construct a cabin for his cousin.

Wincing slightly, he pulled his suspenders up onto his broad shoulders, and he made his way over toward the cabin's fireplace. He absently ran his hand through his dark and tousled curls. The cabin had begun to cool somewhat, as the fire had dwindled down during the early hours of the morning. He added a few more logs and stoked the flames until the fire was roaring and blazing rosy red. The red fingers of flame flickering in the rock hearth darted quickly up towards the chimney. John paused for a moment, seemingly mesmerized by the red and orange glow of the flames. John's mind drifted back to the day of Jesse's funeral. Somber faces and bleak expressions, along with a dark and brooding overcast sky had set the scene for the sadness that they all had felt that day. *It just ain't right to outlive your brother. It just ain't the way that things are supposed to be in the natural order of this life.*

Jesse was nearly three years John's senior, but John had always felt as if he were the elder brother. Jesse was smaller than John in stature, and a world more meekly mannered. John had always felt overly protective of Jesse, even from an early age. Living still, when your brother is dead way too young, can make a man feel mighty guilty for even drawing a breath. Seeing his mother so distraught over losing Jesse was just about more than he could take, that day. John had never seen her hurt like that in his whole life. That day was the blackest day that John had ever lived through, and he seemed forced to recall it, much too often. Dark overcast days and flickering flames were all it took to bring it all back in a flood. Sometimes just the smell of burning wood did it.

The old horse barn that his father had built many years before had burnt to the ground on the very same day of Jesse's funeral. Someone had forgotten to put out the torch that lit the barn, and somehow it had fallen over and caught the hay on fire. No one person had taken the blame for the fire outright, but just the same, they all felt responsible for it. The sadness and melancholy over the loss of Jesse soon turned to complete panic and disbelief as the barn quickly went up in smoke. Thankfully, the livestock had been gotten safely out and just in the nick of time.

The agony of losing his brother had caused the loss of the old barn to be of little consequence to John. But, his mother sure had taken it hard. It was a terrible day from start to finish, and John would just as soon forget about it. But forgetting was something that had just never happened, not for any of them. *Guess it never will happen, either,* John thought with a somber expression. *Momma's heart will never mend. She's just torn up over it.*

His brother Jesse had been born with a terrible limp. He had a weakness that ran along one whole side of his body, and a foot that was just wasn't quite right. The bones didn't align properly and it drew to the side awkwardly. Jesse had tried to cover it up, always making light of it. He had also learned to walk in such a way that only a very observant eye would have ever noticed it. But, it was certainly there, and it had remained.

Even as a young child, the limp became more and more visible as the day wore on. But Jesse and John never talked about it much. John could tell that it pained Jesse considerably to discuss it, so he just didn't bring it up. The tendons were overly stretched in his leg, and this malady adversely affected his gait, but not his demeanor. It certainly never bothered his attitude or his outlook on life. Jesse was a happy soul, and he constantly provided a much-beloved ray of sunshine within his family. Jesse had continuous pain in his leg and a severe ache in his foot that never left him. But, that intense pain was something that he would not have ever admitted, to anyone. He didn't want to be pitied; and even more so, he didn't want to be given any special treatment because of his infirmity.

John, who was most sympathetic to his brother's plight, would try his best to help Jesse without Jesse ever realizing it. Over time, John thought that he had gotten his occasional slight deceptions down to quite an art form. But, the truth was that Jesse had known all along what John was doing and he loved him all the more for it. John often did his brother's chores before his own, going at it hard, even before the sun had fully risen. John had never minded it. The bond between these two inseparable brothers ran deep and true. There were strong ties of love between all the children of James T. Hensley and Eliza Crowder Arrowood. Eliza was John's beloved mother's given name, but most folks that knew her well, just called her 'Lizey'. James and Lizey had a strong love for each other, and they passed that love down to their six children that made it through to adulthood. And eventually, they passed it on to their extended family made up of many nieces and nephews.

Jane lowered the journal that she held in her hand and gazed out the window. She saw the mountain that stretched out along the horizon and she smiled wistfully. *James and Lizey hadn't any clue that they would someday become my fourth great-grandparents. They didn't know that their son, John, would soon marry pretty little Frances and that they would eventually have a son, themselves, named Samuel Augustus. I wonder what they would tell me now, if they only could? Would they approve of me living here, up on the Roan? I would love to tell my third great-grandpa, John, that I fully understand the discomfort of being fenced in and cooped up like a brooding hen. I'd like to tell him that the same need for open spaces is something that has been passed down to me, as well. And for that, and many other traits that I have inherited, I am very thankful. Samuel and Sarah Ellender certainly had the love of these mountains ingrained deep within them both.*

Jane felt pride well in her heart for the amazing and loving family from whom she had descended. Jane bowed her head and offered up an earnest prayer of thanks for all of the many blessings she has been given.

Soon, Jane reluctantly decides that she has read quite enough for one night. She had nearly fallen asleep, and the journal had slipped from her hand, twice. *Sometimes, you just have to get some rest, no matter how much you're dying to find out what happens next, girlie,* Jane thought to herself with a slight grin. She snarled her upper lip comically and then smiled as she unsuccessfully tried to stifle a yawn. She padded off in her socked feet to the bed. With yet another sleepy yawn, she reached out and clicked off the light.

Once she was covered up and the pillow was tucked up nicely under her chin, just the way she liked it, she was out and floating into dreamland in almost no time at all.

10

*I took a day to search for God, and found Him not; but as
I trod, by rocky ledge, through woods untamed, just where
one scarlet lily flamed, I saw His footprint in the sod. ~*

~ WILLIAM BLISS CARMAN

*Yet you do not know what your life will be like tomorrow.
You are just a vapor that appears for a little while and
just vanishes away.*

~ JAMES 4:14

THE WINDS BLEW gently high atop the Roan. Floating along
in those winds, were low murmuring whispers that made
their way down the mountain, and straight to the house where
Jane slept. She dreamt restlessly as the wind continually whispered
to her, from just outside her window. The whispers repeated and
seemed to almost chant in the wind, but they were never heard by
human ears. The tree branches scraped against the window-panes,
as if they were long, spindly fingertips reaching out, and scratching
for attention.

The wind fueled the movement of the limbs, so it seemed as if the wind itself, was reaching out toward Jane, seeking her. Jane slumbered silently, behind that glass pane. She was covered up snuggly under the old quilt, and she simply dreamt on. The tree reached out toward her again, but the seeking fingertips never touched her. Jane continued in her deep sleep, not moving even as much as an inch all night. Lately, her dreams had been very intense. When she slept, it was as if she had fallen off a ledge into a black, bottomless chasm. In that deep and dark chasm of sleep, she was motionless and almost catatonic. It was in this state that the voices came to her more easily, and the whispers in the dark recesses of her mind echoed over and over.

Jane heard someone call out her name repeatedly, and she struggled to answer through the thick fog. Although she could hear them quite plainly, she couldn't see clearly from where the voices came. Answering seemed nearly impossible, but somehow it seemed not to matter at all. Her name was called again and again throughout the long night, but she never remembered it at all come morning.

The wind slowly subsided and the branch appeared somewhat elongated and distorted in the shadows, still reaching out toward the window. In the dim light, it seemed almost to retract and morph slowly back into its original shape. Later, as the early morning's light took on its familiar rosy glow high atop the ridge, it was nothing more than an ordinary branch. Jane never saw anything of this nature, outside of her dreams. She only saw the same familiar tree standing just outside her window. Jane saw the same tree that had been there for many years, standing almost as a guard over the house. Out of the corner of her eye, she caught the movement of the tree branches in the wind right outside the window. *After all these years, the wizened old tree still stands guard right outside this old house that is now, my very own,* Jane smiled with the thought.

She stretched out languidly, and her pink toes slowly peeked out from under the edge of the quilt. Her troubling dreams and the whisperings of her name were completely forgotten in the bright morning sunshine. She didn't know that the old threadbare quilt that she had slept beneath had once been wrapped around the 'other' Jane, of long ago. It had once covered *the* Jane of the balds as she had shivered from the extreme cold of that miserable, frozen night out on the mountain.

The old hand-stitched quilt had been stored away for many years and then it had slowly made its way to Ollie as a gift. Ollie had wrapped the quilt up lovingly in paper and placed it in the trunk for safe-keeping. Then, Jane had found it, still tucked away, all these years later. It was almost as if the quilt had known who it should belong to, and it had waited upstairs in the shadows, for her to find it and cherish it, once again. The latch on the old trunk clicked audibly in the shadowy house. Then, the other latch clicked, just as if someone had opened it. The creak of the hinges sounded out into the darkness, and the moonlight fell on the old gun and glinted. The idea was in Jane's head as soon as she had opened her eyes that morning. It had somehow formed without much thought, and she quickly knew that she was going to take a hike, even if just for a short way, out on the Roan. She didn't know that someone had told her in a whisper to go up on the balds that sunny early morning. She only felt the undeniable urge to go.

The sun was shining bright and despite an unexpected coolness to the air, a walk seemed greatly appealing. Jane grabbed an extra jacket from the chair near the trunk, just in case it was windy and maybe just a tad too cool, and she tied it around her waist. She stopped short in mid-motion, and glancing back she saw that the trunk lid was open. She thought, *Well, now, that's odd. I don't remember leaving that open.* She stood and stared down at it, pondering over it for a few moments as she pensively bit her lower lip. She was positive that she didn't open the trunk looking for anything. The gun was lying on top of the folded quilt, and she distinctly remembered that she had wrapped the gun up in the cloth and tucked it away, down beneath the quilt.

Jane didn't like to touch the gun but she didn't know why, not exactly anyway. She just knew for sure that she didn't like it. She decided to wrap the gun back up in the cloth and place it back underneath the quilt. She just somehow felt better knowing that it was hidden from sight. She knelt down in front of the old steamer trunk and stared closely at the gun. Suddenly, and without any conscious memory of doing so, Jane found that she was holding the gun as if she planned on firing it. Her hand was firmly wrapped around the trigger.

Bewildered, she stared down at her hand that held the cold metal grip of the gun. Jane felt dizzy and somewhat disoriented. She shuddered and dropped the gun. It fell from her hand and landed on the quilt, which effectively cushioned it from the fall. Jane's state of panic rose immediately, and her heart pounded heavily in her chest. *Why in the world did I pick up that gun like that? What was I thinking? That's just so crazy.* She reached out and then suddenly pulled her hand back with apprehension. Jane quickly pushed the gun over and into the cloth, trying to touch it just as little as possible. She tucked the bundle down deep between the folds of the old quilt. She reached forward, closed the trunk lid, and snapped the latches closed quickly.

Still trembling, Jane held her hand to her chest and rubbed it. The hand that had held the gun tingled oddly and throbbed. Jane stood up and backed slowly away from the trunk. She sat down on the edge of the bed, still staring at the trunk and tried to sort out her thoughts. She tried, but she couldn't come up with a plausible explanation for what had just happened.

Later, after resolving to put the incident behind her, Jane stepped into her slip-on sneakers and headed out of the house. Standing on the porch, she drew in a long full breath of the clean morning's air. As usual, Jane was instantly struck with the unmatched beauty that the Roan possessed. Even when the blooms are not quite ready to burst forth onto the scene, the mountain has boundless beauty to share with those who care to venture out. Colors are abundant no matter the season up on the Roan; even the drab grays of winter when the land is still slumbering, varies greatly.

The hike proved to be quite invigorating, and she soon realized that the extra jacket wouldn't be needed, after all. She made her way up Carver's Gap and suddenly emboldened, she was inspired to trek out over the balds on the Roan. She had been instinctively making her way to Jane's Bald all along, but she didn't consciously realize it. Whenever she heard the mountain call out to her, Jane simply had to go.

She didn't question it; she simply had always figured that it was some ancestor's blood droplet coursing through her veins that caused her to hear the quiet, still call of the mountain. She loved this mountain with all her heart, just as surely as if it were *her* mountain, entirely. Sometimes she felt down deep, that it truly *was* her mountain. *Just as Sarah Ellender felt that it was hers*, thought Jane with a smile. Suddenly, the phrase *'blood memory'* echoed in her mind. Jane silently figured that a 'blood memory' was just some innate tiny bit of some substance or other; that was passed from each generation down to the next. She felt certain that her own daughter-to-be would someday hear the same quiet call from the mountain. It had to be that just one tiny microscopic bit of blood bound you, to wherever it was that you belonged. *There's an invisible band of considerable strength, contained in that tiny speck of blood*, she mused to herself. She tried not to over-think it; it was, simply, what it was. *It is, what it is, Girlie.*

The Roan was in her, and she was a part of the Roan, and she really wouldn't have wanted it any other way. *Maybe I am a little possessive when it comes to this wonderful old mountain, but somehow I think even that's perfectly normal*, Jane laughed lightly. *Maybe as an Arrowood I'm not the only one that feels protective of one of God's perfectly beautiful creations. I feel sure there are plenty others that would fight fiercely to protect the Roan. This mountain is a gem; without a doubt, a wonderful, precious gift from God. I am so blessed to be able to call this mountain, my 'home'.*

The sun softly illuminated the higher peaks and smooth grassy areas of the mountain, and transformed them into a golden and green dappled vista. It stretched out for as far as you could see. The various hues of the new green of spring bursting forth high up along the ridge were brilliant against the deep blue of the sky. *The sky looks almost as if it has been photo-shopped into that amazing color. It looks like it couldn't possibly be real*, Jane thought with a sigh. *God's perfect creations cannot be rivaled.* The Roan's beauty lives on. She is ageless and timeless. The same beauty before Jane now, was also seen through the eyes of Jane's ancestors. She walks along the same path that they, too, once followed. Now, that same trail connects with the Appalachian Trail and winds its way northward, right along the North Carolina/Tennessee border.

Jane stops as she gazes out at the misty beauty before her and breathes a heartfelt prayer of thanks. The Roan just somehow does that to you. *It humbles you and puts you smack-dab right in your place; right where you belong. You are only a speck in this vast, sprawling universe, and you surely feel that, here. You are only just a fleeting vapor. You simply cannot stand on her majestic rolling ridges and not feel the presence of the mighty Creator of this wonderful place. Be still and know that I am God*, Jane heard the familiar words echo in her head. *Surely this is why the people of the mountains laid their dead to rest high atop the peaks and rolling hills. They wanted them up where they would be closest to God, our creator*, thought Jane with conviction.

Allowing herself yet another pause to try and take it all in, Jane sighs and stretches out her arms, reaching upward toward the heavens. She always feels closer to God up here, where the wind blows freely, and the gnarled pines whisper ancient secrets quietly among themselves. Somewhere deep within Jane is indeed a blood memory. This mountain remembers her children and continually calls them all back home. Only a few can still hear the call echoing deep within their cells, but the call is always there. Jane made her way over to the bald on the mountain known as 'Jane's'.

Jane remembered the story told to her by her father many times, about two young girls that crossed the mountain, late up in the fall one year. The two sisters, Jane and Harriet, were hoping to cross over into Carter County, Tennessee, to visit with another sister. Jane had taken sick with the 'milk sickness' and had been quite ill for a time. She had postponed the trip, but, she felt that she had recovered enough to make it over the mountain. Early on, the mountain folk didn't know what caused them to become sick after drinking cow's milk. Many theories evolved alongside the old wives tales, but eventually it became known that the sickness came from drinking the milk from a cow, or eating the meat from a cow, after the cow has eaten a plant called 'White Snakeroot'. Snakeroot is a shade loving plant that grows in the area. It was this very same 'milk sickness' that killed the mother of Abraham Lincoln in the fall of 1818. Many of the cows were herded over the mountain for grazing, and some occasionally ate the poisonous plant in passage. When it was finally known what the cause was, the cows were fenced in, to prevent them from eating the snakeroot. Jane had recovered somewhat and wanted desperately to see her sister, so she set out to make the trip with her sister, Harriet. So, the two sisters struck out on their journey, but they had unwittingly waited too late in the season to make safe passage over the Roan before the cruel winter weather descended.

Weather changes real quick up on the mountain, quicker than you can just about shake a stick at it, her Dad would say with a curt nod. The wind turned bitterly cold and blew with a vengeance around poor Jane and Harriet. It quickly blew up an early snow storm that swirled the snow up into high drifts overnight. This simple, early snow storm soon turned itself into a full blown blizzard. Not only the frigid cold temperature endangered these two sisters, there were also hungry wolves and panthers prowling out on these ridges, as well. Jane had often shuddered during the retelling of the story by her father, as she thought of how unbearably frightened those two sisters had to have been, huddled together under a pine tree that offered little protection on that terrifying and bitterly cold night.

Jane's Dad could tell the story so well, that you could almost see it all unfolding as if it were happening right before you. Jane was sure that she could smell the cold crisp snow in the blowing wind as the story unwound. Her father would get all caught up in the moment, telling the tale. Jane's wide-eyed and rapt attention only fueled his fervor in the storytelling and everything seemed all the more real and intense. Jane smiled and shook her head remembering how delighted her Dad had seemed, telling the stories that kept her spellbound. *Only Daddy could tell a tale quite like that. The Arrowood's have a gift for storytelling, that's for sure*, Jane smiled.

Harriet had suffered terribly from exposure on that cold, snowy night. *With the first light of day, Jane had made her way back down the mountain to try and search for help. Her sister was just too weak to go any further, not even another step. Jane finally made her way over to the very first house she had come across and it turns out that they hadn't even made it very far from Carver's Gap. But by this time, Jane was nearly frozen solid herself*, Dad had sadly conveyed. Every telling brought sadness to his eyes, and he had certainly told the story more than once to Jane. *The man she found at the house was a Young if I rightly recall, or maybe he was a Clark, I can't remember which now*, her father often paused and reflected here, while telling the tale.

Jane smiled wistfully as she remembered how intense his expressions got as he ventured deeper and deeper into the story. She remembered the way that his brow would knit together and his blue eyes would cloud over when he got to the sad part of his stories. *Now, that fellow that Jane had managed to find up on that snowy mountain, why, he said nary a word, and he hitched up the horse to his wagon right away. Then he went straight on up that snowy old mountain, to try and fetch poor Harriet back down. She was just barely alive at that point, but not for very much longer. The poor thing just couldn't hold out after what she had endured up on that mountain. She just faded away and died, the very next day. It nearly broke Jane's heart to lose her sister. But after that, the bald became known as 'Jane's'. To this very day, it's still called 'Jane's Bald'.*

Jane's father would always look out into the distance at the end of the story, and a mist seemed to veil the sparkle of his blue eyes. All through the years, Jane had often wondered what caused the mist that settled over her dad's eyes from time to time. She'd never known what he'd been thinking about. She had never asked him outright, and he had never offered up an explanation. But Jane chose to let some things about the father she adored, remain a secret, just as he would have liked it to be. *Odd that this bald would eventually be named for me, as well*, thought Jane with a melancholy smile. *I think that I love it even more, because of it. It's definitely special to me, maybe more than all of the other beautiful ridges on this old mountain. I never thought that it was possible to love one area more than the other, but it seems I do.*

Jane breathed in deeply of the clean mountain air and again spread her arms outward and reached up to the sky as she hiked along. A huge blue expanse of open sky lay before her, and the rolling ridges stretched out as far as she could see in every direction. She was in her very own heaven at the moment, and she reveled in it. Not another soul was in sight.

Jane remembered that the Jane of 'Jane's Bald' lived to be way up in years. She purportedly lost her hearing as the years progressed and couldn't hear even very loud noises, or so it was told. Jane shook her head in sympathy as she imagined how it had to have been, not to be able to hear the wind whispering among the pines from high up on the mountain that she knew, and that she had to have loved, as well. Once you have heard that beautiful sound, it would be so sad never to get to hear it again. Jane longed to hear the Roan's whispering song, more than just about anything else. *Except for the ringing laughter of my sweetheart Jake, of course*, Jane smiled.

She walked out onto the huge outcropping of rock that stands just at the ridge overlooking Jane's Bald. Jane thought once again about the stories about the singing of the mountain. The Roan sings and it has for centuries. Even the Indians heard the song, way before the first settlers ever arrived on the Roan. *This mountain has been singing to anyone that will only listen, for countless centuries before my ancestors from Scotland and Ireland even found their way to her.* The eerie music that she makes has been likened to an animal's sound. Some don't hear it at all, but to many, it's very real. *Maybe it's the wind humming through the high grasses out on the balds. Maybe it's the wind singing over the ridges' edge and on through the trees.* No one really knows what causes the Roan to sing. But those that love her, know that she does. Jane made her way off the huge rocks and continued along the trail that leads down along Jane's Bald. The view was beautiful as the grasses swayed to and fro in the light breeze.

As she walked along, she wondered about the trail and where it led beyond the expansive view that stretched out before her. Maybe one day she and Jake would hike the trails over the mountain together. It would be a fantastic hike. She grinned to herself, thinking of how Jake will protest when she first casually mentions it to him. *He will groan loudly, in his usual, overly dramatic fashion. Then, after some time goes by, and he's had some time to digest it, eventually the idea will slowly grow on him. Then he will come around to the point of actually being excited about it.* Jane chuckled. She thought she surely knew him well enough to gauge his responses to most things, now. *What a wonderful man I have found for myself! Who knows what other gifts the mountain has in store for me? I honestly can't wait to see them, each and every one,* thought Jane with a wide grin.

As she made her way further up the trail, she saw the color of bright red dotting the green of the grass, off in the distance. The tall grass tips brushed her fingers lightly, as she held them out as she walked along. As she drew nearer, she could hardly believe her eyes. Jane broke into a run and quickly covered the short distance. There were dozens of lilies, blooming happily in the meadow grass. The red lilies danced in the breeze with their heads bowed low. Their heads gracefully dangled downward on their slender necks. These were Gray's Lilies. Precious and rare beauties, they graced the mountain from time to time, when the conditions were just right. It was a treasure to behold their timeless beauty, once again. Jane squealed a tiny bit, in spite of herself. It was hard for her to contain her excitement. *These are Ollie's beautiful lilies; the very same ones that were carved on her rocker.* What an unexpected treat to see these beautiful lilies blooming abundantly on either side of the path.

Jane turned slowly in a full circle where she stood intently scanning the horizon, and not another living soul was in sight. She so wanted to be able to share her wonderful find with someone. Sometimes beauty is just too special to not share, and this was certainly one of those moments. She felt as if this moment had somehow been reserved just for her and her alone. *How very blessed I am to see this,* Jane smiled with the thought.

The flowers seemed to be nodding their heads, and it reminded Jane of children's heads bowed reverently in prayer. She thought, *This certainly has to be the reason that I was drawn out here to walk the balds this morning.* Jane hung her own head just like the beautiful lilies and was thankful for being allowed to experience it. *It's such an amazing sight. The beautiful rolling green meadow with its grasses dancing in the sunlight, accented with the deep crimson of the lilies, is almost too much beauty to take in all at once.* A tear welled in her eye as she stood looking in awe at God's handiwork. *God has made this mountain so intensely beautiful, and now he has chosen to adorn it even more, with these beautiful lilies. God chose to make all this beauty simply for his children here on earth, to enjoy. What a wonderful, unimaginable love he must have for each and every one of us.* Jane marveled at the thought as she stood looking through the prisms of her own tears. She stood mesmerized for quite some time, watching the nodding heads of the lilies surrounded by the dancing green grass. As Jane stood quietly still, some moments later on the beloved ridge of the Roan, she reflected on the beauty that surrounded her.

Her thoughts quickly turned back to Ollie, and how she had lived such a terribly tormented life. *Why must she have suffered so? She suffered one excruciating loss after another. I hope heaven holds vast mountains and endless fields full of Gray's Lilies where Ollie can wander without a single care or hurt in her whole heart. The poor woman was never shown much mercy in this life*, Jane reflected. *She was always standing right on the edge of mercy, but almost never experienced any for herself. Standing right there at the edge, but somehow it had eluded her. It's just heartbreaking*, thought Jane.

Turning slowly, she took one last look out over the mountain before she headed back up the winding trail toward home. She made her way slowly, not wanting to rush, at all. As she walked, she pondered the strange sounds she had heard recently in the house. The reason for her being up there at all, among the spiders in the attic, was because she had somehow felt led to be there. *There is a time for everything. A time for every season*, Jane surmised. *Sometimes you just never know what each season holds in store for you. Sometimes even spring cleaning can bring you way more than you ever anticipated, and that's for certain, girlie. I really never thought that even more about the family would be revealed to me. Especially after finding a wonderful trunk full of treasures*, thought Jane as she walked along. *But, that just goes to show you that this life is full of surprises. Some surprises are good and some are bad. God never promised anyone, all clear sailing through this life. Things will come at you, from right out of the blue. You just have to trust that God will see you safely through any storms that may blow your way. I feel sure that Ollie held fast to her faith despite all the hard times she faced. God's love and mercy along with her strong faith saw her through the darkest times. I am so glad she had her faith to turn to. If God leads you to it, He will lead you through it, and that, girlie, is the honest truth. Now, what needs to happen next in my story, is for me to marry the man that I love more than anything before someone else comes along and snatches him up.*

Slowly a huge smile dances across Jane's face as she realizes that she would never have gotten to experience the joy of seeing the lilies had she stayed at the house as she had originally planned. She suddenly realized that she could very well miss out on her life's most wonderful moments, by not sharing them with the man that loves her so much. Jane felt sure that it had been God's plan, to send her up to the balds today. His plan was to show her finally, the way to go, and she felt positive about it. She knelt down in the sweet smelling grass warmed by the morning sun's rays and prayed a prayer of deep gratitude. Moments later she stood and quickly walked the rest of the path back to the house. A smile that was nearly as bright as the morning sun never left her face.

Breakfast was on her mind, now. She was nearly starving. Then, Jane's mind suddenly returned to the open trunk and the hold that the gun seemed to have had over her. Jane shuddered and absently rubbed the tingling hand that had held the gun. *I'm just not going to worry about this right now*, she thought. *There'll be plenty of time to worry over that, but not today, girlie.*

The sun's path illuminated the mountain in a golden swath as she took one last admiring look over her shoulder, as she stood on the porch before going inside. Upstairs in the nearly empty attic, the old rocking chair slowly began to move back and forth, and the floorboards beneath it creaked noisily. It was as if someone had sat down and started rocking slowly and contentedly. The squeaking of the chair was barely audible down below, as Jane puttered happily about in the kitchen.

Jane made herself some breakfast and poured herself a steaming hot cup of coffee. Jane reached over and turned on the radio and sang along as Patsy Cline crooned out 'Walking After Midnight' as it played on the local oldies station. She never heard a sound as the rocking chair slowly rocked up in the attic above her.

11

Then I set my face toward the Lord God to make request by prayer and supplications, with fasting, sackcloth, and ashes. And I prayed to the LORD my God, and made confession, and said, O Lord, great and awesome God, who keeps His covenant and mercy with those who love Him, and with those who keep His commandments, we have sinned and committed iniquity, we have done wickedly and rebelled, even by departing from Your precepts and Your judgments.

~ DANIEL 9:3-5

JOHN HENRY WAS *a tall and lanky sort of fellow. He had a strong jawline that was often set with determination, but he had kind and gentle eyes. I'd say that he got those gentle-looking eyes from his momma, Sarah Ellender, for sure. They were every bit as blue as hers were. They were every bit as blue as the sky in May. He was a God-fearing, good-hearted man, and there was never a doubt about that.*

John Henry was certainly an obedient and faithful servant of the Lord. He had heard the call to preach God's word at an early age, and he had accepted it, just as his father, Samuel, had predicted he would. The Reverend John Henry Arwood was a natural at bringing in the lost sheep of the flock, and no one could argue it. Honest words of conviction rolled easily off his tongue each Sunday as he stood tall in the pulpit delivering yet another fiery sermon to his devoted church members.

The House of Welcome Church was packed, as usual. The ample bosomed church ladies sat elbow to elbow in the wooden pews, with their paper fans flapping back and forth in time with the music. Their cheeks were rosy patches that grew even rosier as the service wore on. The children were packed in between the ladies like sardines in a tin. It was easier for them to keep a close eye on their broods that way. The heat inside the small church was stifling. It was hard for a body to even draw an easy breath, because the air was so heavy. Not even a hint of a breeze stirred through the open windows.

The women's pin curled hairdo's wilted fast underneath their store-bought hats, decked out with ribbons, flowers, and netting. Many hats were slightly faded and not exactly what you would call 'up-to-date' with the latest fashion trends, but the ladies in the isolated community were quite oblivious to this fact. The latest trends in fashion were always years late in coming to the isolated regions of the North Carolina and Tennessee high country.

The year was 1932 and boy-howdy, was it ever heating up fast in the House of Welcome Church. The humidity hung heavy in the air like a damp shroud on the lush green North Carolina mountainside. John Henry's fiery words were pouring out conviction onto the hearts of each and every backslider in attendance that morning. *A body could hardly tell if it was the intense heat of the hazy mid-July day or the fiery blast of the minister's words that caused the sweat to bead all along their brows and upper lips.* On this particular Sunday morning, each and every soul in attendance was sweating it out. *Reverend John Henry was practically on fire and nary' a one there could deny it.*

John Henry eventually got so wound up in the preaching of hellfire and damnation to the souls that sat in the sweltering heat before him, that he got winded several times and had to lie down on the front pew. He laid there until he had rested, his breathing had slowed, and he had gathered up enough strength to continue on with the sermon. He would wave a hand at the choir and they would spring into song as he slipped down on the pew and extended his lanky form out for a few minutes, to recover. *Why, he surely did stretch right on out on the pew, the entire full length of him. Now, he surely did that very thing. I tell you, he did. Now, preaching to a congregation of believers up in the mountains was not a thing that a body took lightly. No Sir-ee. Now, when the good people came out to hear themselves a'preaching, well, an honest preaching is what they got from John Henry. There just weren't no two ways to Sunday about that. It was hard work a'chasing the devil out from the hearts of hardcore backsliders. If anyone knew about that, now, why, Reverend John Henry Arwood surely did. The Devil's a black-hearted fellow. He's mighty mean and crafty. That Devil doesn't just up and run away when he's confronted, either. That ol' devil wants those souls and in the worst way, now. So, John just dug in his heels and made sure that the sermons that he was a preachin' were hard hitting and fast. His sermons had to be mighty powerful to get that mean ol' devil to budge an inch; I tell you. Conviction has to be felt in the very hearts of those afflicted, and it has to run deep and true. But if there was ever a preacher man up on that mountain or beyond, that could preach the devil completely gone; it was surely Reverend John Henry Arwood.*

John Henry had, of course, started out as an 'Arrowood' to begin with, then John's son, Spencer, shortened the name a few years back, and 'Arrowood' had become 'Arwood' in this branch of the family. It was easier to spell, and it was, of course, how the mountain folks pronounced it. *So, they just figured it was the natural thing to do, you see.* The preaching sometimes carried on until way up into the late afternoon hours. Baskets of delicately tender fried chicken; green beans seasoned with rich bacon drippings, and crispy pan-fried potatoes were tucked into the baskets lined up underneath the pews. That wonderful food was just waiting to be spread out, for a regular 'on-the-grounds' feed. *The smell wafting up from those baskets was enough to drive the little ones crazy, but not one dared to poke nary a finger in any one of those baskets. It was simply not done, and the children in attendance knew that better'n anyone. Waiting for time to finally eat was sure hard, and little ones drew mighty impatient, just as little children will do. If I were to tell the honest-to-goodness truth, there were even quite a few of the grown-ups that felt those mighty hunger pangs in their midsections as well, along about three o'clock in the afternoon on a Sunday.*

A cold biscuit slathered with Aunt Nora's wonderfully thick homemade apple butter was on the minds of just about everybody, as the afternoon wore on. Nora was John Henry's sweet little wife. She was every bit as fiery a preacher as John Henry was, when she hit her stride. She had felt the inclination to give her husband some pointers on how to go about the preaching, on more than one occasion. She loved John Henry with all her heart, but sometimes, they just didn't always see eye to eye on how to attend to the needs of a congregation. But, mercy me, that little woman could cook. I tell you what, now. My heavens, but she sure could. Even if the church members didn't feel any special heartfelt need for getting themselves all good and preached up, many came just so they could taste a bite of whatever delicious dish it was that happened to grace Nora's basket on that particular Sunday afternoon. That is, if the 'honest-to-goodness' truth was told, you know.

Reverend John Henry's wife, Nora, was sitting right down in front, as always. She seemed so demure and content sitting with her head bent slightly down, apparently lost in earnest prayer. By all appearances, she appeared quite meek and mild, but those that knew her well enough, well, they knew the truth to be a different story, altogether. She was a tiny woman in stature, but her demeanor was anything but passive. She held strong to her convictions and would often argue adamantly with Reverend John Henry. She would stand her ground when she thought he needed to preach on something in particular or in a certain fashion and certainly when she thought what he was preaching on was wrong.

Nora was brought up in a secluded area to an old mountain family where many strange superstitious ways were still closely practiced.

This difference in opinion caused minor rifts to brew occasionally between the couple. They had weathered many storms in their long marriage. But, even though the storms came, their love stayed strong and true. But that doesn't mean they didn't have occasional heated discussions that kept things lively in the Arwood house.

Nora believed in the old ways and was known as a 'dreamer' by many in the community. That, of course, meant that she had what you call the 'knowing dreams" Not all of her dreams would turn out to be spot-on, mind you, but some were actual foretelling dreams. Just as sure as the world, they were, now. She was not so quiet about it either, which caused John Henry some mighty distress on more than one occasion, I tell you what. He felt that the old superstitious ways went against God's teachings and sometimes he felt compelled to settle down her 'goings-on' about such nonsense.

Nora quietly went about her way, holding fast and adhering to many of the old ways of the mountain area, without John Henry hardly noticing most of the time. She had many odd ways, such as she believed that ghosts hated new things. *So, if it so happened that you were being haunted, you hung something new up over your door.* She was convinced that all the clocks in a house will stop at the exact moment of death of someone in that household. If they don't, you must stop them or else the spirit of the deceased will remain in the house. *She never laid her hat down on the bed, because that would sure as the world bring on bad luck, and in the worst way, I declare it would.*

It was her dreams of foretelling that caused this couple the most trouble, but she couldn't bring herself to keep quiet about something as compelling as her dreams. They were terribly real and lifelike to Nora, and she felt sure that not telling anyone, when she full-well knew what was about to happen, just surely had to be sinful. If she had been given the gift so that she could warn a body beforehand of impending doom or even significant trouble, then it was her duty as a good Christian to do so. So, that was Nora's private quandary. At least it was, until Reverend John Henry finally had his own foretelling dreams to begin as well. Things started to change quite a bit, after that.

12

A child's world is fresh and new and beautiful, full of wonder and excitement. It is our misfortune that for most of us that clear-eyed vision, that true instinct for what is beautiful and awe-inspiring, is dimmed and even lost before we reach adulthood.

~ RACHEL CARSON

LITTLE STEVE ARROWOOD was late getting back home, and he knew that he was most likely in big trouble. Time had somehow gotten away from the boy, yet again. When he was on his bicycle, he simply lost track of what time it was getting to be. He felt as free as a lark when he was flying along like the wind, on his trusty bike. The wind whistled past his ears and lifted his curly, light brown hair up and cooled his brow. The strap of his worn denim overalls slid off his bare shoulder, and he occasionally grabbed it and tugged it back up.

The worn out patches on the knees of his overalls, silently attested to all the 'stump jumping' and 'creek soaring' that he had attempted while he had been wearing them. His feet were bare and tough from going barefoot just about all summer long. Riding a bicycle on a steep downhill run had to be just about the greatest thing he had ever experienced in his young life. There was nothing more exhilarating than speed. The hill down Second Street, which was just a hop and a skip away from Lineberger Park, was his all-time favorite downhill run. It was for sure the best downhill run that Steve had made so far.

He wasn't supposed to have ridden that far away from Seventh Street, but sometimes the hill proved to be just too big a temptation. *He figured that if he pedaled just as fast as he could down Chestnut Street, he would be home before his father noticed he had ever been gone in the first place. Somehow kids always think they are smarter than their fathers, but for sure, they rarely are.* Steve smiled blissfully as he thought about how the wind had rushed past him as he had flown down that huge, steep hill. There was a slight hump in the middle of the downhill run, and if you hit it just right, you could even go a little airborne. *Boy-Howdy, now that was some more fun*, he shook his head smiling. *That was just as neat as anything I've ever seen. It's just about neater than the movies down at the picture-show, sure enough.*

He pumped his bicycle pedals only occasionally, as he mostly coasted down the grade of Chestnut Street and on toward the park. He figured that the downhill coast would help speed things up quite a bit, and get him home faster. His attention turned quickly as a small boy's thoughts sometimes do, and he thought about the creek that meandered through the park. He loved to jump that creek on his bike nearly as much as he loved that wonderfully intense downhill run on Second Street.

He made a quick decision to veer off course and make just one more pass over that creek. He used the 'better to ask forgiveness than permission' logic that sometimes governs little kid's mindsets. He was only seven years old, after all, and quite an adorable little fellow, at that. That cute part allowed him to get away with more than he even realized, especially with his mother, Maude. Now, his father was a different story altogether. Pat wasn't quite as quick to succumb to the cuteness. Lewis William Arrowood certainly had firsthand knowledge about things such as little boys and their ways. He was once a young lad, himself. He had told Steve this before but believing it was pretty hard for a kid of seven. 'Pat,' as his dad was known, had been quite a mischievous little boy. Pat tried his best to oversee all of his kids with a firm and steady hand, but one that was also gentle, filled with kindness and with love. There had been many times when Pat had turned away to keep from laughing out loud at the contrite little upturned face, as Steve pleaded his case with seemingly repentant, actual tears. Pat knew the score and he knew all about little boy's crocodile tears, but little Steve was unaware of this. Little Steve was certainly aware that Momma was the one that you turn to first; your odds were much better if she was there and standing by your side. Nobody was as quick to understand as a Momma was.

This day would prove to be altogether different. Steve had made this jump plenty of times and felt confident that he could do it once again. *Why maybe even blindfolded or with just one hand on the handlebar.* As he turned into the park he saw 'Old Man' Coletta, as Steve knew him, stopped over at Long's liver mush plant delivering a large block of ice. He had the ice hoisted up with a large hook and strap on the back of the wagon. An immigrant from Italy, Carmine Coletta was a kindly soul and very well-liked in the community, by both young and old. Most of the time, he walked along behind the wagon, as his horses led the way through town on his route.

Sometimes when the amiable Mr. Coletta stopped to talk to folks that lived along his route, the horses would grow impatient while having to wait. Then, the horses would start up all on their own, walking off down the road without him. Mr. Coletta would have to run after them to catch up. The horses could practically make the route by themselves; they knew the way so well.

Well, it just so happened, that on that particular day, Mr. Colletta was running a bit later than usual, on his weekly run. Carmine pulled his pocket watch out and checked the time. *Maybe, I was chatting just a bit too long today,* he silently admonished himself. Steve, meanwhile, had made his way up to the slight bluff that overlooked the creek in the middle of the park. He backpedaled his bicycle just a bit and gave himself a bit more height by rolling up the slope of the hill behind him. He imagined that his flaming red cape was glistening in the sun and flowing out behind him in the light breeze that suddenly stirred. He felt that the moment was just like the story in the comic books, when the hero with his cape billowing out behind him, saves the day. In his mind's eye, he saw the crowd of adoring spectators that lined the creek on either side, loudly cheering for him. He felt the excitement of the impending jump down deep in the pit of his stomach. The throngs of people that he imagined lining the creek were chanting his name, over and over, just like he had seen down at the show at the State Theater on Main Street.

Steve bowed slightly at the waist, while still sitting on the bicycle. He raised a hand to wave to all his imaginary adoring fans. Little Steve was grinning ear to ear. He got off his bicycle and walked it further still, up the steep hill behind him. He was hopeful that it would help provide him with enough extra momentum to make it across the creek and safely to the other side. He had done it before, but that knot that formed in the pit of his stomach was there again, large and solid feeling. It was quite a jump to make, especially for a small boy of seven. He knew that he had to get up enough speed, or he just might not make it over to the other side. He peered back at the ten-foot drop down into the rocky creek bed below, and the knot in his gut seemed to tighten up even further.

Steve had just about decided against trying the jump, but he turned back again and saw the crowd of screaming fans in his little boy's imagination and exaggeratedly saluted the crowd with a big smile plastered on his freckled face. With all the forced bravado he could muster, he nodded curtly to the screaming crowd down below. Steve decided just to go ahead and do it. At the top of the hill, the slope into the creek looked as if it closely rivaled that of the Grand Canyon. But, the screaming crowd of his imaginary fans eagerly awaited his triumphant deed. So, he took a deep gulp and jumped on the bicycle as his handlebars skewed wildly. He steadied the wobble as best he could. Then he held on tight and peddled that bicycle like the very devil himself was hot on his heels.

His speed built up fast as he practically flew down the slope toward the creek bank's ledge, and then it happened. The worst possible thing that could've happened went and did. He tried valiantly to control it at the very last second, but it was just too late. Steve hit a bank of soft sand that lay just at the edge of the drop that was hidden behind a large clump of Johnson grass. The bicycle careened wildly. The bicycle went airborne, wildly flinging skyward, and the little boy that was on the seat was suddenly lurched skyward as well. Steve was flung mostly separate from the bike, but one hand still held desperately to the grip of the handlebar. Steve had time to let out a frightened yelp of dismay and then came crashing down with a thud. He landed hard in the rocky creek bed. He tumbled and flailed about, head over heels, before finally releasing the considerable momentum he had built up. He came to an abrupt stop. Steve's head had taken a hard hit on a good-sized rock, squarely on the forehead. Little Steve was knocked out cold.

Old Man Coletta had stopped to watch the tiny daredevil's spectacular creek jumping feat from his vantage point across the way. He was up on the hill, out by the edge of the road. From there, he had a clear view of the creek and the hill.

When he saw the sudden turn of events, Old Man Coletta led his horse pulling the wagon quickly down the slope of the hill from Chestnut Street and into the park. As he made his way to the creek, his thoughts were in upheaval. He was frightened of what he might find once he got there. *Oh my goodness, but that little fellow took himself quite a nasty tumble, for sure he did*, he thought worriedly. He quickened his steps and made his way to the creek. The sight of that tiny sprawled out boy knocked out cold, nearly scared the living daylights out of Mr. Coletta. He yelled out frantically, "Madonna Mia!" as he took in the frightening scene below. Quickly he scrambled down the embankment. He gently gathered up the bloodied boy and cradled him in his arms. Carmine climbed up the uneven creek bank, slipping several times, as he fought to find traction in the sandy loam. He quickly laid Steve gently on his ice cream wagon. He knew exactly where to take him. He had made deliveries to Steve's parents before and he knew Maude and Pat well. He hurriedly turned around the wagon.

Once at the house, he called out from the yard, and Maude met him at the door. Alarmed, she took one look at the ashen face of her little boy and her knees buckled underneath her. She prayed aloud, "Lord Jesus, Please don't let my baby die." Maude was nearly six months pregnant and terrified beyond words. She hugged her belly and tried her best to breathe. She cleared the way as Carmine laid little Steve gently down on the bed. Maude sent Hilda to find Pat where he was working out by the barn. Little Ann stood trembling and holding on to her mother's dress tail. She watched with wide eyes as the frightening scene unfolded.

Maude cried out pitifully in a muffled sob as Pat came quickly to her side. Pat softly told her, "Everything's going to be alright." "Now, you're just going to have to get ahold of yourself, Maude, the children here are nearly scared to death." Maude calmed herself somewhat as his words registered and she motioned for the children to gather around her. She held them all close to her and whispered that everything was okay, and that God was in control. Hilda was ten, and she held reached out and took Ann's hand. They were both trembling with fear at the sight of their brother lying there, lifeless. Steve was unconscious, but still breathing.

The doctor was summoned and concluded that there was little that could be done at that point. These were the days when you just didn't go automatically to the hospital. Concussions or not, you just waited for the doctor to come to the house. The doctor was called to attend to you, and more than likely, he was the same one that regularly made house calls. Little Steve was unconscious all the rest of that day and through the night. Maude and Pat kept a bedside vigil and Maude prayed with intense fervor. The prayers were sent up nonstop and that very next evening the earnest prayers were, without a doubt, answered. Little Steve slowly opened his eyes and announced that he was hungry. He appeared to be okay. Maude breathed a sigh of relief and told him to lie still and not move around much. She had to explain to him that he had taken a nasty tumble. Steve closed his eyes and remembered. The imaginary crowd of adoring fans had simply vanished the moment that his bicycle had skidded in that sand. *No one much wanted to stick around to see what was gonna happen after that*, figured little Steve to himself with chagrin.

The good Lord was without a doubt watching over little daredevils in Lineberger Park, that day. Maude rejoiced and prayed prayers of earnest thanks that her little boy was alright. She knew that God had saved him, with certainty. Steve remained in bed for a few more days and eventually he returned to his old self. He did refrain from creek jumping, for awhile. Well, at least for the better part of a month, or so. Old Man Coletta had been rattled almost as much as anyone had been and continued to show his concern for the little daredevil. He made regular visits to the house to check on him, in the weeks that followed.

Maude and Pat became close friends with Old Man Coletta and were thankful he had been there for Steve, that day. After being told what had been done for him on that fateful day, Steve was very appreciative and credited Old Man Coletta for saving his life for the rest of his days. After his 'adventure' there have no doubt been many other misadventures by the tiny daredevils that came after him through the years, many right in that very same spot of the park. That creek seems to call and coax out the 'stunt man' in most of the local boys and year after year; it claims its victims, one right after another.

Jane remembered back to the first time her Dad had told her about his ill-fated jump back when she was just a child herself. They were attending a family reunion there at the base of the steep slope that overlooked the creek. It was the very same spot where he had made the jump many years before. Standing there, her Dad had wistfully looked over the edge of the bank, and at the creek bank down below, and shook his head with a light chuckle. He must have seen once again, that little red cape flowing out behind that little freckled face boy in his mind's eye, as he told me the story. *There's no doubt about it*, Jane thought with a smile, *he saw himself there, just as sure as the world.* Jane looked up from the journal that she held in her hand. She stared out into the room, looking at nothing, lost deep in thought. *This must have been written years after the incident had happened. The land wasn't called 'Lineberger Park' until years later, after it was donated to the city. Before that, it had been privately owned property. Of course, 'Seventh Avenue' was eventually renamed 'Laurel Lane'. Carmine Coletta continued to deliver his ice cream, in that old horse-drawn wagon. Then, he opened the store. Tony's Ice Cream is still on Franklin Boulevard. It's the favorite ice cream of the local folks, and that's for sure. And that certainly includes me. Thinking about it sure makes me want some of that delicious butter pecan.*

Jane slowly shook her head, thinking to herself, *Strange to think how close I came to not being here at all. Thanks to a tow-headed little daredevil and his trusty bike. Wild to think about it, but that same precious little boy, with visions of airborne bicycle stunts and leaps of fancy eventually became my dad.*

Jane heard her dad's words echo in her mind as she thought about her own first bike. *Janie girl, now don't you ride off too far from the house on that bike. Don't you go on off and do something crazy. I don't want you to get yourself hurt on that thing.* Jane laughed out loud at that thought. He had known all too well how easily a kid can think that they're invincible and that all superheroes can fly.

All you really need is a glistening red cape, after all.

Carmine Coletta

13

Trust in the Lord with all your heart, and do not lean on your own understanding. In all your ways acknowledge him, and he will make straight your paths.

~ PROVERBS 3:5-6 ESV

JANE HAD WANTED to go and explore a cemetery near Mountain City, Tennessee, for quite some time. She had begun searching for her ancestor's final resting places and in just a short time, it had become quite a quest. The Winters family that had lived on the mountain had a large brood of fourteen children. Seven of the children were good, so they were called the 'angels', and the other seven were pretty ornery, so they were considered the 'devils', or so the family legend went. Jane wanted to see if she could find them all; hoping to find her second great grandmother, Sarah Ellender's, siblings at the cemetery she had researched. She especially wanted to find Martin's grave. He was considered to be one of the Devil's. She decided to go ahead and go before Jake returned home, so she packed some cokes and a couple of sandwiches in a small cooler and struck out extra early one morning. The winding road in the country was so picturesque and beautiful that she couldn't help but stop a few times and snap photos of the old barns and country houses along the way.

As she was nearing the main part of town, she turned off onto a road that meandered around through the rolling hills and then down into a hollow. The small hidden hollow was tucked snugly between two small mountains. The road winded itself around and around, with each turn offering a progressively more beautiful view of the pristine valley, down below. Suddenly, there appeared immediately on her left, an exceptionally lovely view. The view was overlooking a white small farmhouse complete with a flagpole out beside the driveway.

Old Glory rippled in the light breeze, its stars and stripes shining brightly in the morning's sunshine. Jane's heart quickened at the sight. *Oh, sweet Americana, at its best,* thought Jane with a grin. *Gotta get that picture for sure!* She pulled the little red car over and rolled slowly to a stop on the side of the country road. Her tires crunched on the gravel as she pulled up onto a side road and switched off the engine. She got out and retrieved her camera bag from the trunk of the car. She tossed her keys into the bag as she pulled out the camera and quickly removed the lens cap. She pulled the bag's strap over her head and adjusted it on her side with one hand. The movement was made with the fluid ease of familiarity. With her camera in her hand, she made her way over to the overlooking hill, just above the quaint farm.

Picture taking was one of her favorite pastimes. She snapped a few pictures from this vantage point and quickly decided to go a bit further down the hill and closer to the farm. She wanted to try and locate a better angle for the picture. As she descended the hill, she heard an extremely strange noise that seemed to be coming from somewhere high above her. There was an electrical tower nearby, and Jane wondered if the sound was being emitted from it, or maybe from the lines attached to it. Jane glanced quizzically skyward and pivoted her head around and around trying to determine the source of the strange sound. It was almost an 'other worldly' type of sound.

Whatever that is, it's certainly bizarre. The noise was like nothing she had ever heard before in her whole life. It started out low, and it gradually grew to a deafeningly loud crescendo, reverberating off the hills that surrounded her. Then, all of a sudden, she saw it. There, cowering over on the hillside was a small donkey with its head hung low. The donkey was looking at her with one single eye that was opened widely, staring in her direction. It was apparent that the poor donkey was in a state of extreme distress. *Oh, my, it looks positively terrified*, Jane thought compassionately. The little donkey kept its head down low. It almost seemed as if it were trying to make itself appear even smaller than it was. Jane thought, *If a donkey can cringe or cower, then that's exactly what that poor little fellow's doing.*

Apparently, it thought that by keeping itself small, that Jane wouldn't be able to see it standing right there before her. The little donkey was sure hoping that it was invisible, and it was painfully obvious. Then the strange sound came again, amazingly loud. Still not quite believing, that the unearthly sound could possibly be anything except a humongous hovering alien spacecraft, Jane searched the blue skies above her, once again. Unbelievably, all she saw were some fluffy white clouds. Then she looked once again at the small pot-bellied donkey. It had its mouth opened wide, as it brayed. The donkey sucked in another long breath, and that strange sound suddenly filled what seemed like the whole valley, once again. The sound amplified itself and bounced off the surrounding hills with such force that it was truly astounding.

Jane was so startled that she froze for a moment, standing there wide-eyed. Then, she suddenly backed up. Her feet slipped on the grass and she nearly fell. She clutched her camera close to her. She searched all around for anything that could've possibly made that excruciating racket. She quickly covered the ground between herself and the car, still backing up the hill. She never turned to flee; she was too afraid to turn her back to whatever it was that had made that awful noise. Instead, she kept her eyes focused intently in the direction that she believed the terrible sound had come from. Once she had clamored to the top of the steep hill, she was puffing from exertion. The donkey sucked in air and brayed once more, and the deafening sound filled the hollow.

The light bulb flickered to sudden life above Jane's head. *The little donkey was making that racket, all along! A tiny pot-bellied donkey had me scared so silly that I nearly wet my pants.* A slow smile slid onto Jane's face. Then she grabbed hold of her waist and laughed out loud when she realized that she had 'just had the mush scared right out of her' by a little-bitty fat bellied donkey. *All of a sudden that little fellow must've looked up and there I was, standing there, holding my camera. It thought I had just appeared right out of thin air,* Jane thought giggling. *So, then the little donkey had done all it knew to do and had screamed out in fright in its peculiar donkey scream.* Jane came to a sudden revelation. *Donkey screams sound very much like a huge 'Martian mothership' is trying to land, right there beside you.* Still holding her midsection, Jane belly laughed at how silly she was. *Good grief, girlie. Well, whoever watched that, sure got themselves a show.*

The photo she intended to take was completely forgotten at this point. She reached over and leaned on the car as she tried to catch her breath, still giggling. As she was wiping tears from her eyes, she saw a quick flash of red through the trees. A red truck was passing by on the road that lay just below her through the trees. Her giggling quickly subsided, replaced with a sudden quickening of her heart. It was a truck that looked almost like Jake's, but she was soon sure that it wasn't his. Her heart quickly fell, and she suddenly realized just how much she missed him. *Soon, girlie, he'll be coming back soon,* Jane thought. A light smile played on her lips, and she chuckled once again, thinking about the tiny donkey. *You're honestly not right.*

Once back on the road, she made her way up to the tiny cemetery, situated on a knoll. The grass swayed in the bright sunshine as she made her way along, amongst the headstones. She didn't find a marker for Martin, but she knew in her heart that he was there.

There were numerous other markers with the name 'Winters' scattered throughout the cemetery. They were all descendants of his line. She paused and said a prayer as she wandered among the graves, just as she always did. *I am becoming a regular graveyard rabbit*, Jane thought with a grin. *These old cemeteries certainly fascinate me. They are truly 'outdoor museums', each and every one. Each grouping of stones can tell you the story of those souls buried here.* Jane remembers something she had read some time back, about death being the greatest equalizer of all. *No one is more special than anyone else, here. Nothing distinguishes the wealthy from the poor here, in this nearly forgotten cemetery.* Even the lofty grandiose achievements of some of these long-gone souls are not compared to those that seemingly squandered away their days on earth. Both prince and pauper all buried side by side in the same plot of ground. *Sure does make you think*, Jane mused.

Jane looks wistfully back, once again, at the old crumbling and leaning headstones. She turns and slowly makes her way back to her car parked just down the hillside. Many thoughts run through her mind as she contemplates the drive back home. Jane thinks, *I've had quite a day, and I still have a huge decision to make. I can't put this off any longer. I have to get over this fear and move forward sometime. Life just won't wait forever.* It's a decision that's going to have to be made soon, and she realizes it. It has to be made before Jake comes back home.

Jane sits in the car, with her hands resting on the steering wheel for a few moments. She glances back up the hill at the cemetery and finds herself lost in thought, once again. Then after a few moments of reflection, she reaches in and pulls her cell phone out of her purse. She wonders about the reception and if she can even get a signal. She looks to see if there are enough bars on the screen. Wonder of wonders, up on this knoll there is a slight signal.

She dials the number of her girlfriend, Patti Duncan. *Patti always knows exactly how to say whatever it is that I need to hear. That sweet girl always knows how to tell me, with crystal clear simplicity, which path is the right one. She's seen me through tough times in my life, and I haven't even taken the time to talk to that sweet soul, in months.* Jane felt instantly ashamed of herself. *Seems we don't reach out to those we truly need in our lives until our desperate moments demand so. Why is that so messed up? Why does life always seem to come at you so fast?* Jane waits for Patti to answer the phone, listening to the purr of the phone in her ear. *Hello?*

And with that, Patti, the sweet and familiar 'voice of pure reason', is on the other end of the line. Jane smiles and closes her eyes as relief washes over her.

14

THE NEXT MORNING, as Jane walks down the hallway, she pauses when she comes to her Grandmother Maude's photo. It hangs on the wall beside her grandfather's picture. Jane had hung a collage of pictures on the hall wall, of her ancestors down through the generations just a few months back. She was fortunate to have found most of the old pictures in the house. Each one was precious to her.

Jane often paused at her grandmother's picture to say a quick prayer for her or to simply reminisce about her. Jane had always firmly believed that prayers help everyone, no matter what the person's circumstances may be. *Even if you are already on the other side, you still need prayers sent up every now and then,* thought Jane with misty eyes. *Surely it can't hurt to pray.* She missed her grandmother terribly, in so many different ways. The bond between them was undeniable. Some people simply connect on a whole different level than most do in this life, and she and her grandmother just always had that special connection.

Jane missed the way her grandmother's long dark hair smelled like flowers after she had just washed and rinsed it with the cool rainwater she had gathered up in a basin. That smell was one of Jane's fondest memories, she supposed. Jane remembered combing her grandmother's dark long tresses and gently twisting the lengths and fastening them up with bobby pins, in what Maude called laughingly, 'kissy-curls'. They had spent many hours together in the cool of a summer's evening sitting in the rocking chair together as her grandmother read to her from her worn Bible. Jane sought that wonderfully warm and secure place, tucked deeply into her grandmother's side, whenever the world threw more at her than she could handle.

Grandma's love had always been there for her. That love, constant and reassuring, was always right at the end of Jane's outstretched fingertips. Like a rock, her love anchored Jane. What a comfort it had brought her, to know that her grandmother would always be there for her. Nothing quite compared to that feeling of complete security. She missed the smell of the sweet lilac sachet that Maude wore whenever she got dressed to go out. Sometimes she would hold the sachet jar down to a level where Jane could reach it, and she would allow her to dip her tiny finger down in the jar. Jane would dab a bit of that wonderfully luscious fragrance behind her own ears, as well. Nothing was quite as wonderful as smelling just like your grandmother, or at least thinking that you did.

Her hands were always gentle and soothing, especially when Jane ran a fever or had some sort of sickness that seemed to come almost weekly in her younger years. Grandma always knew what to say or do, to ease the misery, without even giving it a second thought. *A grandmother just naturally knows these types of things. It must be a special gift from above, which God grants only to them.* Jane unknowingly had a tear to escape and slide down her cheek as she gazed at her grandmother's smiling face peering out from the photograph. She missed the way her bare toes would pat the rug to rock the chair back and forth, in her soothing methodical fashion. Maude was barefoot almost always, but she did love to wear her high-heeled shoes, from time to time. Jane missed the way her material and lace, that she stored on the back porch in the summertime, smelled. The whole house smelled like chicken and dumplings simmering on the stove and magnolia blossoms floating in a bowl of water sitting by the kitchen sink. It always had that 'lived in' and comforting smell. It always smelled just like 'home' to Jane.

The whirr of her grandmother's sewing machine could lull Jane into an instant state of bliss. *Oh, that wonderful old Singer sewing machine.* Jane often perched down beneath it and insisted on pushing the pedal back and forth while Maude tried to sew. *Just imagine how annoying that had to have been. But, she only smiled sweetly down at me and allowed me to do it. She knew that I thought for sure that I was helping,* Jane thought with a shake of her head and a sigh. Jane remembered each corner and every nuance of that house filled with love on Seventh Street in Gastonia. The house sat on the street that eventually came to be called 'Laurel Lane'. It was her destination of choice for comfort, and she had traveled back often, through the years, in her mind, as well as in her heart.

It was where contentment and peace still lived in the heart of the child that she once was. That same child from years ago still lives down deep within the now, all grown-up, Jane. *I guess there's still a small bit of the child that we once were, tucked away down deep in all of us,* Jane thought. *It's like a precious piece of heaven tucked safely away, saved for another day.* Her grandmother Maude was truly like no other. Jane was certain that she was the best grandmother in the whole world. *If anyone knew Maude at all, why, they would have no other choice than to agree wholeheartedly with that statement,* Jane smiled genuinely at that thought. *Although, I'm sure that everyone must think the same about their own beloved grandmother. Oh, Grandma, how I miss you. How I wish I could step back in time and walk right into that photograph to be with you. I have so many things that I would so love to talk over with you. So many things that I would love to tell you; so much has happened. I may be grown up now, but a girl always needs her grandma.*

Maude Rose Hull Arrowood

The days stretched on for Jane, as she waited for Jake to return. She read from the stack of journals and letters, almost every evening. The reading helped the time to pass by, much more quickly. She read the journals and letters intently, and each time she read, she was instantly transported back to the years of long ago. She stepped back into those days, with each turn of the page. Jane realized that it was a true gift that she had been given, to have such a rare glimpse into the lives of those that came before her. She opened a new journal and sighed softly, as she read the words written on the page. *Grandma.*

Maude pushed the loose strands of hair up off her flushed brow and felt around, patting her hair. Then, she pulled out a bobby pin, hidden deep in her thick hair. Her dark hair was twisted up into a bun, secured loosely at the nape of her neck. She was a beautiful woman, but she honestly didn't know any such thing. The year was 1940, and Maude was thirty-two years old. She had flowing dark tresses that spilled down over her shoulders and fell nearly to her waist. She was a timeless beauty with an easy, unassuming grace. The depth of her beauty was enhanced with her sweet and easy-going temperament. Maude was an understanding and forgiving soul. She loved life, and it was just as simple as that. With that abiding love within her, her free spirit found joy in even the most mundane and routine tasks of life. She easily found the intrinsic joy of simply being alive, and in turn, gave joy freely to all those who were lucky enough to find themselves around her.

Maude was looking out the door absently, with a far-away mist in her dark eyes. It was the very same look that she often had when she was lost deep in thought. She had a hidden intensity within her that was often most evident when she was passionately sending up prayers for others in need. She brushed her hair up off her neck with the side of her left hand and reinserted the bobby pin deftly with the same hand. Maude's right hand was clutching her starched apron hem. She held it up, to form a makeshift tote for the large ripe peaches that filled it. She had just been out to pick peaches off the little tree that was down just below the house. She had thought about making a pie. *That is, if the day somehow manages to cool itself off a little.*

The heat was nearly intolerable. *Nearly hot enough to bake my bread right out here in the yard*, Maude thought with a grin. The field shimmered and wavered in the heat. The North Carolina humidity this late in the summertime made you feel positively sticky all over. The thought of taking another tepid bath was surely inviting, but the kids would be coming in from school in almost no time at all, and she knew that dinnertime wasn't that far off. *Pat would be home from the mill soon, as well.* Pat and the kids would all be clamoring to eat, just as they usually were. *They'll be terribly hungry and nearly half-starved to death, just as sure as I'm standing here*, Maude smiled broadly with the thought. *Better get started on making us some dinner before they make their way home and my babies wake up from their nap.* Oh, how she dearly loved her brood of babies. It didn't matter to Maude how old any of them ever got; they'd all still be her 'babies' to her. Nothing in the world seemed to make Maude happier. Her family was everything to her. God had blessed her with each and every one of her children. Having them all gathered around the supper table, was her absolute joy.

That's not to say that it wasn't a job, because it surely was. Looking after the kids, and managing the house was hard, but she'd never minded it. Motherhood was something that just came easily to Maude, just as easy as her peach pie. She never much thought about anything else, but being a mother. She was just born to it, as she would've said. She never was one to dote too much on herself, or even take herself all that seriously and maybe that was the key to it all. She was always worried about everyone else and whatever it was that they needed, but not ever about herself and what needs she may have had. God would provide her needs. He always had. She had never needed much, anyway.

It was just her nature to be how she was and who she was. She was a kind, nurturing soul and the passel of kids she had, sure needed all the nurturing that she could muster up, and then some. She smiled to herself as she thought of them, one by one. Maude laughed softly.

She thought good-naturedly, *Mercy, what a cackling little flock of geese I have myself these days. Little Steve, the spitting image of his Daddy. My little sweet Stevie, always into something, but always taking the time to think of others. Never stops talking for even a minute. My, how handsome he's getting to be. Of course, there's sweet little Hilda, my little 'mother-hen' of the kids. She's such a wonderful help to me. Always there to help out in whatever way she can, quite grown up for her eleven years, already. So funny and so very smart, someday she will be quite the lady. With that smile, she'll win a thousand hearts or even more. And my sweet little Ann. Smart as a whip, and quite an artist as well. She's so inquisitive and dainty. With her sun-streaked hair, she's becoming quite a little beauty. She must surely have taken after her father. Ann's about to turn five years old this coming March. Goodness, can that be right? Yes, for lands' sake, she's almost five now. Then there's my little Bennie, with those flashing dark eyes. He's just about always getting himself into something or other. Now, with Ray gone out west to make his way in the world, the burden of watching out for little Bennie will fall squarely on Steve's shoulders. Steve is grounded and will watch out for his brother, so I guess I shouldn't worry so much,* Maude pondered this with slightly narrowed eyes. *Bennie's dark hair and complexion must have surely come from me. Maybe even his streak of fierce independence came from me, as well,* Maude thought with a chuckle, shaking her head slightly from side to side.

Little Patsy is just over two months old now, sleeping peacefully in her bed in the front room. Maude walks into the room to check on her and gently brushes Patsy's dark curls back off her face and leans down and places a light kiss on her tiny forehead. *What will my little babe, Patsy, turn out to be like?* Maude wondered aloud in a soft whisper. Patsy's hair was dark and promised to be almost the color of little Bennie's. Patsy slept on, only making a slight cooing sound in reply. *Little Ann and Bennie will be up from their nap soon, as well.* Then the clamor of the family will raise the sound within the house to a deafening level in no time at all. Maude smiled as she thought, *My precious family. God has blessed me so much.* Little Ray had grown into quite a handsome young man. He was the reason that she had become 'Mrs. Lewis William Arrowood', in the first place.

Maude had been just seventeen, and somehow little Ray had found her while he had wandered away from his Poppa one day, and Ray had decided almost instantly that she was to be his new Momma. *Poor little fellow*, Maude thought with pursed lips. *He lost his momma, Edith, way too early on in life. Don't reckon he would even remember what she looked like or even being held by her.* He was just too little when she passed, not quite two years old. Maude had fallen instantly in love when she first laid her eyes on little Ray. *That little fellow was 'ripping and romping' all around, nearly every minute.* He gallivanted all over the neighborhood just about every chance he had; whenever he could steal away from the watchful eyes of his Pa. But, his Pa really wasn't to blame. He was still a grieving widower and not used to having to watch after a rambunctious toddler all by himself. Maude figured that it was all just meant to be. She believed that was why he had wandered right up to her house that late afternoon in May. Wandered right up and stole away with her heart. *That was just exactly what had happened. Little Dickens, he just ran his little self right up to me and stole my heart. It was as if he knew full well what he was a'doing*, Maude chuckled as she nodded her head in complete agreement with the thought.

Ray was just about the cutest little boy she had ever seen. Now, he was such a handsome young man. *How can that possibly be so? Time sure flies past you when you're not looking*, lamented Maude. Ray had gone out west to live with his momma's family out in New Mexico. Hopefully, it was just temporary. There was plenty of work to be had out there and better prospects all around, for a smart young man such as Ray. After much thought, his father had reluctantly consented and let him go out west and try himself, if only for a short while. Maude sure missed him. And she knew that Pat did, too. The house seemed quite empty without him. But that's the thing that you have to learn to accept about your children. Eventually, they grow up and strike out to find their way in the world. They leave you behind and go their own way; it's just the natural way of things. *It hurts your heart so badly, and makes you so happy and proud, all at the same time,* thought Maude. Now that the sun was beginning to dip a little lower in the sky, the heat of the day seemed to lessen, somewhat.

Maude emptied her apron full of peaches out onto the kitchen counter and deftly caught one as it tried to roll off into the sink. She untied the apron from her waist and laid it on the counter, as well. She walked through the kitchen and out onto the back porch. There was a slight breeze beginning to blow through the higher branches of the trees, down below the house. Maude saw the movement high in the branches of the trees and sighed. She wanted to catch just a bit of the cooling breeze if she could. Standing at the back screen door with it flung wide open, the sudden gust of air brought a much welcomed coolness to Maude's flushed face. She stood there for a moment longer until the breeze died back down. She smiled, feeling a bit refreshed. Maude then turned back toward the fresh peaches and looked at them scattered about on the counter. She sighed. She paused and turned back around once again to face the back door and searched the sky quickly for any sign of coming rain. The wind was quite blustery, and more often than not, that signaled a storm blowing up. The leaves on the oak tree were showing their pale backs occasionally, so that was a very promising sign, as well.

Her thoughts quickly returned to the moment, as she turned and began preparing supper. She figured she had just enough time to get the peaches peeled and sugared down, before the kids would be flying in the front door, each raising a little ruckus of their own. She smiled when she thought about how not one of them could come in quietly, or at anything less than a full-tilt run. Each always had a story to tell of the events of the day and sometimes it seemed they were all in a heated race to spill their story first. It usually all came flying out, tumbled and jumbled, in a fast torrent of excited speech. They were almost to the point of yelling, more times than not. But,

Maude didn't mind it, not even one little bit. She doted on each and every one of her babies, and listening to all they had to tell about their day, was something that she simply relished. She thought to herself, *I wouldn't take a gold monkey, for any one of my kids; I sure wouldn't*, smiling broadly.

Children just have their special way of attaching themselves to the people that they love. When they feel welcomed and that their love is reciprocated, you just about can't get them to stand back, even if you wanted them to. It would take a crowbar to separate these children from their precious mother, Maude. The bond between them was just too strong. Maude wouldn't have had it any other way.

This was about three years before her last child was born. Little "Bill Boy", William Augustus Arrowood, thought Jane with a smile.

Ray, Ben, Steve, Ann, Hilda, Patsy, Bill

15

In the night of death, hope sees a star, and listening love can hear the rustle of a wing.

~ ROBERT INGERSOLL

PAT WORKED LONG hours down at the Dunn mill, but Maude kept herself busy and the hours of the day just seemed to fly past for her. Maude smiled wistfully and thought, *My handsome little Irishman.* Pat played baseball for the mill's team, and he was a mighty fine shortstop. The other players had dubbed him the 'Little Irishman' and the nickname had stuck. Pat dearly loved playing baseball, and he had grown into quite a gifted ball player. In those days, the Claire, Dunn, and the Armstrong Mills in the town of Gastonia had a combined baseball team that they called the 'CDA'. Pat and the kids kept Maude's life full and quite busy. She washed their clothes in an old wash bucket, scrubbing them clean on a washboard. She hung them out on the clothesline to dry in the morning's sunshine. *Nothing quite compares to the smell of clean cotton sheets dried outside in the warm sunshine,* thought Maude with a smile. *There's just something about that crisp, clean smell of the summertime air in a sheet that's just wonderful. One deep sniff can carry your troubles right off of you.* Maude often thought about this as she drew the water up from the well that was out back of the house. They didn't have running water, and they had an outhouse down below the barn.

Life was simple and easy in some ways, and hard and tough, in many other ways. But, Maude didn't want for very much. You just don't seem to miss the things you've never had; it was just the way that life was. She knew they didn't have very much money left over at the end of each week, but they somehow always made it work. That was all that really mattered, anyway. *Maybe we don't have a lot of money like some folks do, but we sure make up for it with love a'plenty.* But, Pat sure fretted and worried about the lack of money, at times. He did what he could to make sure they had enough.

The country was drawing near to the end of the Great Depression, and most everyone had good enough reasons to worry about money. Maude knew deep in her heart that God would provide them with what they needed. And God surely did. Maude was a woman of deep and unshakable faith, and she rested her worries on the knowledge that God knew their needs before they even knew themselves. So, she never let herself worry about such things. With her houseful of babies and Pat as well, to look after, she honestly didn't have enough time to worry about such things. *God would provide what they needed, and He did.*

Maude had a good husband, and she knew it. Pat grew a large garden to feed them all, and they had plenty enough to eat. Pat had a big heart and he often shared his bounty from the garden with others in the area that had even less than they did. So, for the most part, they considered themselves to be doing just fine, even better than most. Hilda and Ann excitedly competed for Maude's attention as she cooked dinner and readied it for the table. Steve was still outside. He had run straight through the house, following his father as he went out the back door with the screen door slamming behind him. He had stopped just long enough to kiss Maude on the cheek as he had made his way, dashing through the happy, noisy kitchen. Bennie was playing on the floor with wooden blocks, and Patsy was lying in the bassinet, wide-eyed and well rested from her afternoon nap. There were five happy children in their household, and there was never a dull moment in the Arrowood house.

But, there had been seven. *With Ray gone, it sure makes the house seem mighty empty*, thought Maude. Then she thought of her little Bert. A tear spilled down her cheek. Maude brushed it gently away with the back of her hand. It was still hard to accept, but little Bert had gone on to be an angel, and it still seemed like it was only just yesterday. *It'll be six years come the 13th of August since we lost our sweet little baby. My little Bert. Precious little thing was only two years and eleven days old. Goodness, he'd have been eight years old, now. I can't help but wonder who he would have become if he had lived. What would he have been like, all grown up? There are so many things that we'll never know. I pray that the sweet angels gather around him and give him comfort.* Maude's eyes misted over as she traveled back in her memories to that horrible time.

They had all been so terribly sick. Dysentery had run its course through just about every household in Gaston County that year. Children were sickened the worst, and quite often, it turned deadly, quickly. Little Bert had been terribly sick. He had held on longer, there at the last, than Maude had thought he possibly could have. It was a horrid ordeal. The whole family had it, and the neighbors had come in and taken care of them all when it was at its very worst. They were all so weakened that they couldn't do much of anything for themselves. Slowly, they had all gotten some better, and when Pat thought he was finally well enough to go back to work, he went. He went even though he wasn't completely over the sickness.

The steady work at the mill had slacked off, so Pat had to take whatever job he could, to put food on the table. He'd been offered jobs working at concession stands at different fairs, during the summertime before, so he decided to head to where the fair was going on and try to get work there. He made his way down to Columbia, South Carolina to where he knew that the fair was operating. He soon got a job cooking and serving food in one of the concession stands. The pay wasn't very much, and it was hot work with long hard hours, but it was a job. Pat was very grateful to have any job at all.

While Pat was working, the little ones were still quite sick. Maude nursed them as best she could, but little Bert, the youngest of the children, seemed only to worsen with each passing day. He was so frail and had lost so much weight, that it frightened Maude. She knew that he was going further and further downhill, and fast. She called in her fellow church members to come to the house and pray over him. They came to the house that night and stood over the sick child and prayed for him to be cured of the terrible sickness. They also prayed for him to be allowed to live until his daddy made it home from South Carolina. While they prayed over him, he seemed to take progressively shallower breaths until eventually, he appeared to stop breathing altogether. Pat's twin sister, Esther, grabbed up a bottle of camphor in a panic and rubbed his tiny body down with it. After a few agonizing seconds had passed, little Bert gasped audibly, and started breathing, once again. Maude cried out to the Lord, begging Him for mercy. She laid her hand on his beautiful head of blonde curls and bowed her head. She was beginning to fear the very worst. She was afraid that Bert just wouldn't make it and that Pat wouldn't get to see his baby boy one last time. She sent word to Pat that he needed to come back home, at once. As soon as he got the news, he left the fair and came home as fast as he could.

When Pat got to the house, he went straight to Bert's bedside. They all stood around the bed, holding hands and praying for a miracle. But, sadly, baby Bert stopped breathing one last time, and they couldn't revive the poor child. Maude was devastated.

It was an unimaginable heartache that Maude endured when she lost her sweet baby. She felt just as any loving mother would have felt. He was just so tiny and frail, there at the last. He was weakened to the point that he couldn't go on. His loss nearly broke Maude's will to live. The doctor cited the cause of death as colitis.

They took Bert's ravaged thin body and washed it carefully, in preparation for the funeral. Then, they dressed him in a tiny dress that had belonged to his sister, Ann. They buried him in the small church cemetery of Mount Olivet on the outskirts of Gastonia. Maude came home from the funeral inconsolable. She took straight to her bed. After a few day's had passed, and Pat went in and gently sat down on the edge of the bed where Maude laid. He talked low and quietly so that the other children wouldn't hear him. *Maude, I know losing little Bert is the hardest thing you've ever done in your life. I know because it was also the hardest thing I've ever done, besides burying my Edith. But, if I have learned anything in this life, it's that you can't just lie down and die, too. Even though dying seems like the easiest way out of your pain, maybe even the only way out, you just can't do it. You have to get up now and help me tend to our children. They need you, too, you know. We all want you to come back to us. We just can't lose you, too, Maude. You are going to have to let God hold this grief for you. You can't hold it all yourself, right now. Let the good Lord carry it. It's just too much for a body to carry alone. Just ask the good Lord to take it from you. You just have to do this thing, now Maudie. We have to keep on living on this earth, until the day finally comes, that God decides to take us home. You know that we'll all be together once again, up in Heaven. You have to hold on to that. We'll be all together, one day. You know that just as well as anyone. Just grab hold of that with both hands and with all of your heart, and let's get on with living. We've got our young'uns to tend to, you and me.*

He kissed Maude gently on the cheek and patted her hand as he held it. Maude had listened in earnest to his words. She sighed and dried her tears, got up and did her very best to try and get on with living. Sometimes it's just what you have to do in this life. She still grieved fiercely, but God held the worst part of her grief, just as she had asked Him to do.

Jane thought to herself, *Grandma Maude did the best she could. It's what we all do to get through the hard times that life sometimes hands us. We grieve, and we push on through it. Somehow, with God holding our hands and carrying the bulk of the hurt, we push through it. When we stumble, He holds us up, and when we regain our footing, He is still holding our hand. He is always there, supporting us. Always comforting, and always gently guiding.* Jane sighed heavily and closed the journal.

She hugged it close to her chest, thinking over all she had just read. *What unimaginable pain my precious grandmother must have suffered through. What agony to lose your baby boy. A precious little life lost. To an illness that could easily be taken care of with a simple dose of medicine, today.* Jane hung her head and cried.

Maude and Pat

16

It's not only children who grow. Parents do, too. As much
as we watch to see what our children do with their lives,
they are watching us to see what we do with ours. I can't
tell my children to reach for the sun. All I can do is reach
for it, myself.

~ *JOYCE MAYNARD*

THE NEXT EVENING, Jane picked up an unread journal. She settled in on the couch and opened it. She eagerly began reading
the words that had been written down so long ago.

Little Pat was running in the tall grass along the dirt road, smiling
ear to ear. The morning's sky was brilliant blue and cloudless. The
air was sweet with the heady scent of honeysuckle that grew tangled
in the ditch nearby. Even though it was mid-morning, the heat of
the day was already beginning to build. The little boy's name was
Lewis William Arrowood. He was named that by his father, Welzia.
Welzia Augustus was a preacher man born into a family with a long
line of preachers. Occasionally, Welzia would call little Pat, 'Lewis

William'. He called him by his given name only when he was in trouble for something or other. Most often, it was just 'little Pat'.

Pat was currently on an important errand for his mother, Isabelle. She needed a package of sugar from the store, so she had tasked Pat with it. It was the first time he had been allowed to go over to the store, all by himself. He was very excited and knew that it was important to get the sugar and get it back fast, so that he could make his Ma proud of him. Pat was a smart lad with an endearing smile. His blonde hair was tousled and it blew back off his forehead as he ran. The store was not too far away from their house, up on the mountain.

The Peterson's from the area had owned and operated the general store for many generations, but little Pat didn't know very much about this. He just knew that he had a shiny coin in his pocket that he surely shouldn't lose, so he kept his hand cupped over that coin as he ran, for safe keeping. It just would never do, if he somehow lost it somewhere along the way. His Ma had told him twice not to run and lose the coin out of his overall pocket, so he ran as hard as he could with his hand clutching the coin through the denim of his overalls.

It was mighty hard for a boy like Pat to walk anywhere. He mostly ran instead. Like the wind, he ran. He was barefoot, and it was summertime up in the high country along the North Carolina and Tennessee border. The sun was shining high in the blue sky over the mountain. He loved this time of year, just as most kids do. On either side of the steps leading up to the store's door were brightly colored hollyhocks in full bloom. They were beautiful, but Pat paid them no attention at all. He ran up the stairs to the store and the bell on the door tinkled merrily as he turned the knob and pulled it open. He struggled a bit with the heavy door and then went inside. The mercantile was a magical place for a little boy of seven. It was positively mesmerizing. The shiny utensils and interesting hardware hung just about everywhere; even from the high ceiling.

There were wonderful things to see, just about everywhere you looked. The building also housed the Post Office, where letters and cards could come from amazing places, all around the world. That thought stopped Pat in his tracks. He stared at the wall where the letters were kept. *Maybe one day I'll get a postcard from somewhere way far off, too. Maybe even as far as South Carolina. Boy-howdy, but that would be ever-so-fine.* Pat stood in the doorway with wide eyes, totally entranced. Mr. Peterson peered down at him from behind the heavy glass display counter and cleared his throat. He said, "Ahem. Can I help ya' with somethin' today, son?" as he peered down over his spectacles. Little Pat turned and stared up at the rail-thin Mr. Peterson. Pat stammered and struggled to remember why he'd been sent there, to begin with. The heady swirl of excitement had simply wiped the memory from the small boy's mind. Being in the store all alone for the very first time ever, was about too much to take in, all at once.

Pat gulped, and in a voice that came out small and barely above a whisper he said, "Shh-sugar, please, sir." Mr. Peterson pursed his lips slightly and nodded curtly, closely eyeing the small boy standing before him. He pushed the small spectacles that were sliding down the bridge of his thin nose back into their proper place and turned to retrieve the sugar package from the shelf. The year was 1907, and it was early in the month of June. Little Pat Arrowood was about to make his very first financial transaction ever, at the Peterson's General Store in the tiny town located not far from the Roan.

The store sold many wonderful items and to a little boy, it was fascinating to see the shiny merchandise lining the shelves, row after amazing row. Not to mention all the brightly colored candies that were all lined up in huge glass jars. Each and every jar of was enticingly calling to him from behind the counter. When you're only seven years old, the world is an endless, vast array of wonderful things to both see and smell. It was very hard to maintain focus on the task at hand. He tried his best to concentrate on the sugar. "Remember, sugar, Pat, just get me the sugar." His mother's words echoed in his thoughts.

Mr. Peterson peered over his spectacles questioningly at the boy. Pat suddenly snapped back to his senses, and he clumsily fished the coin out of his pocket and handed it over to Mr. Peterson. Pat had almost forgotten to pay for it, and his face grew red with embarrassment. Mr. Peterson accepted the money and nodded with satisfaction. The transaction was complete. *Mr. Peterson's face seems to be a might too thin to hold up them thick glasses,* thought little Pat. *He keeps on having to put 'em back up on his nose, where they belong.* Little Pat suddenly smiled up at Mr. Peterson, victoriously. *Little Pat was completely lost in the shining moment of his first glorious business transaction.*

Pat turned to quickly run home and tell his mother. He made his way over to the door and pulled hard on the knob with both hands. The bell hanging high on the door tinkled once again as Pat struggled with the heavy door. Mr. Peterson yelled out, "Stop, son!" Little Pat froze in absolute terror. *Have I went and done something wrong?* He couldn't think of a single thing as his thoughts raced. He couldn't figure for the life of him, what it could possibly have been. Mr. Peterson peered once again down at him over the rim of his round spectacles. Seemingly in slow motion, he took his index finger and pushed his glasses back up to where they should be on his nose, once again. Then he said, "Son, you done forgot your sugar." With his face flushing beet red with embarrassment, little Pat walked sheepishly back over to the counter and took the small package that Mr. Peterson held down to him.

This time, Pat walked sedately back to the door and quietly closed it behind him, as the bells sounded. Once outside, he took a deep breath and cautioned himself to be careful with the sugar. This was important, after all. He remembered not to run this time, and he walked home. Walking is excruciating to a little boy of seven, but Pat somehow managed to do it, anyway. He knew that dropping the package of sugar while running would prove disastrous and bringing the sugar home safely was of utmost importance. *He was just about to bust his britches, he was so proud of himself.* "I just can't wait to get home and tell Esther all about this." He smiled broadly, holding the package tightly to his chest with both arms as he made his way back toward the house. Esther was Pat's twin sister. His older brothers and sisters wouldn't necessarily be all that excited about his mercantile adventure, but Esther sure would. She would understand; she always understood things like that. He was as close as any brother could be to his sister. Little Pat didn't know what he would ever do without her by his side. Twins just have a natural bond; a bond that is truly like none other.

Isabelle tried to covertly hide the smile on her face as she listened intently to Pat's story about the sugar and the thinness of Mr. Peterson's nose. She patted his slender shoulder and told him how very proud she was of her little 'man'. Pat smiled up at her blissfully and towed the ground with his stubby bare toes, slightly embarrassed at the sudden attention.

Little Pat instinctively knew that he had been tasked with something very important, and he was proud that he had performed the task successfully. *And it sure felt good. Yes, Sirree, boy-howdy, did it ever feel mighty fine.* It was a milestone in his young life, and he intuitively knew that it was something special. *There's just no telling what all Ma will let me do for her, after this. She knows for sure that I can be trusted and that I can do things, and it feels purty good,* Pat thought to himself, beaming ear to ear. Esther did, indeed, want to know every single detail of the adventure and Pat purposely spun the tale out much longer than needed. He did it mostly to entertain Esther, more than for any other reason. He knew that his twin would want to hear every detail.

Life up on the mountain was not usually all that exciting for a young boy. But sometimes, amazing things did happen. Actually, there was something amazing that had happened just a few days back. Pat remembered this in detail and relayed it all to Esther, as well. She sat rapt with attention, listening to every word as the story unfolded. *There was this here big ol' rock that had smoke just a'coming out from right underneath it. The ground was just'a smokin'.* Esther's wide eyes and slightly open mouth only served to fuel Pat's fervor in the telling of the tale.

The crevice beneath the rock had been barely noticeable. It wasn't anything that a passerby would've given a second look. *There weren't really nothin' all that special about that rock, not nothin' that I could tell anyways,* said Pat with an air of authority. Actually, no one had noticed anything, until someone saw the smoke curling up from the ground. Then it got all sorts of attention.

People came from all over to take a look-see at that smoking rock. People began to wonder about it, and speculate. *Why people started up to speck-a-latin' all over the place, about that smoke comin' up from nothin' but a hole in the ground,* Pat said emphatically with comically raised eyebrows. The news spread quickly, and it was too much for a little kid to ignore. Little Pat had gone over bright and early one morning, to check out the smoking rock for himself. It seems that no one ever did figure out exactly what was going on with that rock. When the smoke or steam or whatever it was, quit coming up from underneath it, the interest just sort of died down. It was just the natural way of most things, people got interested pretty fast, and disinterested nearly just as quickly. Maybe there was a cave deep down underneath that rock. *A big cave where the hot rocks are stacked up high, way down, way at the bottom of the world, close to China, even, and all that steam just would come right up out of the ground whenever it rained real good,* Pat thought with widened eyes.

It had certainly caught the imagination of nearly every little boy on that side of the mountain, and even some of those 'boys' that weren't so little anymore. Little Pat's imagination ran wild for years about that smoking rock. It occasionally happened down through the years, with no reasonable explanation ever offered up for the strange phenomenon. *Things like that are not very likely to ever be forgotten by the little boys that actually see it, in person. And for certain, it never was.* Jane smiled. She had heard the story about the smoking rock while sitting at the feet of her grandfather. He had even raised his eyebrows while telling the story. In her imagination, she saw the sweet young face of the little blonde boy with wide eyes that he had once been.

Still chuckling lightly, Jane turned the page on the journal and began reading another chapter from the tattered and faded pages.

Pat Arrowood

17

For you created my inmost being; you knit me together in my mother's womb. I praise you because I am fearfully and wonderfully made; your works are wonderful, I know that full well. My frame was not hidden from you when I was made in the secret place, when I was woven together in the depths of the earth. Your eyes saw my unformed body; all the days ordained for me were written in your book before one of them came to be.

~ PSALM 139:13-16

Babies are bits of star-dust blown from the hand of God. Lucky the woman who knows the pangs of birth, for she has held a star.

~ LARRY BARRETTO

SARAH ELLENDER WIPED her brow with the back of her hand. She was miserably hot. The heat was stifling, and nearly intolerable in the back room of the small cabin. The air hung thickly in the house and boiling water over the roaring fire for the past hour hadn't helped, not even one bit. But, it had kept the young man busy, and that was a big help, for sure. The day had dawned overcast and drea-ry. The weather matched Sarah Ellender's current thoughts exactly. Even the mountain itself seemed to be downcast and glum. Sarah Ellender got back up from where she had sat for all of five minutes, and she sighed heavily. She placed a hand on her aching lower back as she slowly straightened up and stood. She walked over and reached into the bowl on the nightstand and wrung out the cloth that was floating in the clean water. Sarah Ellender gently laid the cool rag on the forehead of the young girl that lay on the bed beside her.

It had certainly been a long, hard night. It was turning out to be a terribly painful labor for this girl. She was extremely thin, despite the large baby she was carrying. The baby had taken just about everything out of her, and she was plainly suffering. It was times such as this that made Sarah Ellender truly question her decision to ever have become a midwife in the first place. There was only so much she could actually do to help, and she knew it. She wasn't a doctor, and she'd never be, plain and simple. She didn't have the proper schooling, and she just didn't have all the doctoring ways and know-how that she wished she had.

Had she been born in another place and time she would have made a fine doctor. But, she had no fancy ideas about any such fool-ish notion, now. Sarah Ellender was a patient and kindly soul. Caring for others came easily to her, even from an early age. She knew her remedies, herbal tonics, and such, just as well as her grandmother, Polly Shell, had known them, and that was saying quite a bit. It was true that her grandmother had taught her everything she knew, but there was just a lot more known in medicine, nowadays. *But, this is here, and this is now,* Sarah Ellender silently admonished herself. *Stop your wool-gathering and figure out a way to help this poor girl.* She was up on the old mountain, miles away from a regular hospital with new fangled medicine and doctoring ways.

The year was 1873, and Sarah Ellender was nearly thirty-three years old. Still a quite handsome woman, her blonde hair had turned a shade darker, but it still had the sun-warmed blonde streaks that it always had. Sarah Ellender felt that since she knew more than most about healing sickness that it was her duty to help out the women on the mountain. Most of them did need help, and desperately. She felt the need to step up and do her part. Those with the knowledge of birthing and midwifery naturally felt obligated to help others. It had been this way for many years. There were babies being born just about all the time, and women folk most always needed help during their time. Especially when it was a young girl, having her first, like the one lying on the bed before her. She had no mother and had no one else to help her. If anyone needed help, this poor girl desperately did on this miserably hot and humid morning. *Ain't much air to be had, in this here house. There isn't enough windows for any air to come in,* thought Sarah Ellender with a tired sigh. *The air was heavy, making it hard for a body to even draw an easy breath.* She had been up for two days straight, and it looked like there was yet another long day stretching out ahead of her. She may have to call for some help before this one was over. Normally, there were two or three women that helped one another out during a birthing, but it so happened there were two others in labor just over the mountain, and another down in the hollow on the other side of Buck Mountain. So, in a situation such as this, you just did the best you could with what you had. It was the mountain way, and always had been. You make do with what you have, and somehow or another, you find a way to make it work.

Life had never had been any different, not as far as Sarah Ellender had known, anyway. *It is, what it is,* Sarah Ellender thought dolefully. So, she was on her own, at least for the next few days. Sarah Ellender had told the father of the child, to keep boiling the water. He was beside himself and constantly asking what he could do to help. It was Sarah Ellender's years of experience that told her that the best thing to do with a worried father was to give him some busy-work. A chore that would keep him busy, as well as let him feel somewhat useful. Often, there was really nothing at all that he could do to help. It was hard enough dealing with a momma that was in a world of pain, but when you added in a worried pa, it made things a lot worse. Eventually, though, she'd have to tell him to stop. *The steam is making it harder and harder to breathe in here*, sighed Sarah Ellender. *Poor fella, he's worried plumb sick over her. I bet he's burnt through nearly five trees by now. If he keeps it up, the mountain'll be bald in no time.* Ellie moaned, and Sarah Ellender stepped quickly back over beside the bed.

The girl lying beside her was just barely old enough to be having a baby of her own. *They grow up so fast. It's hard to believe that pretty little Ellie is soon to be a momma.* Sarah Ellender remembered her as just a teeny-tiny thing running around, and it seemed like it was only just a few short years ago. But on the mountain, babies grow up quickly. Sarah Ellender had waited until she was 19 years old before she had married, but that was considered to be quite old. She'd been thought of by most, to be nearly an old maid.

Ellie murmured and fretted, her pain was quite evident. The girl moaned, turning her head from side to side. Sarah Ellender reached over and laid her hand on her forehead gently, to try and soothe her. Sarah Ellender whispered, *Now don't you fret, sweet girl, we're goin' to get you through this. You're doing fine, now Ellie girl, just fine. That baby's goin' to be here, a'fore you know it.* Ellie nodded and moaned softly in reply. Sarah Ellender hoped that the baby wasn't coming in breech. She had seen that happen more than her fair share of times, and it wasn't something that she would've wished on anyone. It was a terrible thing to suffer through during the childbirth, and then there was a lot of pain, in the days that followed. It was dangerous, as well. You had to move quickly in a situation like that. Ellie whispered again, softly, and Sarah Ellender bent down closer to hear her. She said, "Tell Marty to go fetch the axe. I just can't take this much longer." Sarah Ellender didn't quite make out what she was saying at first, but she soon realized what it was that Ellie wanted her to do. "I'll go get it right now," Sarah Ellender said with an understanding nod.

The mountain folk were just about all a superstitious lot, and many of the old beliefs and ways had been handed down through many generations. One such belief was that if you placed an axe underneath the bed of a woman in labor, it would 'cut' the pain and ease the suffering. Sarah Ellender believed in no such thing herself and tried her best to dissuade others from believing in such non-sense. But, in this particular case, she felt certain that it couldn't hurt a thing. The girl was so painfully young, and she was scared some-thing fierce. *Sometimes, just believing in anything helped.* It sure didn't matter what it was if it could help you get through the ordeal you are faced with, so Sarah Ellender complied. She went to the doorway of the bedroom and lifted the quilt that hung over the doorframe as a makeshift curtain. She quietly asked Ellie's young husband to go get the axe.

The look of bewilderment and shock in his eyes was instant. Sarah Ellender stepped completely out of the room and let the quilt fall, effectively closing the bedroom off behind her. She laid her hand firmly on the boy's shoulder, trying to comfort him as best she could, as she quietly explained the purpose of the axe. The look of relief on his face was almost comical and had it not been so stressful a moment, Sarah Ellender may have even laughed out loud. But, she was too bone-tired to laugh at anything. She asked him to leave the front door of the cabin open, hoping that it would let in some air.

As she placed the axe underneath the bed, and you could see the girl's face relax, almost instantly. Sarah Ellender also went and found a large butcher knife. She placed it under the pillow on the bed and made sure that Ellie saw her do it. These things were all a part of an effort to soothe and help, and Sarah Ellender understood the impor-tance of that, more than most.

The hours passed, and it was late in the day before the baby fi-nally came. Sarah Ellender gently washed the tiny pink newborn and wrapped it up in a clean bed sheet. She washed and bathed the new mother, as well. Sarah Ellender was exhausted, and as the new mother and newborn rested comfortably, she sat in the chair beside the bed and slept soundly for at least an hour. She wrapped up the afterbirth and took it outside that evening, and buried it.

As she dug a hole in the ground, she thought about the new young mother, just starting out. *They are both so young, and already a brand new family. Between the two of them, they haven't even learned how to spell the letter 'A' yet. But they will learn, and quick enough.* They would most likely have to learn most things the hard way, but they would learn, just the same. That was for certain. They were well on their way, now. Just why the people of the mountain didn't seem to want the young ones to learn the lessons of life, was beyond Sarah Ellender's understanding.

Sarah Ellender Winters Arrowood Miller

The old timers didn't seem to want the young to know about the facts of life and everything that goes along with it, until they were grown. Most were very closed-mouthed about such things. That sure didn't make much sense to Sarah Ellender. She had told her own brood the facts of life, from an early age. *Why, knowing is a helpful thing. Knowledge is a gift from God. When you know what's to come, you aren't as fearful of it. And you can make sound choices with the knowing. Now, that's what makes perfect sense, don't it, now?* Sarah Ellender pondered as she dug. Sarah Ellender chuckled lightly to herself as she remembered what she had been told as a child. "When you decide that ya want a baby of your own, why, you just walk right on out into the woods and find yo'self one that you cotton to, and ya jest bring it on back 'ere to the house," her mother smiling broadly, had said.

Sarah Ellender had endlessly searched for babies in the woods as she ran over the mountain and she had never, ever found one. She had thought that very odd, for many years, as she did her growing up. The woods were thick and plentiful up on the Roan, and she had thought as a child, that the soft cushioned floor of the forest, where the pine needles fell thickly would have been the perfect place for a baby to be. But she had never found one, lying in the soft moss. And she had sure looked hard enough. Shaking her head, Sarah Ellender wondered why her mother had told her such nonsense. She surely didn't understand it. *Why, it made no sense, at all,* she thought shaking her head, smiling.

18

*As you do not know the path of the wind, or how the body
is formed in a mother's womb, so you cannot understand
the work of God, the Maker of all things.*

~ ECCLESIASTES 11:5

BEING A MIDWIFE was appealing work to many of the mountain women, even if it was hard. Helping out another woman in her time of need had its own rewards. Just knowing that someone was there to hold your hand while you birthed your baby was a tremendous comfort and blessing. The women all knew this to be true because nearly all of them had all been in the very same predicament, themselves. The bond between the women of the mountain was strengthened by this, and they often requested the same midwife with each new child.

Sometimes, no doctor could be found for miles and having someone that cared for you and someone that could help you should you need it, gave great peace of mind. The pay surely wasn't the reason why women were midwives. More often than not, there was no pay at all. People on the mountain were poorer than most. They had very little money, but if they did, they paid you maybe just a few dollars or so. Mostly the pay was a sack of whatever it was that they had on hand. Sometimes, it was something that you didn't have or something that you could use. A simple sack of potatoes or onions was often the payment. Some had nothing much at all to give, and Sarah Ellender understood that completely. She went to help them, just the same.

Sarah Ellender stayed for almost a full week after Ellie gave birth. She taught her how to care for her new baby girl. Ellie caught on quite fast. She was a kind, nurturing soul, and Sarah Ellender was happy to see that side of the girl. *She's going to make a fine little ma for that sweet baby.* Sarah Ellender was proud of her patient's burgeoning mothering skills and was especially glad to see how she so lovingly interacted with her tiny newborn. The joy that shone in Ellie's eyes made Sarah Ellender all the more eager to get back home to her children.

Her youngest, John Henry was now nearly three years old. Her oldest, Welzia, had recently been hired on as a farm hand over on the Garland farm, and he sent money to his mother regularly now. *It was such a blessing to have a little extra money on hand.* He was a good son. She felt sure he was destined to preach, just like his father. He had the calling and there was no doubt about it in Sarah Ellender's mind. There was a certain way about Welzia that instantly soothed others and put them at ease. You could sense that the hand of God had touched Welzia; it was as plain as it could be. God was watching over Welzia and for that, Sarah Ellender was very grateful.

Welzia would go on to do plenty of the Lord's work in his life, and she felt confident of it. Samuel had seen the calling in young Welzia, many years ago. Sarah Ellender was happy that his father had known. *Samuel was way too young to die, but God's plan isn't always made plain to us. We just have to trust in Him. God always knows what's best, for each of his children.*

Life had been especially hard on Sarah Ellender since her Samuel had died, but she was determined that they were all going to be alright.

She was committed to holding her family together, no matter what. She left the kids to stay with her parents, Eliza and Billy Winters up on the Doll Flats, when her services were needed as a midwife. The kids were there, up on the Roan with them now, at her beautiful old home place. She loved that mountain, with her whole heart and soul. *My kids are roamin' those same rolling ridges that I did, as a child, and why that just tickles me plumb pink.* It was a place of indescribable beauty. Sarah Ellender knew each of those rolling hills as well as she knew the back of her hand. It was truly home and always would be. You never leave the Roan entirely, not when you are part of her, as Sarah Ellender surely was. *The Roan is always there, deep within you. She calls out your name, and you'll always hear it. The Roan never forgets.*

That was a phrase that she had heard her father, Billy, say many, many times. Then, as she grew up, she began to realize just what he had meant back in the sweet days of her childhood. She knew in her heart of hearts, that it was true. *The Roan never does forget.* She smiled as she thought of her favorite spots and how the evening fell on the mountain in a blaze of rich color. The colors swirled in the clouds and bathed the hills in a wash of peach and pink. There was no other place on earth quite as beautiful to Sarah Ellender as her beloved Roan. Life had taken many twists and turns for Sarah Ellender; ones that she could never have foreseen. She knew for sure that everything had happened for a reason. She felt sure that God's plan was always meant to be. She didn't know why her sweet Samuel had to die so young. Each day her heart and soul still ached for him. There would never come a day that she didn't think of him. He was her intended soul mate in this life. She had never been surer of anything than she was of that.

But now, she had to think of her children and their welfare. She couldn't rely on her parents to supply a roof over their head and food for her children. Sarah Ellender's parents had always been there to help, but the time had come for Sarah Ellender to make some hard decisions for herself. *Sometimes life just seems to have a mind of its own.*

Dave Miller was a widower that was having a time trying to raise his children up, all on his own. Her mother, Eliza, had mentioned that fact more than just a few times to Sarah Ellender. Dave had some land and a comfortable home. Sarah Ellender knew that she couldn't continue shuffling the children around and burdening her parents with keeping them. They had raised their children and now they were getting up in years. They shouldn't have to raise their grand-children, too, at this stage of their lives.

Dave had married Margaret Jane Callahan early on in his youth. She was quite a beauty with a quick smile and a mane of flaming red hair. Margaret was a force to be reckoned with and to say that she was a handful, would have been a dreadful understatement. In fact, she had turned out to be more trouble than Dave could have ever imagined. *Margaret was an exceptional beauty, certainly, but she did have some quite peculiar notions about a lot of things. She was more than just a tad superstitious and that woman held on tight as could be to some pretty strange notions.* Dave tried his best to dissuade her, but her strange beliefs only intensified as the years went along.

The notions and signs that she held so firmly to were all the usual, run-of-the-mill ones, with a few really strange ones thrown in, as well. There were ones such as hearing 'a rooster crowing at night', that meant somebody in the family would soon be sick or dead, or the notion that you were 'not to rock an empty cradle' or the baby will surely die. And, of course, she had some even more outlandish ones that set the town's tongues to wagging something fierce. Dave loved his wife dearly and tried his best to understand her, but as hard as he had tried, things only worsened over time. *These superstitions of hers had been passed down from generation to generation, and mind you, ones such as that tend to die mighty hard up here on the mountain. Margaret Jane was only thirty-two when she died and poor Dave took on something terrible, I tell you, he did.* He was left with five small children to raise up, all alone. *The eldest twin girls were grown and out on their own, soon enough. When Margaret came up pregnant* with the eighth child, she had been so happy. Then she saw that dad-blasted 'news bee', and she was convinced that it was only the first bad sign that was set to befall her. She told Dave that it had been right outside her bedroom window when she had first seen it. "That bee flew straight up to the window to let me know, just as plain as day, that somethin' bad is fixing to happen," Margaret lamented with tears streaming down her face. *The bees tell you the 'news' of what's to come, and you can be sure that woman believed that those bees never lie. Oh, Lord a'mercy, but that woman took on so, the likes of which you've never seen. Seems that if a regular yellow bee happens to fly up to you, why now, everything's fine, but when one of those big black bees come right up to you, with a purpose, it's never good. Something dreadful is surely about to commence.* The bee had stopped poor Margaret in her tracks as she was pulling up the bedspread. She had just gotten finished fluffing up the feather ticking on the bedstead that morning.

Then, the blackest bee she'd ever seen in all her live-long days flew straight up to that window and bumped itself directly up against the window pane. Then, it flew straightaway down the holler from the house and straight toward the cemetery that lies up on the ridge, just over yonder. Margaret ran herself right over to that window, to watch and see which way that ol' bee had flown off to. Margaret's breath had caught in her throat and then she'd let out a choked gasp. *When she had enough air to manage, Lordy, now, but did that woman ever let out a blood curdlin' scream. That scream she let could've woke up the long-dead that lay up along that ridge, way on over yonder in that tiny cemetery. But, it just so happened, that Dave wasn't there to hear it. Now, that was a blessing; I tell you it was. It would've scared that man nearly out of his skin. It sure enough would've. Those children were afraid of their own shadow, just like their mother. Why, they couldn't help themselves from being that'a way. She didn't even realize just how scared they all were. But they were; they sure were. Children learn fast, and they learn exactly what they see. Just sure as the world, they do. Why, they learned to be afraid of pert near everythin' after watching their momma. Even the drawing on of an evening caused their hearts to quake in their little chests. Evening meant oncoming darkness, and with the darkness, came the haints and lost souls that wander about, roaming the land. Little children follow closely in your footsteps; they watch your each and every move. Everybody needs to pay a mind to that. Lordy, they sure do.*

Each generation does pass their fears down to the next. After a time, these beliefs became a way of life for the people that lived so isolated up in the mountains. The unknown was terrifying, so anything and everything became a foretelling, and just about anything out of the ordinary was considered a 'bad sign' by people. Even the little ones turned somber-faced and quiet come evening time, for everyone knew that if you went to bed laughing and acting silly or having too much fun, somebody would turn up sick come morning, or maybe even dead.

Ollie had begun to write her own thoughts down as well, as she wrote the story that had been told to her long ago. It seemed to Jane as if Ollie was talking straight to her. Jane nodded her head in agreement as she read the words written down many years ago. "Sometimes the boogey man that lives right under your own skin is way more frightening than anything that might be bumpin' around outside your window in the coal black of the night." "Then, when they lost pretty little Lucinda the way they did, well that nearly put poor Margaret clean over the edge and halfway into stark, rank madness. She was gone for sure, after that. She loved that darling little girl more than she loved life itself. I tell you now, Margaret surely did." *Little Lucinda was only seven years old, and she was just about the most darling little girl that you ever did lay eyes on. Now, that there was the honest truth.*

Below the Roan

19

Oh, the golden age of the barefoot time,
While life was a fairy tale sung in rhyme,
When phantoms grim of a future day
Were hid in the mists of the far away...
Off for a swim on an afternoon,—
The moments—why would they fly so soon!
The rosy skies of our barefoot days
Lie hidden from view by a misty haze.

~ ADELBERT FARRINGTON CALDWELL (1867–1931)

He will wipe away every tear from their eyes, and death
shall be no more, neither shall there be mourning, nor cry-
ing, nor pain anymore, for the former things have passed
away."

~ REVELATION 21:4

DAVE HAD GONE *out a'huntin', way before daylight that morning. It*
was snowy and icy out, but he went, anyway. Margaret had begged
him something fierce not to. She kept telling him that she had herself a

terrible 'bad feeling' about it. But, Dave was more than used to hearing about her goings-on, and he had just about heard his fill about all those 'bad feelings' she was always a'havin'. It was always first one thing and then another with that woman. It's a wonder he put up with it. I reckon he had finally just learned to shake it all, right off. Seems after all those years had passed, ignoring Margaret's rantin' and ravin', had become just as easy as could be for that man. He sure put up with a lot of bally-hoo from her, but love does sort'a make you blinded to another's faults.

If ever a man truly loved a woman, now that there was a man that did. I guess everyone should know what it's like to have someone love you that a'way, at least once in their lifetime. It's sad, but hardly anyone ever really does. Well, not very long after Dave had set out into the woods to go off a'hunting, the shot rang out. That morning just seemed sort of strange from the very start. It was extra still and quiet. It was foggy, you know, and the heavy fog in the air will always sort'a muffle a sound comin' from a long ways off. But, now that shot was certainly easy enough to hear. Back up at the house, Margaret wailed out like some wild animal caught up in a trap when she heard it. She just knew that Dave was dead. But he wasn't. Dave had stepped on an icy log and lost his footing. He'd slid off and fell backwards. The gun just went off, and why, he nearly shot his foot clean in two. The older kids jumped up and went a'hollering and a'running right off toward the sound of the shot, not even a minute after it had rang out.

Margaret was beside herself and in no condition to be of any help to anyone. That was what she usually did, poor thing. She just fell plumb to pieces. She worried and fretted over ever little bitty sign that she thought she saw a'comin'. Then, when calamity actually struck, why goodness alive, she wasn't one bit of help to nobody. She was absolutely hysterical and acting right wild and crazy. It was something else; I tell you. It was quite the spectacle. The poor woman went loony, and there wasn't any way to reach her when she fell apart like that. You couldn't talk no sense into that woman, not in the state that she had gotten herself worked up into, that day. No, matter what you tried, you just couldn't do it.

As soon as the children had managed to get their daddy back on up to the house, and Margaret saw that he was alive, after all, she sort of came to her senses enough to help the kids dress his wound. She seemed dazed, but at least she helped the poor man. But, poor Dave never did walk quite right after that. That's why they called him 'Crippled Dave,' I'm pretty sure. Many thought it was because he had been injured in the war, but the limp was from him nearly shooting his own blessed foot off. My, but that poor man got himself an ear full from Margaret, that day. She lit into him like the dickens and let him have what-for, now I tell you, she did. She started in a'yelling at 'em and ending up crying and a'heavin'. Lordy help, but that woman was upset. Some of what she said, why he couldn't even begin to make it out. No one could've, but he stayed his quiet and meek self, and let her have her say. He knew full well that the ear chewing was goin' to come no matter what, so he just let her get it all out. I reckon she just couldn't keep from letting her mouth overload her tail. There wasn't nary a thing on God's green earth that was ever goin' to change that woman, and if anybody knew it, Dave did.

You see, she had heard the crowing of the rooster, that very night before. The children had all heard it, as well. The crowing had started up right around midnight, and the racket eventually woke the whole house. Then, later, it went at it again, and that rooster crowed itself silly until around three o'clock that morning. The second time Margaret had gotten right up out of bed and went to pacing back and forth on the bedroom floor. She figured at first, that it was a bad sign, but she certainly knew it the second time. Once could have been overlooked because Dave had told her that they sometimes do just up and crow at midnight. But, crowing twice? Now, that there surely wasn't no accident. She knew then it was an omen; a dark sign. So, after Dave had fell and shot his foot, she calmed down, somewhat. She naturally thought that the bad thing had happened and that the dark shadow had passed on by them. Lordy, but that's when it happened. It was just when she wasn't expecting anything else bad to happen.

Sometimes, that's the way it is in this life. Right out of the blue, with no warning at all, death snatches up and takes what it believes it's owed. Death creeps in like a sneaking low lying mist, just when you ain't watching for it. Lordy, but it does. Little Lucinda had gone outside to check on her chickens. Why, my word, that little one sure worried and fretted something awful over those ol' chickens. She mothered them and loved them just like they were her own babies. She thought that something had maybe just scared that rooster into crowing during the night, and whatever varmit that was about, may have gotten into the chicken coop. So, she snuck out in the icy cold weather to have herself a look-see. She slid on an icy patch, they think, and she fell. She fell hard. Somehow, she landed just right and the fall snapped the poor little thing's neck like a twig, just like that.

Jane could see Ollie in her mind's eye as she snapped her fingers for effect, and Jane blinked and recoiled in response. Jane swallowed hard with the terrible image flashing in her mind. *That precious little girl was lying there in the icy snow like a limp doll, with her head cocked off at a slightly peculiar angle. Just one look told you that her neck was broken, and just sure as the day is long, it was. She was staring right off, up at the sky, they said. Just lying there staring right off, but seeing nothing. It must've been a terrible sight to see your young'un just a lyin' there like that. Must've happened real quick-like and that was surely a divine blessing sent straight from God. It would've been even more terrible for that sweet child if she had just laid there and suffered.*

But, she didn't suffer, or it didn't seem like she did. Her face was serene and beautiful. Like a beautiful china doll that had been dropped and broken, laying there in the pure white snow with her hair framing her precious face in ringlet curls. Lordy, did Margaret ever take on, when she saw her baby girl a' layin' there dead. There was wailin' and going on like you have never seen in all your days, I tell you. Margaret was like a woman possessed.

Sometimes people just can't accept it when bad things happen, and they go straight off into the deep end of the pond. It seems like their mind just leaves them. Well, it seems that's just what happened to poor Margaret. Once they got her up off the frozen ground you could see that she was pert near gone. When they got her on inside the house, she took to her bed and never got up, again. That woman grieved herself something fierce. She was just a pinin' away, for her sweet little Lucinda. If you don't believe that a body can will its own self to die, well, you had better just rethink your way of thinking. Folks can surely talk themselves right into dying. If they want to die bad enough, they can force it to come on. They can, just as surely as I am writing this, this very moment.

Margaret didn't want to live not even one more day without little Lucinda. So, she decided it was time to go. She just simply up and died. Dave had tried everything he knew to get her to get up and had tried to get her to eat at least a bite of something, but there wasn't no use. No use, at all. She had made up her mind she was going on to be with her little girl. Back then, there wasn't any mental hospital that would come out and get somebody like that. You just dealt with whatever life handed you, the best way that you knew how. Sometimes you would call a neighbor or someone to come over to help you, that is, of course, if you had anybody to call.

In Dave's case, he didn't have a clue as to how to make her understand how much he loved her and needed her. Not to mention the baby she was carrying or the other poor kids she was leaving behind, motherless. It was a sad thing to see Dave's state of being after she died. He was a ghostly shadow of himself. Yes, Lordy. It was a sad sight to see. Margaret nearly killed him off, as well. He wandered around aimlessly and didn't eat hardly anything for a nearly full-on fortnight. Of course, sometimes men have their own way of grievin', and sometimes you can't tell what they are going through just to look at them. Folks began to wonder if he was going to go mad just like her, for awhile there. The children were scared and worried, too. Time rolled on by, as time somehow or other just knows how to do. Way back up in those mountains, the harsh wintertime passes slowly and eventually, the blessed springtime rolls back around again, with the melting of the deep snow. Little Lucinda and her mother, Margaret, were buried up in the small cemetery that rested up on the ridge above the Miller farm, as soon as the ground had thawed out enough to allow it.

They were buried in the very same cemetery that the bee had foretold when Margaret saw it right outside the window. Dave placed fresh meadow flowers regularly on both of their graves, and he spent many hours up there alone, sitting quietly. The children saw him sitting there, but all were too timid just to walk up and ask him why he sat there so often. Dave saw that the grass was beginning to come in on the bare earth that covered the graves, and was somehow comforted by that.

He grieved himself for many long months, and then one day he realized that it was summertime. He just all of a sudden, knew what it was that he had to do. So, he gathered the children around him and announced that they were all going over to the Holtsclaw's corn shucking that had been planned for the following week. *The children had all been so sullen and quiet, just moping around, keeping off to themselves. They were worried they were about to lose their daddy as well, I suppose.*

Like the notion had just come from out of nowhere, Dave just decided that the living were supposed to be doing exactly that; getting on with living. It had to happen sooner or later, if nothing else but for the children's sake. So, he finally put his own heartbreak aside, and he did what he felt was best for the children. He gathered the children up close around him, and he led them in a solemn prayer. They all grasped each other's hands and prayed for God to send his angels of mercy to attend to Lucinda and Margaret. He prayed that they had been flown straight up heaven on the wings of those angels and that they were safe and sound. He told the children that the time for being sad was done and over with and that it was time to try and be happy again. He told them that they should remember the happy times and think fondly of their sweet mother and sister. "Remember to pray for them every day, because we all need prayers, no matter where we might happen to be." "Life will get better for us all, directly," Dave told them with conviction. Life had been hard for this family, and it continued to be for quite awhile, but they had love, and that was the main thing. *Love is a world more important than a body ever truly realizes.*

Jane was convinced that it was Ollie that was telling the story about Dave's family, many years ago. *It's so sad to think that this actually happened. Amazing, what people had to endure. It's a wonder that people even survived. Love endures all things, it surely does.*

20

I can do all things through Christ who strengthens me.

~ PHILIPPIANS 4:13

*Sorrow is a wound. It cuts deeply, but sorrow is a clean
wound, and will heal unless something gets into the
wound, such as bitterness, self-pity, or resentment.*

~ CHARLES L. ALLEN

THE DAYS THAT led up to the Holtsclaw's corn shucking had
passed by fairly quickly. Everyone in the Miller family was still
trying to deal with the devastating loss of Margaret and Lucinda, as
best they could. They had all loaded onto the wagon and made their
way over to the farm. The children were happy about getting to play
with other children, and that was how it should be. It was there that
Dave Miller first met up with Sarah Ellender. There, while the others had commenced with the shucking, Dave noticed pretty Sarah
Ellender standing there alone, watching the festivities.

Every corn shucking was looked forward to with great anticipation, by just about everybody up in these mountains. The corn was

picked fresh from the field and placed in a large pile right out on the barnyard. Most of the times, they piled it up real high. Hidden down deep in the pile, nearly every time, was a half gallon of corn squeezing liquor and the first one to reach the jug of spirits always got the very first sip out of it. Then the jug was passed around, and the merry-making commenced in earnest. Sometimes, the first man that found a red ear of corn while shucking, got to kiss a pretty girl of his choosing. *When that prize was announced, the young men started shucking that corn like the devil himself was a'chasing right along after them. All of them was a'trying their best to find that red ear first.* The red ears of corn were sometimes called 'pokeberry corn,' because the corn kernels were as red as poke berries. *Those boys had a fire burning hot inside them to find that red ear, and it was always quite entertainin' to watch.* Sarah Ellender couldn't help but chuckle when two young men both dove for the same ear of corn and nearly gave each other a cracked skull to show for it. *Goodness, but their heads came together mighty hard. You could only imagine how badly that had to have hurt.*

She shook her head in dismay over how heated the competition was getting to be, and after awhile Sarah Ellender distanced herself from the cheering crowds. She wandered away to where it was quieter and found herself a bale of hay to sit on, underneath a large shade tree some thirty feet away. She sat there quietly watching when Dave walked right over and spoke to her. She knew that he had lost his wife not very long before. He had always seemed nice enough, but he was a notoriously distant fellow. She didn't exactly dislike him, but she knew that he was a person that was hard to get to know, or at least he had the reputation as such.

Dave still walked with a limp but was able to get around well enough, considering the seriousness of his injury. Women in a small community always talked, and she had heard various conversations about the man, from time to time. But she was polite enough, as he talked to her, watching the corn being shucked. She figured being polite couldn't hurt a thing. It usually didn't, anyway. The kids were happily off playing nearby, and little John Henry was with his grand-dad and grandma. Everything seemed quite peaceful at the moment, so she let herself relax a little, and made light conversation with the man. Dave spoke quietly to Sarah Ellender, with his head bowed and his eyes downcast. Then, the conversation between the two suddenly turned quite serious. He told her all about losing Margaret, and how the children were beginning to learn how to cope, a little better, almost every day. He also told her that he had recently come to the decision that he and the family sorely needed a woman's touch around the house.

He went on to talk about how the girls would soon need the guidance that only a woman could give them, and how the boys needed to be schooled by a gentler hand than he, himself, possessed. Sarah Ellender's eyes widened as it slowly dawned on her, just exactly what it was that Dave Miller was getting around to, in his own peculiar way. *He was trying to ask her for her hand in marriage! Just like that, with nary a minced word. No courtship, no sweet words, not even one flower. It was nothing of the sort; this was just a 'shoot from the hip' business-like proposal of a marriage union. It sounded more like a marriage of convenience than anything else. Her mind reeled over the startling prospect. She barely even knew this man that stood before her.*

Sarah Ellender drew in a deep breath. She sighed with resignation. Then, she thought sternly, *Now, Sarah Ellender, you've got to put aside your silly schoolgirl notions of candy and flowers, and sweet stolen kisses. This is now, and that was then. You can be certain that those days are over and gone for good. The days of long courtships and starry-eyed school girl dreams, have long since passed you by, and you need to come to understand that. Your own future, and most certainly your children's, hangs in the balance. The children's well-being is all that really matters now.*

Those silly notions of the love-smitten little girl, still hiding somewhere deep inside you, have simply got to be put aside where they belong. They need to be stored away with everything else that belongs solidly in the past. Better yet, they need to be taken high up on the Roan and let the winds blow them away, once and for all. Time only moves forward in this life. Time spent looking back is a sad waste of a precious gift.

She finally allowed herself to exhale slowly, and her breath released softly. Sarah Ellender's mind raced with the speculation of how life would be if the two families were suddenly blended as one. She knew that Dave could easily provide the things that she alone, could not. He owned a nice home, on a good-sized, working farm. His was a home that would be warm, come winter time.

Sarah Ellender slowly realized that she was actually beginning to consider the union, long before she had even heard the final words of his conversation. She had almost made up her mind in just seconds flat. She waited a few moments silently. As soon as she thought it was proper, she turned to face him and said, *"You're alone, trying your level best to raise your children up right, just as I am. Blending the two families together seems to be the most sensible thing to do in this situation. I know our children seem to tolerate one another well, and that is a blessing. It seems we should be able to learn how to tolerate one another if the children can. With the Good Lord's help, we can raise them all up to be fine and decent Christians."* Dave looked at her with one slightly cocked eyebrow and then seemed to relax somewhat. He smiled a seemingly genuine smile, one that effectively hid the bulk of his mixed feelings. After a few moments of considering it, he said, *"So, I'm to believe, that this matter has been agreed upon?"* Sarah Ellender whispered her reply. She heard herself say 'yes' and could hardly believe that she was the one that had said it.

It sounded like the voice of someone else coming from somewhere far away. And that was the beginning and the end of the courtship of Sarah Ellender, for the second time of her life. It had been completely devoid of sweet words of love that one would expect to hear, but still, she felt sure she had made the right decision. It was a business agreement basically, devised for the betterment of all involved. Both parties obviously stood to benefit from the union and both were in total agreement over that fact. At the time, it seemed to be more than enough for Sarah Ellender. She drew another uneasy, shaky breath and forced her quivering lips into the nearest resemblance of a smile that she could muster, under the circumstances.

Sarah Ellender had never been so scared in all of her life. She knew without any doubt that life with Dave would provide them security. It meant food for the table and the surety of shelter over her children's heads. She knew that all of her children needed new shoes and in the worst way. She had noticed that Dave's children always had on better shoes than she could have ever have afforded herself. Sarah Ellender felt that she'd had very little choice, but to accept his generous offer of marriage. Sarah Ellender knew deep down in her heart that he never would really love her. Dave had deeply loved Margaret, and he would forever love her. But, at that moment, love was just about the last thing on Sarah Ellender's mind.

Winter was coming on, soon enough. A woman all alone on the mountain with small children is something that anyone with even a lick of common sense would know is a sure-fire recipe for disaster. Life together as a family was hard enough, but without a man in the household, it could be near on to unbearable. *Sometimes life takes you down dark roads that you'd just as soon not go down, but often there's just no choice in the matter.*

Sometimes the dark roads need to be traveled, just to take you on in life where destiny and the good Lord above, has determined that you belong. Dave had told the children that God was in control and that He knew best when they asked him why their mother had to be replaced. He tried his best to answer the questions that they had asked and consoled them when they needed consoling. He did what Margaret had always done for the children, as best he could, and he tried to be the father that they so badly needed. He explained to the children that it would take some getting used to, on everyone's part, but that they would all be a family soon enough. The news of the upcoming nuptials was met with raised eyebrows by some, happiness by others, and of course, all the children were a bit skeptical, at first.

Tongues in a small community will wag, just as sure as the world. But Sarah Ellender paid no mind at all to the stories that were quickly being passed down the hollows and over the fences. *Rumors fly around just like June bugs in the warm winds of June, especially when something comes along that's interestin' and not just your average, 'run of the mill' gossip.* Sarah Ellender knew this and didn't think badly at all, about the tongues that wagged that month. *That's just the way that things are, sometimes. Every trying situation in life just somehow comes along on its own. You can't always avoid it, so you deal with it the best that you know how to, and you move on.* This was no exception.

Sarah Ellender had on her best dress and had carefully braided her long blonde hair up in delicate strands, adorned with clusters of tiny white flowers that circled the crown of her head. She had wound the braids loosely around her head, and the effect was stunning. She was breathtakingly beautiful, and she had never even once entertained the thought that she might be even slightly pretty. *It's almost time,* thought Sarah Ellender nervously.

Suddenly, her pretty little daughter, Mariah, appeared quietly beside her, and gently thrust a delicate bouquet of sweetly scented wildflowers into her hand. Mariah had just picked them from the meadow, just down from the house. She had slipped into the room so quietly that not even the air was disturbed. *She moves just like a mountain lion, quick and quiet-like, hidden in the shadows high up on the Roan,* thought Sarah Ellender. Mariah Elizabeth smiled coyly up at her mother.

Mariah was a good daughter, and she always had made Sarah Ellender very proud. She was strong and quite sure of herself, even at the tender age of twelve. She would make a good wife to some lucky young man one day, God willing. The thought that her girl's own wedding day was not that far off, caused Sarah Ellender to purse her lips slightly. *She has grown up so quickly, just as all my babies have.* Mariah knew full well why her mother's heart was heavy. She could sense the apprehension that her mother felt, but she wasn't quite sure how she sensed it. She also knew the reason that her mother was marrying up with 'Crippled Dave Miller'. She didn't need much explained to her, and she never had. She understood and respected her mother for putting the needs of her family before her own wishes. Mariah was soft spoken on the rare occasions when she did speak, but usually, she kept her words and thoughts to herself. She was especially quiet about the matters that adults generally think of as something that's 'not fit for children to be concernin' themselves with'. She knew her place, and she knew that she was only twelve. *Grown-ups just don't feel the need to explain themselves to little children.* But, even so, she was a sharp girl, and a lot wiser than her years allowed. She knew exactly why her mother was marrying up with a man she hardly even knew.

Sometimes life just isn't always the way you want it to be, and you just have to make-do with whatever life hands you. So, when Mariah looked up into her mother's eyes that day, it seemed to be just a casual glance. But in truth, more transpired between them in that brief exchange than any observer could have possibly guessed. Sarah Ellender quite often read Mariah's thoughts because they were so much alike. She was sure that her daughter had inherited much of her savvy. Sarah Ellender simply nodded her head gently and smiled at her. Mariah smiled back. There was no need for words between them.

Mariah reached out and took her mother's hand. She patted it softly and then she whispered, "You're sure a beautiful bride, Mother. Don't fret yourself, now. Everythin's goin' to be all right." Mariah smiled a smile that could have lit up the heavens in the middle of the darkest squall. Mariah turned quickly and ran back outside to play with the other children. Sarah Ellender knew that she had glimpsed a rare and precious glimmer of the fine woman her young daughter was destined to become and she was suddenly filled with an overwhelming sense of pride. Her eyes brimmed with tears as Sarah Ellender turned back to check her reflection once more, in the beautiful oval mirror that hung on the wall beside her bed. Samuel had given her the mirror as a gift. He had given it to her back when she was still the happy girl that she once had been. He had hung it up on the wall with a wire, covered with a strip of cloth. It was still hanging from the very same nail that Samuel had placed there, so long ago. The cloth on the wire had begun to fade over time.

Her mind floated back, and suddenly she was back in that happy moment of long ago. Samuel's smiling face was peering over her shoulder as she looked into the mirror that he had just hung. He wrapped his arms around her waist and rested his chin on her shoulder. Samuel said, "Now, you can see the beautiful sight that I am so blessed to behold, with the first glow of the morning's light, each and every day." "Each morning I wake with the sun to find a vision lying beside me in the peach-colored glow of sunrise." "God has blessed me in so many ways." "He gave me a wife that I couldn't have even imagined in my dreams." She turned and kissed his cheek and turned back to look in the mirror and said, "God has blessed me just as much, maybe even more, with you, my love." The memory faded, along with Samuel's smiling face. Sarah Ellender was instantly transported back to the present, once again, but the smile lingered on her face.

21

What we are is God's gift to us. What we become is our gift to God.

~ Eleanor Powell

A daughter is a little girl who grows up to be a friend.

~ Author Unknown

Sarah Ellender's smile slowly faded and she drew a ragged breath and looked solemnly into the eyes of the face that reflected back at her from the mirror. The thin woman that stood before her didn't look the same as she once had, and she barely recognized herself. So much had happened in the last few passing years. Her life had changed so drastically in what seemed like the blink of an eye. The changes hadn't seemed to stop coming, either. Where was the young girl that used to run like the wind over the ridges of the Roan, happy and carefree, with her long blonde hair trailing out wildly behind her? Was she really somewhere in her still, hidden deep inside the thin woman that was looking back at her from the mirror just now? The mirror was the same beautiful old mirror, but was she the same? There were dark circles just barely visible under her eyes, but Sarah Ellender knew why they were there.

Those dark shadows were from all of the seemingly endless, sleepless nights. There were new faint lines beginning to form on her forehead. These lines were from the constant worry about her family having what they needed. There was a deep sadness that lingered in her sky blue eyes. It was that same sadness that hadn't left her even once, since the day her sweet Samuel had died. The sparkle that used to twinkle in her eyes was forever dimmed, and everyone around her had surely noticed it. She had been through tough times of heartache, but she was still here. She had somehow managed to survive, through it all. And with her very own special brand of tenacity along with God's unfailing guidance, she would survive this, too.

She drew in a breath for courage and raised her chin in defiance. She would make this work. She had no other choice, but to make it work. She would be a good wife to Dave Miller, and if he wanted more children, as she full well knew that he did, she would give those children to him, just as promised. Life demands that you keep on living. But, at that very moment, all she could think about was how her life would have been, if her darling Samuel hadn't died. Her eyes misted over, and she drifted back, again. She went back to a happy time when they were sitting on a blanket high up on the mountain, surrounded by the tall meadow grasses. The grasses were swaying back and forth, dancing lightly in the warm late summer breeze. She saw little Mariah toddling away from her; laughing in the tall grass.

How happy Samuel had been, smiling broadly at her. His sweet laughter rang out over the meadow and down into the valley below. The Roan sometimes echoed this same sweet laughter from years long gone, but Sarah Ellender had somehow lost the ability to hear it. Long ago, she'd been able to, but no more. It seemed as if the sadness that had snuffed out the light that once sparkled in her eyes, had also shadowed the light that had always surrounded her. Some evenings she wandered out, alone on the ridges overlooking the valleys below.

She often returned to the ridges that she had so loved as a child, hoping to hear the mountain singing to her, once again. Eventually, she realized that somewhere along the way, she had lost the ability to hear the music altogether.

Sarah Ellender had once known the gift of true love and happiness. Maybe she hadn't known it for nearly as long as she had wanted to, but she had surely known it. God had blessed her greatly. She was very thankful for having known honest and true love. Sarah Ellender turned and took one last quick glimpse of her reflection in the mirror. Then, she walked decisively toward the front door of the house. She heard the music begin to play. The fiddle players had chosen to play a lively Irish tune that she knew well, and the sound of happy chatter drifted up from those gathered out on the grass in front of the house. She would be announced as 'Mrs. Dave Miller' in just a matter of minutes.

Another page is turned, and another chapter begins in her life's book. While the first chapter has surely ended, she takes solace in the knowledge that she can open the book and look once again at the pages, whenever she likes. She can return to those sun-filled days that have long since passed, and stroll back into that beloved green meadow of tall grasses. The book is still her own, and in her possession, and it would remain with her forever. That beautiful meadow still exists, and it's tucked high up on the Roan where her true love and mercy still abides. It still calls out to her at times, but her soul can't quite embrace it the way that it once did.

Her treasured book of memories will travel with her, no matter where this life takes her. As she walks slowly, a single tear forms and trickles down her cheek, unnoticed. She sends up a silent prayer that God will bless this union; she prays earnestly that she has made the right choice for her family. She prays for guidance as she begins this new life. Sarah Ellender has faith that God will be right beside her, every step of the way. *My faith in the Lord is great.* The thought bolsters her confidence with each step. *My faith will sustain me.* She draws a deep breath for courage and smiles a genuine smile. *I can do all things through Christ, who strengthens me.*

As she walks out onto the porch and down the stairs, she sees Dave smiling up at her. They soon stand side by side. Dave reaches down and gingerly takes her hand into his.

They turn and face the Reverend Samuel D. Cox. It is July 20, 1873, and Sarah Ellender marries once again, out under a large oak tree surrounded by her children, her intended, and his children. Together, she and Dave vow to blend a new family and a new life. After Sarah Ellender and David exchange their vows, a loud, happy cheer erupts from the crowd of well-wishers.

Flower petals are tossed up into the air, and they rain softly down over the couple. The petals tumble in the wind and some remain in her hair. Sarah Ellender instantly turns and searches the crowd, searching for the sweet face of her daughter through the falling petals. She breathes easier when she finally settles her gaze upon her. Mariah stands by herself, as the shower of flower petals floats softly down. Her face is stoic and her eyes trail downward. Mariah clasps her hands together, bows her head and breathes a silent prayer of her own. She looks up, and her eyes lock with her mother's for just a few seconds. Then, everyone begins pairing off, dancing to the music, and little Mariah backs away slowly. Quickly, she disappears into the crowd of merry-makers.

Time marches bravely forward and the years slide on past. Some years are happy and some years are peppered with sadness and struggle, but they pass on by, nevertheless. Today there will be another happy wedding. It is October 21, 1877. A sixteen-year-old Mariah is now standing before her mother with her own bouquet of wildflowers, wearing a beautiful wedding dress of pure white. The dress has been hand stitched lovingly, with tiny embroidered rosettes adorning the delicately smocked bodice. Sarah Ellender has done her very best finger work for her beloved daughter.

Mariah looks down at the dress, admiring her mother's fine skills and looks back up at her. She speaks with a tremor in her voice, sparked by the depth of emotion that she is feeling. "Oh, Mother, you have simply outdone yourself with this dress. It's simply the most beautiful thing I've ever seen!" Sarah Ellender smiles and tucks an errant curl back into its place among the tiny flowers that seem to blossom from a cloud of delicate mist on her daughter's headpiece. The mist instantly reminds her of the mountain that she loves so well. Sarah Ellender's eyes brim with unshed tears. Quietly, she says, "No, daughter, you're the most beautiful thing on the mountain, this day." At the same time, both of their heads bow together, and they touch foreheads with matching smiles. They have done this since Mariah was just a baby. Each and every time, it reminds Sarah Ellender how like-minded she and her daughter truly are.

Sarah Ellender thinks to herself wistfully, *I declare, where has my little free spirited Mariah gone to, already? Where is that little freckled face girl that she was, only yesterday? Nearly as quick as a flash of summer lightning, she has grown up into a full-grown beauty. Now, it is her turn, and she is the bride that stands before me. How my heart swells with pride as I look into the eyes of my child that somehow became my very best friend. She's wise, way beyond her years. It's as if God granted my child the wisdom she needed to help me along on my own path. God said, "With aged men is wisdom; in length of days, understanding." But, surely my wise and beautiful young daughter is a precious gift straight from God.*

Mariah turns back to gaze at herself in the same oval mirror that her father lovingly gifted to her mother so many years before. She silently thinks back over the years, since her mother married Dave. He wasn't her father, and he never could be, but he tried his best to do right by them all. He had been severely heavy handed with doling out her brother's discipline, at times. He had pushed them out and on their own when they were each barely old enough.

Mariah had heard Dave lament his hasty decisions concerning the boys many times, and she felt he was truly remorseful of how he had treated them. It was obvious to many that he had mellowed in his later years, as many staunch and stern men do. Mariah slowly realized that she had become truly fond of the man. He was a without a doubt a strict man and there was no one around that would have contested that fact, for even a moment. But, Dave had been charged with maintaining and blending a household of seventeen children all totaled, between 'his,' 'hers', and 'theirs', anyone could see that was a hard 'row to hoe'. But somehow, through it all, they had made it work. She knew her mother had never had the romantic love for Dave that she undoubtedly had for her father Samuel, but they had grown to love one another, just the same. It was something more of a 'well seasoned' love, borne of appreciation and genuine concern for one another.

Sometimes a mature love can form a very firm and lasting foundation, for many years of marital happiness. *You can learn to be just as happy with this kind of love, as you can be with the hot flame of youthful love.* Sarah Ellender had grown to understand this completely over the years, and although it wasn't and could never be, what she had with Samuel, she was content with her life. The children kept her busy and life was never dull, that was for sure. Events came and went and the stages of life appeared and then slowly slipped on past. *Each year brought another year of happy times, as well as its share of the sad.* It was simply put; life. And life was always good, as far as Sarah Ellender was concerned. *It's all good.* Every blessing far outweighed any and every negative aspect of her life. She had learned early on that you can choose to be miserable in this life, or you can choose to be happy. And Sarah Ellender made the choice to always choose happy. She always said, "Life is what you make of it." So, Sarah Ellender had made it happy. *Not perfect by any means, but happy, still.*

Sarah Ellender had become pregnant with their first child, Albert, within the very first month of being married to Dave Miller. Then, on the first of May, in the year of 1874, little Albert Miller was born into the family. Soon after, more babies followed. Lockie Ann, Polly, and David Jr., were born to this couple. Then the last child; little Lydia arrived. One by one, the older children began to leave the nest to begin their lives out on their own. Welzia, the eldest, had been the first of Samuel and Sarah Ellender's sons to strike out. Then, Welzia met Isabelle not long after taking the job on the Garland farm as a hired hand. Welzia had known from an early age that he was called to become a preacher. It wasn't long at all before the ministry called him in earnest, and Welzia followed his heart straight down the path that his father had taken many years before. Meeting Isabelle was a gift from God that Welzia was thankful for, all the rest of his days.

Young Welzia was able to save up some money from his work on the farm so that he and Isabelle could start building a home for themselves. Later, when the Roan called them back, Welzia eventually came to realize that this had been the hand of God guiding them into the right direction from the start. *God was so very good to both of them.*

Now, Mariah was poised to spread her wings and fly from the nest as well. She was a year and a half younger than her brother Welzia, and they had always been very close. They shared lots of good times together growing up, and the thought of being away from one another was difficult. Mariah Elizabeth was marrying Joseph Honeycutt, from Hollow Poplar.

Hollow Poplar was a small community not too very far away, over in Mitchell County, North Carolina. Joseph was a Minister also, and a close friend of Welzia's. They weren't on an even keel over denominational choices, but each had decided that their friendship and brotherhood in the Lord, was far more important than the petty details. You see, Joseph Honeycutt was a Freewill Minister, as was John Henry. Both were staunch believers in the Freewill style of worship. These were not men that could be swayed easily, and neither was Welzia, who was by faith, a Methodist Minister.

The discussion about the particulars of each denomination could easily become quite heated, when Welzia's own brother, John Henry, joined in to express his disapproval. But, all three completely agreed on one thing for sure, and that was serving the Lord with all your heart, mind, body, and soul. They agreed, as well, on living your life as you truly should, according to how the Good Book instructs you. They all heartily agreed on that, with nary a cross word passing between them.

22

Love one another and you will be happy. It's as simple and as difficult as that.

~ Michael Leunig

Submit yourselves therefore to God. Resist the devil, and he will flee from you.

~ James 4:7

Reverend John Henry and Nora were running a tad later than usual, on this warm Sunday morning in August. The sun had begun pounding down its unrelenting heat already, promising a steamy day to come in the small community tucked away on the mountain. Nora dabbed her perspiring face delicately with a lace hanky and then she quickly tucked it into the bodice of her cotton dress. She had hastily decided that maybe with it tucked there, it would keep her perspiration from running down and tickling her so badly in the heat of the day. She was thinking about yet another dream she had, just the night before and of course the meal she would be cooking later on in the evening. She had a few biscuits left over from breakfast that would hold over until dinner. She had covered them up carefully and put them back in the warmer over the stove just before she had left the house through the kitchen.

John Henry had come in from hitching the horse up to the wagon and went straight over to the sink to wash his hands. He turned, narrowed his eyes and studied Nora thoughtfully. He saw that she was ready and waiting patiently by the kitchen table. But, Nora's lips were pursed tightly, and her jaw was set in a certain way, and through the years John Henry had learned exactly what that look surely meant. John Henry knew his wife well. When the woman pursed her lips and set her jaw, just so, it was a sure-fire indication that his ear was fixing to get bent and bent back pretty good. John Henry took a deep breath and sighed heavily as he turned his attention back toward the stream of cold water running over his hands. Nora busied herself with re-tucking the hat pin into her hair more deeply. She had been trying to secure her hat nearly all morning. *Intolerable ol' thing, seems intent on slippin' right on off my head this mornin',* Nora thought with a grimace.

The water ran icy cold and refreshingly over John Henry's work worn hands. His hands were not the ones that you would expect to find belonging to a preacher man, but he was not just your ordinary preacher. The calluses and strength of his hands showed that he had worked hard, most all of his life. It never ceased to amaze him how cold the water from the mountain stream was, even in the scorching heat of a steamy August morning. The water ran continuously through the sink and on out through the drain, eventually flowing back down into the stream that ran along right under the edge of the porch of the house.

John Henry had built this house himself, and through the years, his sons had pitched in and made improvements and repairs. God had blessed John Henry in many ways, but somehow, he never felt truly deserving of all the blessings he had received. God was indeed good, without a doubt. *Our children were all blessed with more than a fair amount of book-smarts.* They had for sure, outsmarted John Henry, even at an early age. They had amazed the man continuously through the years. It had been pretty much decided that the running water idea was going to be put into operation before he had scarcely heard a word about it. His boys had devised a plan to let the natural flow of the creek, carry the water into the house, and gravity would soon take over and do the rest. *The boys set up the piping so that it flowed right on up to the house and through the pipes, into the kitchen sink, down the drain and out of the house. All those boys are simply amazing,* thought John Henry. *They are nothing short of amazing, all these children of ours.* At the time, no one else they knew had running water in their house. Certainly not up in Pigeon's Roost, they didn't, and that was one thing for sure. The electric lights came soon after. *What a miracle that had surely been and continued to be.* The boys had done all that on their own, as well. They planned it all, figured out the details, and put their idea quickly into action. Their house also had the very first electric lights on the whole mountain. *It had surely confounded nearly the whole community. Just screw in the glass light bulb, yank down on the chain and suddenly the whole room was filled with light nearly as bright as day, even in the middle of the darkest night. What other wonders await this old man?* John Henry thought to himself, with a smile and a shake of his head.

As he remembered that he was running a bit late for church, he also remembered that Nora was still waiting silently behind him. He could suddenly feel her steely gaze on him, even with his back turned to her. He grabbed the cotton cloth lying on the counter and hurriedly dried his hands. He turned and resolutely said, *Now, Nora, sweet little woman, I know for sure that you've gone and got y'self somethin' weighing mighty heavy on your mind, but it's just gonna to have to wait until after church service lets out. We're more than just a little late this morning. We have got to get ourselves a move on, and get on over yonder to the church.*

Nora's lip twitched and her eyes narrowed slightly. She reached over and slid her arm through the handle of her purse that sat on the table, gathered it to her and felt around for her hat pin. After three failed attempts, she found it and grabbed the hat pin that was stuck in her hat. She tried once again, taking another hearty stab with the pin, trying to secure her hat. With that, she turned and walked right out of the door. She spoke not even one word all the way over to the church.

Nora sat stoically beside John Henry in the wagon, with her back stiffened nearly as straight as a board. John Henry knew that she was madder than a wet hen, and he knew that he would catch the dickens just as soon as they were back home and by themselves. *Well, whatever it is that seems to be bothering the hound out of that little woman, will just have to wait until after church service is over.*

Pigeon's Roost, Arwood Farm

John Henry couldn't keep himself from grinning when he thought of how obviously mad Nora was becoming. But he was extra careful not to let Nora see it. *Why, land's sake, that woman would light right into me like a hurricane, if'n she saw even the faintest glint of mirth in my eyes. Lordy, but this little woman of mine is something else. She could try the very patience of any sainted soul. But, she is the light of my life, and I don't know that I could've made it through this many years, without her. Surely God knew exactly what he was doing when he sent her off in my direction. It seems as if the day we met was a lifetime and a half ago, and we have been together, pert near, ever since.* John Henry wondered to himself if he could have chosen another and been any happier during this life of his. He quickly determined that saucy or not, this little woman was the one that he wanted for a life's mate.

God chose her for me, no doubt, and God always knows what he's a'doing. John Henry prayed a silent prayer of earnest thanks for the little lady that stewed in leaden silence right beside him. *All this poutin' nonsense and goin's on is her daddy's own fault, more likely than not. He raised her up to think that she could have a mind of her own no matter what and boy howdy, did she learn herself that there lesson, and well.* Her foretelling dreams bothered him fiercely, there was no denying that. It just didn't seem fitting to him that a servant of the Lord, should have a wife that claimed that she saw things that were about to happen in her dreams. *It just wasn't fitting, not at the very least. It was somethin' a'kin to fortune telling and such nonsense as all that*, thought John Henry.

He thought of it as the devil's work and he surely wanted no part of it. He had tried to put his foot down early on about such nonsense concerning the knowing of the future through your dreams. Little Nora held steadfast to her faith, and there wasn't any doubt she was a true believer, but she also held on to the notion that God had given her the gift of 'knowing' and the gift of 'sight'. She claimed that God had told her these things in her dreams. John Henry tried to dissuade her from that way of thinking through all the years of their marriage, but it just didn't seem to bring about any change of heart in Nora. She kept right on thinking the way she always had, and

Rev. John Henry Arwood on his horse, George.

John Henry held close to his beliefs and his ever-true and steadfast faith in the Lord.

Together, they finally just had to agree to disagree, but the heated discussions still came along, from time to time. Try as they might they could never come to a 'meeting of the minds' concerning that one certain subject. As long as Nora kept that kind of talk confined to just within the family, John Henry had eventually come to abide by it. *It was just how it was to be, because there was no changing a woman that was as headstrong and independent as his was.* "Come on George, time's getting away from us, and we need to get over yonder to the church directly, now," John Henry spoke kindly. The horse plodded along the dirt road slowly, not seeming to pay any mind at all to the gentle coaxing words of John Henry. *I could get myself right down off the wagon and beg that tired old horse on bended knee, and it wouldn't hurry ol' George up; why, not even the slightest bit.* John Henry chuckled in spite of himself. The horse had been a good one through the years, and John Henry had a soft spot in his heart for the poor old animal. That was something that he would've never openly admitted to a single living soul. He just couldn't bear the thought of having to trade the horse off to someone.

He had ridden George all along the ridges of the mountains as he made his circuit, ministering to his churches over the years. *They had become close companions, and George had heard himself many fine sermons as they plodded along through the misty hills. John would often practice his preaching, you see, as they went along.* John Henry felt for sure that if he traded the horse off, he would most certainly meet a dismal fate, and most likely, one that would be soon in coming. John Henry just didn't have the heart for that, so they just continued along just as they always had. George plodded slowly up the road in the direction of the House of Welcome Church, taking his own sweet time. It was just as he had done Sunday after Sunday, for many years now.

They finally came to a stop beside the tiny church, and John Henry stepped down from the wagon, gingerly. He winced, favoring his right leg noticeably, as he walked around to the side of the church. He secured the horse's reins to the fence post. He had been limping just about all morning long, having felt the pain ever since rising much earlier that morning, in the misty moments of the first light. His knee was sure acting up, and acting up something fierce. Strangely enough, that painful limp would just about disappear when he got up from the chair that he sat in, near the front of the church. *I never feel any pain in my knee at all, when I set myself to preachin' from the Good Book.* He felt sure that it was something that God simply took care of. He knew that his knee always just stopped hurting and that was an honest-to-goodness fact. God was good to John Henry. Life for him was a glorious blessing, no matter what trial presented itself, with each and every new day. God was up in his Heaven, all was right with the world. The Good Lord was in control of everything. He would take care of any problem, no matter what came.

This service was going to be an extra special one, and John Henry felt it down deep within his being. Sometimes the Lord spoke to John Henry, too, in his own quiet way. *It didn't come with smoke and any of that hocus-pocus nonsense, and it surely didn't come in the form of no old foolish dream, waking or sleeping.* But, God spoke to the Reverend John Henry, and he knew it to be absolutely true. He felt it in his heart of hearts. He knew that God's great power was always with him, and this day was no different. Something powerful was coming today, up on this mountain, and the service would be a service of glory filled to the brim with the almighty power of the Holy Spirit.

The feeling in the air was almost electric. That tingling feeling ran through John Henry once again, and as he turned his face to Nora, she saw it immediately. She saw it as a certain glow about him and knew that something good was about to happen. *The good Lord moved in John Henry.* John Henry went around and helped Nora down from the wagon. He watched her as she made her way around the wagon and up the steps to the church. He thought, *I wonder what in tarnation has gotten that little woman's dander so fired up on this fine Sabbath mornin'?* Nora was thinking at the exact same time, that there would come a better time to discuss what she needed to discuss with him, so she pressed her lips tightly together. Then she pulled her petite frame up to the full extent of her small stature and made her way stiffly past him. She marched up the steps and into the tiny church.

John Henry had made sure to arrive long before the rest of the congregation would begin to assemble. It was always that way, each and every Sunday. He got there ahead of everyone and in plenty of time to pray in preparation for the battle that would soon ensue. He knew what was sure to come. This life on earth was a full blown battle against the devil every day, and he knew that without exception. And he knew that those souls in attendance for the service each and every Sunday morning, fully expected him to come with his heart 'right for the fight'. So he armed himself for the good fight with the heavy and effective armor of earnest and heartfelt prayer.

For John Henry, putting on your battle armor meant 'praying clean through' to the Lord, being fully 'prayed up' and of course, having the words of his sermon already carefully laid out and planned. He walked up to the altar and took the pulpit confidently, just as a man that had done it countless times before.

He gripped the wooden podium solidly with both hands and leaned his thin, lanky frame slightly in, toward it. He bowed his head low and began his prayers aloud. His murmurings of prayer resonated off the walls in the quiet, still country church. Nora took her seat soundlessly in the pew and perched there. She sat, delicately holding her purse on her lap. Then she bowed her head, closed her eyes and began her own prayers. It was the same ritual they had both observed without fail, for decades, throughout all the years of their marriage. It was something that had always been done, but they never really talked about it. There had simply never been a need. They both knew full well what God expected of them. They were steadfast and faithful servants of the Lord, and they had come to God's house to save lost souls.

23

Consider how hard it is to change yourself and you'll understand what little chance you have in trying to change others.

~ JACOB M. BRAUDE

For where two or three are gathered in my name, there am I among them.

~ MATTHEW 18:20

THE LITTLE CHURCH smelled sweetly of old wood. The sunlight filtering in through the glass in the window panes had warmed the benches, year after year. It was mostly from those old pews that the welcoming smell of sweet warmed wood wafted softly up. The old wooden floor was scuffed and worn, from countless scores of shoes and sometimes even bare feet that had crossed over it, throughout the years. The pews were worn as well; they were the original pews, with smooth, curved edges from countless years of use. Church members had held onto the edge of those pews to steady themselves as they had sat down, service after service, and the wood had worn down slowly, over time.

There had been a lot of the smoothing of the seats done by the countless rear-ends that had sat in those pews, all through the passing years. *The skinny rear-ends had smoothed the wood down just as well as the ample ones had, during church services through the decades. Many beleaguered and tormented souls had polished that smooth old wood right on up to a high luster. It had been done one uncomfortable twitch, twist, and fidget at a time.*

Reverend John Henry knew this to be an honest-to-goodness fact. He had witnessed the spectacle, throughout his many years of standing up in that pulpit. Looking down, he had seen the squirming. He had watched the offenders become antsy as the words of his sermon hit an uncomfortable bulls-eye on their black hearts and dark sinning ways. *The backsliders polished up each and every one of these pews, just'a squirming around in the misery of their very own makin',* thought John Henry when he had first noticed the pews. *Why, they each and every one know firsthand, the dark sins that they have committed! They got themselves an up-close view of the hellfire and damnation their sinnin' ways were heading them straight toward. Praise the Lord, they saw it!*

John Henry could almost see the very flames of hell reflected in the eyes of those that were the worst of the lot. He prayed fervently for their souls daily, and when they stopped coming to church services altogether, he would pay them a visit, never wasting too much time in doing so. The devil just seemed to be after some people worse than others, and it was just how things were in this life. *There are always a few souls that seem as if they are bound to be bad, no matter what.* John Henry could show you the most polished pews in the church, the ones that were really shined up, and tell you right away which church member had been the main 'pew polisher'. *The devil sure doesn't rest a'tall when he gains himself even the slightest foothold in your life. If'n you let him in, you won't be able to get him out for nothing in this entire world. Sure as can be, he's goin' to stay right there and torment you till you make it right with the Lord Almighty.*

Reverend John Henry knew that he surely didn't know everything there was to know in this world, but he knew that the ol' Devil had never once backed himself down from a fight. So, he prepared himself as best he could, before each and every service. He fought the good fight, winning back the lost souls Sunday after Sunday, at the tiny House of Welcome Church nestled up in the rolling hills of Mitchell County, North Carolina. John Henry came down from the pulpit after he had finished his prayers. He reached down as he walked past and straightened one of the pews that sat slightly askew, near the middle of the church. John Henry looked up and saw that the members were just now beginning to arrive. They were all milling about and starting to gather up and tote in their wash pots, just as he had asked them to do at the previous Sunday's service. Just about every family had a pot or wash tub, as they made their way into the church.

Nora, John Henry, Robert Henry, Pat, Maude, Hilda, Stevette, and Walt.

John Henry noted this with smiling satisfaction. Brilliant daylight flooded the little church through the open front doors. As each church member passed through the open doors, the light within the church was manipulated; drastically dimming and then suddenly brightening back up. Light talking and banter were exchanged as they happily greeted one another and made their way inside. The congregation's members slowly drifted down toward the front of the church, and each took their seat on a pew. The pews in the tiny country church were only benches with no backs. As the service began, it was announced that everyone needed to fill their washtub at the water spigot, out behind the church. They orderly filed outside and filled the tubs.

What was about to commence was an 'old-fashioned foot washing'. When everyone had brought their filled washtub or basin back inside the church and placed them between the pews, silence slowly fell once again. The eyes of the faithful believers in attendance were all fixed on the Reverend. Reverend John Henry stood and walked with solemn resignation to the podium. He knew the task set before him. John Henry had stood before this same congregation for countless Sundays over the years, and he felt very at ease doing so. He turned his face toward the congregation, earnestly searching the faces of the church members. He scanned them intently, row, by row. When John Henry felt confident that he had everyone's full attention, he began to pace back and forth. He took two long strides and then quickly pivoted taking two strides back to his starting point on the small platform on which the podium rested. He began to preach with a slight tremor in his powerful voice. He spoke with a voice that easily conveyed the strong conviction and deep-seated belief that he held deep in his heart for his words.

The sound of his deep voice resonated off the walls of the small church. *Would you wash the dusty feet of a complete stranger, if'n he was to wander into our midst on this very fine morning? If right here, this very minute, our precious Lord and Savior, Jesus Christ, was to sit right down in front of you, right on that very same pew in front of you, would you dare let him wash your feet? My good brothers and sisters in Christ, are you listening to what I'm saying? What I'm really saying? Would you feel worthy enough to allow the Holy Spirit, the Holiest of all that is Holy, to stoop right down, grab up your feet and wash them? Do you flinch right now, at the very thought of it? You, yourself, a time and time again, sinner? Do you think yourself worthy? Could you in all good conscience, allow the most Holy One to touch your feet? Could you, my friend? Even though, you know in your heart that you are guilty of countless black sins of the flesh, mind, and spirit? Would you be able to sit just where you're sitting right this minute, and let God himself, wash your dirty feet?*

There was a ripple of murmurings that bubbled up throughout the congregation and then slowly died back down again. Silence fell softly in the church. Many heads were bowed and eyes were downcast. Rev. John Henry paused for effect. He picked the Bible up from the edge of the podium in his right hand and he held it aloft, turning slowly, for all to see. *Do you read your Holy Bible, my good friends? Do you really read it faithfully, now? Do you study it as we as Christians, are supposed to study it? Do you breathe the word and let it settle into you? Do you understand the words and the teachings in the Good Book? Do you understand fully what God is trying to tell us? If God Almighty himself were here right now, He would bend down right in front of your ol' black and sinning heart and wash your feet, lovingly. I said with love! He loves us that much, my friends! He sees our sin, but he still loves us. He is a loving Father to each and every one of us. And you, my dear friends and family, are the blessed Children of a loving God. We are all the children of a precious loving Father.*

Several distinct and hearty 'Amen's!' were heard as they rippled through the crowd of worshipers and Rev. John Henry smiled with deep satisfaction. *Please open your Bibles, my dear sweet brothers and sisters in Christ, and let's read the precious Word of our dear Lord.* There is movement and a small flutter of noise, as the congregation all reach for their Bibles, open them, and prepare to read. Rev. John Henry said, *Turn in your Holy Bible, friends, to the book of John, chapter 13.*

Then, while holding the Bible aloft in his right hand, John Henry took out his hanker-chief from his breast pocket of his jacket with his left hand and quickly mopped the perspiration that was beading on his brow. He quickly poked the hanker-chief back into his pocket, deftly, with two fingers. He began to speak, *It was the time of the feast of Passover and Jesus knew that "his hour was come that he should depart out of this world unto the Father, having loved his own which were in the world, he loved them unto the end." After the supper had ended, Jesus knew already, full well, that the devil had made his way deep into the heart of old Judas. Jesus surely knew that his time on earth was coming to an end, dear people. Oh yes, friends, he surely knew it.* John Henry sighed and hung his head. Then he raised his head slowly and said with determination, *Jesus got up from the supper they had eaten, and He laid aside his garments. Then, He took up a towel and girded Himself with it. He poured water into a basin and then Jesus began to wash the disciple's feet! He then wiped them dry with the towel he had girded up about himself! Why in the world now, would He have ever done such a thing as that? This is a question that you'd full well be expected to ask yourself. Dear church family, He washed the feet of the disciples to give us an example of how to be humble! Can I get an Amen?*

And then a chorus of hearty 'Amen's' rose in unison from the crowd. *He gave us the example and we, as his children, are being led to follow that example! We, as children of the Living Almighty God, are goin' to follow, not just some of them, mind you, but all the examples, that were given to us!* Another spattering of 'Amen's' and a couple of enthusiastic 'Praise the Lord's' immediately went up in unison from the crowd before him. The male church members quickly shucked their shoes or boots, along with their socks, and rolled up their pants' legs. The females did likewise, and they slipped off their sandals, shoes, and stockings. The backless pews allowed those in front to turn around to face the row directly behind them, and each set of pews followed suit. Then, with all facing one another, they took turns washing the feet of the person seated in front of them. The sound of happy voices, praises, and low singing bubbled up from the crowd, as they joined together in the ancient holy ritual.

It was an act of pure faith, done in love and complete humility toward one another. The foot washing service was an act of joy and worship, performed by those devout brothers and sisters in Christ, in that tiny church tucked into a hidden cove in the beautiful mountains of North Carolina. Each person there felt the divine power of the Holy Spirit on that fine sultry day in August. Everyone could feel that God himself was there among them, seated in amongst the sunshine and believers.

Jane looked up from the journal page that she held in her hand and blankly stared straight ahead. She could almost smell the sun-warmed wood of that sweet old church. The words that Ollie had written down all those years ago were written as if she were talking straight to someone. *Did Ollie know that someday I would come and find all this? Did she know that perhaps I would seek out the journals to know the full story of this wonderful family of mine?* Jane pondered if it really could be true.

Could it be that it was all something that had been planned out many years before she was even born? The hair on the back of Jane's neck stood on end, seemingly, one by one. The words on the page she was holding blurred through the tears that were welling up in her eyes. *It's all just so amazing.*

She instantly thought about the old mirror that she had found while cleaning out the house. It was in that same mirror that she had seen the reflection of Sarah Ellender, while she had been working in the hallway. Jane saw in her mind, once more, the image of her beautiful great-grandmother, Sarah Ellender. She had been wearing a high-necked black dress, gently waving her hand, beckoning Jane toward her. *Did it all have some deeper meaning? Should it mean something to me?*

The mirror was stored safely in the hall closet. Jane had thought that she would take the mirror to a 'fix it' shop and see if they could repair the thin hairline crack and maybe re-gild the frame. She'd been afraid to hang it back up in the condition that it was in currently. *Maybe, I haven't hung it back up because the darn thing just about creeped the bejeebies out of me,* Jane grinned sheepishly. *You have to admit; it's not just an everyday happening. Ladies in black dresses don't usually appear out of nowhere and wave right at you from a reflection in a mirror.* Jane sat and thought about it for a moment. *You silly ninny, that beautiful old mirror is not possessed, you are just afraid of what you might see next.*

It does seem like the angels, well, my angels, like to hang out in that mirror. She slowly bobbed her head up and down and a lopsided grin formed on her face. *You are such a ninny, girlfriend. Now, just what would your Dad say about all this malarkey?* she wondered to herself. She heard his voice almost instantly in her mind. *First order of business for you, girlie, is to get that mirror back out of the closet where you've hidden it away.*

What good is there in hiding it, anyhow? Jane smiled. She wondered if the mirror held any more secrets and if she was honestly ready to find out. *Could there be more secrets from the past, patiently waiting for me to come and discover them?* She wondered if her heart could take the excitement from it all. *For just inheriting an old house, I've certainly gotten a lot of more than I bargained for so far,* Jane smiled to herself. *It's been quite a roller coaster ride. Not to mention that I hadn't the slightest idea that I'd even bought myself a ticket,* Jane thought with a wry chuckle.

In the closet where the mirror sat, the darkness enveloped it completely. No light at all filtered through the old blanket that had been wrapped carefully around it. Right outside the door, two small shadows suddenly cast themselves along the wall. Just a few moments later, two little girls, giggling and holding each other's hand skipped down the hall, but Jane didn't see or hear a thing.

24

A man finds room in the few square inches of his face for the traits of all his ancestors; for the expression of all his history, and his wants.

~ RALPH WALDO EMERSON, CONDUCT OF LIFE

Time heals what reason cannot.

~ SENECA

JANE SPENT THE next few days resting. She had somehow contracted a rotten cold that had only gotten worse as the days had worn on. She got out of bed to fix herself some hot soup, but she felt so bad that she went back, after eating only about half of it. Jake called constantly to check on her, and had even offered to come home to take care of her, but she just wouldn't hear of it. She appreciated his concern, but the truth was she looked pretty terrible. Her nose was beyond just being painfully red and had entered that crusty stage of miserable, icky ugliness. The relentless dripping had finally taken its toll. She thought she might be able to actually rest if she could only breathe. The sleep she had gotten over the last few days had only come in short snatches. After a few days of this, she finally succumbed and fell into a deep sleep almost immediately.

Jane was totally exhausted but almost as soon as she had slipped into slumber, she began to dream. Deep in her dream state, Sarah Ellender suddenly appeared right before Jane as she stood on the ridge overlooking the valley behind her house. The light in the sky was beginning to fade, and swirls of peach and gold filled the sweet few moments before full twilight. Sarah Ellender, bathed in the rosy glow of sunset stood before her, smiling. She appeared to be about the same age as Jane, somewhere in her late twenties. She was beautiful. Her flowing locks streamed out behind her, blowing in the sweetly scented air that blew down off the higher elevations and along the ridge on which they stood.

Jane stared at her in awe. She could scarcely believe the moment. It was just too magical, and she was afraid she would ruin it, somehow. She had a passing thought that this dream seemed somehow more real than her dreams usually did. Jane thought, *This wonderful woman that stands before me holds deep within her heart a huge amount of strength and knowledge.* Sarah Ellender did indeed hold the knowledge from another time and place. *She holds the collective knowledge of my ancestors. She holds all the knowledge of the old ones that has been lost in the misty passage of time.* For this brief moment, Sarah Ellender was almost close enough for Jane to reach out and touch her. Jane's tears flowed freely. *How I would have loved to have truly known you, sweet grandmother,* Jane thought without speaking. Sarah Ellender turned away as if she hadn't noticed Jane's tears at all.

Jane tried to speak, but she found that she couldn't. Her emotions proved to be too much. The moment was overwhelming. Sarah Ellender raised her hand toward the Roan, seeming to reach out beseechingly toward it. Then she quickly dropped her hand and turned back to face Jane. Without speaking aloud, she spoke, but Jane heard her voice just as if she were speaking directly to her. *Dear granddaughter, I know you, child, just as you know me. I know your heart. We are one and the same, you and I. My heart beats right along with yours, deep within you. You are the girl child of a thousand or more of your ancestors that all walked this earth long before you. The very same love that was in their once warm hearts now lives on, deep within your own. You need only be still to hear us, and we will speak. You know more than you can fathom. The knowledge that you seek is within you already and well within your grasp. You need only to listen to the quiet, still voice inside yourself. It has always been there for each of us, down through the centuries. If I can leave you with anything of worth from my experience of life, it would have to be this - don't forget to stop and allow yourself to enjoy the moments that bring you joy. We, as children of the Living God sometimes forget and get ourselves all tangled up in the details of life. Those details don't amount to a hill of beans; I tell you right now, that they don't. Turn your attention to what truly matters.*

Sarah Ellender smiled tenderly and said, *Trust your heart, Jane. You are the keeper of your generation, and you should be ever mindful of that. Know your place. You have always known it, deep within you. Each generation produces a Keeper. There is always one that will remember and pass it all forward, to the next generation. You have inherited the love of your many ancestors, just as surely as you have inherited the golden flecks in your blue eyes, and the color of your hair. You come from people that held strongly to life, no matter how difficult the journey became. Be proud of who you are, and secure in the knowledge of where your family drew its incredible strength and perseverance. It was, without fail, our faith, dear girl. Our steadfast faith in our Creator saw us through our tough times. You are a child of God, and God's tender mercy will surely see you through this life's tribulations, just as He did for all of us. Your journey has only begun, but mine on earth is long over. I will continue to watch over you and try my best to help you along your way. Don't worry so about your way in life and the things you think that you don't know, because you already know all that you need to.*

The knowledge is your gift from your ancestors. Remember that, dear Jane, and keep it tucked safely down in your heart. The time of your life is now, so live it to the fullest. Your best years are yet to come. Every minute of every day of this life, live it, dear girl. There is so much more after this and believe me, sweet granddaughter, it only gets better. Sarah Ellender's beautiful face was positively radiant in the peachy glow of the sunset. She turned and looked out over the twilight as the sun began its descent, settling down slowly over the Roan. Sarah Ellender smiled a knowing smile of deep contentment.

Jane had so many things she wanted to ask. Her mind raced with questions. Each question swirled and with so many new questions rolling through, she couldn't help but feel somewhat bewildered. The tears were flowing still, as she looked lovingly at Sarah Ellender and she looked back at her, with the same love. Jane reached out to grasp Sarah Ellender's hand, and she watched as her own hand faded into the mist that was suddenly forming before her. Sarah Ellender faded suddenly and she was gone, just as quickly as the glint of a twinkling star. Jane awoke immediately.

When she opened her eyes, she realized that she still had her hand extended out, reaching out into the darkness for Sarah Ellender, but she just wasn't there. She had suddenly faded and become one with the mist that settles over the mountain in the first hours of the morning's light. Jane tried, but she couldn't stop herself from crying. She laid there while the silent tears rolled into her ears and soaked the pillow beneath her head. She finally took a deep breath and shoved back the covers and sat up on the edge of the bed. Her stomach was in a hard knot, and she felt almost like wailing out loud. She sat up on the side of the bed, holding her head in her hands, as her mind raced with thought. *Sarah Ellender had said 'goodbye'. That had to be it. She just couldn't stay any longer, and she had come to say what she needed to, before she left. Why couldn't she stay, at least until I know more? Why couldn't I have at least been allowed to ask her the questions that I needed so badly to ask? I just stood there like a complete ninny and let her fade away, back to wherever she came from,* Jane murmured aloud while shaking her head. *Why do I feel so terribly empty inside?*

Jane breathed deeply and sternly thought, *Girly, will you kindly get a grip on yourself? This has to be the scene in the movie where they cut to the men in white suits, coming to get the poor girl that just went completely bonkers. You've been spending way too much time alone, and way too much time up in the attic, girlfriend. Just take a good, long, deep breath and get yourself a drink of water. It was only a dream. Hello? It was really only a dream, now, come on. I can easily chalk this up to all the strange things that I have seen in this house. Yes, as crazy as it sounds, my family is somehow still here. I totally get that. It is, what it is, but you can't cry your eyes out over a dream. People live with ghosts all the time, and at least these ghosts are family. You can't drive yourself plumb stark-ravin' crazy, and I won't allow you to. I can hear Daddy laughing for sure, this time.* Jane smiled widely, then she chuckled low under her breath, and then she laughed heartily right out loud.

Jane's merry laughter rang out into the empty house in the early hours before the dawn, and somewhere off in the distance she could have sworn that she heard a scream. The sound seemed to be carried from the ridge not too far off. Jane froze. It had sounded very much like the scream of a large cat. *Could it have been a cat? Was there a mountain lion that close to the house?* She wondered to herself. Slowly shaking her head, she got up and went down the hall to get some water, but decided upon milk and a handful of chocolate cookies instead. *A calorie loaded snack is perfectly in order after all this, no matter what hour it is,* she thought glumly. *Maybe the chocolate will soothe your hormones and mellow you out a bit, you crazy girl.* She sat there on the couch in the dark, with moonlight streaming through the curtains and falling softly across her face. She sat there, munching on the chocolate cookies and sipping the cold milk, as the scene from her dream repeated itself over and over again, in her mind.

Jane thought absently, *First thing in the morning, I need to make myself a strong tea out of honey and black pepper.* Sarah Ellender had told her this remedy would help her terrible cold, and Jane soon found out that it surely did.

Steve Arrowood

25

May flowers always line your path and sunshine light
your day. May songbirds serenade you every step along
the way. May a rainbow run beside you in a sky that's
always blue. And may happiness fill your heart each day
your whole life through.

~ IRISH BLESSING

"When the wind calls, you know that somewhere in the
mountains, it has found the answers that you were looking for. The pull of the horizon overcomes the inertia of
reason…And you just have to go."

~ VIKRAM OBEROI

THINGS ALWAYS SEEM to somehow or another, have a way of sort-
ing themselves out come morning. *Situations do always seem to
smooth themselves over, sometimes just a little and sometimes a lot, come
morning,* Jane mused to herself. *It must be the hope-filled promise of a
brand new day; or that you have a clean slate and a fresh start. It has to be
hope, no matter how elusive, that makes you feel so much better, come light of*

morning. This morning proved to be no exception. The new landline phone rang early, and Jane ran to answer it. She skidded precariously on the hardwood floor of the hall, barely catching herself before she fell. She had only gotten halfway dressed, wearing her socks and Mickey Mouse shirt, when she heard it ring. The phone was sitting on the end table by the couch in the front room. She picked up the phone and tried to answer without seeming so out of breath, but she really couldn't. She stammered slightly breathlessly into the phone with a grin, "H-Hello?" "Jane, is that you, sweetheart? Is everything ok there?" Jake asked. Concern was obvious in his tone. "Yes, sweetie, it's me. Everything's ok, I, I mean I'm fine," Jane stammered. "How are you, sweetheart, and when are you coming home?" "I'm missing you even worse than I ever thought possible, and I need to hear you say that you're coming home and soon." Jane spoke in a torrent of heartfelt truth. She truly needed him to come home.

Jake was quiet at times, but he was the best listener in the whole world. Jane needed that right now, more than she had ever realized she might. Jake sighed into the phone and said, "Well, babe, I hate it, but there's been another snag." "There's a delay in our cabinet order, but the supplier says it won't be too much longer." "But, I feel almost sure that it's going to be at least another week, maybe two." "I hate this. I'm so ready for this one to be over with. You just have no idea how much." "But you know that things like this can and will happen with special orders and especially with all the oddball special features involved in this one." Jane sighed and said, "I know you hate it, sweetheart, I do too. But, you're right. Things like this *are* going to happen from time to time." She took a big breath as his words slowly sank in. Her hand went to her forehead. Jane gripped the phone and put on a brave front, trying her best to hide the deep disappointment from her voice. It wasn't his fault, and she knew it. It just seemed that everything was conspiring against them, of late.

After speaking to one another for a short while longer, Jane slowly clicks the phone off and lays the receiver down on the end table. She stood and stared down at the phone for a few long seconds. She sighs dejectedly. "So, Missy, that's just how the cookie crumbles in the 'world according to Jane'." Jane crossed her arms over her chest and puffed out her breath with lips pursed comically. *Why can't anything just be the way that it's supposed to be? Just for once? I miss you so much, Dad,* Jane thought for about the millionth time. *This world's just not the same, without you. You always knew how to pick me up, no matter how low I felt. You always had the words that I needed to hear, primed and ready. Even in the worst times, you could always make me laugh. How you were able to do that always amazed me. I miss you so much. And I miss my Jake, too.*

Jane walked over to the front window and looked out at the rolling ridges bathed in sunlight. The day is clear and beautiful despite Jane's heavy heart. Her thoughts once again return to the beautiful old mirror that Ollie had written about in the journals. *So, Samuel had gifted that mirror to Sarah Ellender all those years ago,* Jane reflected. *It was certainly beautiful in the old ornate oval frame. It was very intricately carved and despite the old mirror's silvering being missing in spots, it still retained a regal quality about it. Wonder where Samuel had gotten that mirror from, so long ago? It had to have been an extravagant gift to the woman that he loved with his whole heart and soul. Surely a humble preacher didn't have much money to buy fancy things. Samuel and Sarah Ellender had the kind of love that everyone dreams of having in this life. It was the very same love that Nancy and David had for each other. My family had love, even if they had little else. Faith, hope, and love, and the greatest of these is love,* Jane thought with a smile. *All that love is what has held us together down through generation, after generation. It held us through the good times and the bad. God gave us all such a precious gift.*

Jane was thankful to have been gifted with the intimate knowledge of all the true loves in her family, through the journals and letters she had found. She was proud to have descended from all the wonderful people that had come before her. Jane smiled softly, and as she raised her head, her gaze fell on the closed closet door across the hallway. *It's high time to get that mirror fixed, missy. Now that I know just how important that mirror was to Sarah Ellender, it deserves to be restored back to its original state. It belongs hanging on the wall of this beautiful old house, and very soon, it will be. And that, Janie girl, is a fact,* Jane smiled broadly.

Later, Jane asked the waitress at the diner where she should take the mirror to be repaired, as she ate her 'blue plate special' lunch. "Well, your best bet, Sugar, would be to tote it on over to the hardware store, at least that's where I'd take it, if'n it was mine, and all." Susie propped a large deeply veined hand with scarlet fingernails on her ample hip as she appeared to study on her reply. After staring upwards through her thick fake eyelashes and thinking a minute or two, she leaned down close to Jane and cast a furtive glance out the diner's window. Jane looked up at her quizzically and then arched her eyebrows in surprise when Susie said, "Scooch, girl." "Go on now, scooch," with a flick of her scarlet fingertip. So Jane 'scooched' over, sliding quickly over on the seat of the booth, just as instructed. Jane hadn't ever been to restaurant, in her entire life, where the waitress had told her to slide over in the seat so that she could 'take a load off'. But apparently, up here in the mountains, it wasn't considered to be that far out of the norm for a waitress to do such a thing.

Jane quietly observed that no one around them was staring or seemed to have paid it even a moment's worth of attention. But, Jane had certainly witnessed the scene with widened eyes. She was amazed. Her arched eyebrows stayed up, right where they were, for the duration of the whole exchange. Jane couldn't stop the smile that slowly spread across her face. Susie sat down heavily and leaned back in the seat with a sigh. She had sat down so quickly that it caused the air to blow forcibly out of the cushion beneath her, making an odd high-pitched 'whoosh' noise as it made its exit. Susie appeared not to notice it. "Lordy now, don't ya know that feels some kind of good? I gotta tell you what, it sure does," Susie said in a quick release of her breath. She then stretched out her spine against the back of the diner seat, pressing even deeper and yawned widely. "Whatcha need to do, now, is take yourself and that mirror right on over to Sam, right on up the road here, to the hardware store." Then, while stretching out her legs under the table in the booth, she said, "Now, he'll fix ya' up real fine and proper-like. He redoes that stuff on the backs of mirrors, and everythin'." "You know, that silver stuff; or whatever ya' call it. When he's done with it, why honey, it'll look brand- spankin' new."

"You listen to what I am telling you, now he's the man that can do it. I saw one that he had done before. Might be that no one else has the proper know-how around these parts, but ol' Sam, now, he sure enough has it." So, Jane waited a few moments after the bell on the counter chimed out, and the cook had hollered, 'Order up!' twice, before Susie had made any move to leave. Begrudgingly, Susie finally got up to go after the order, with her wide hips sashaying back and forth between the tables. Jane left the money for her lunch along with a generous tip, lying on the table on top of her bill. Jane placed her empty glass on top of it, to keep it from blowing off. As she walked out, Jane turned and smiled, waving her hand to Susie. Susie winked and nodded in her direction while putting down a steaming hot plate of veggies on the table in booth number eight.

Jane walked out into the sunshine and over to her car, dodging large mud puddles left from the heavy rain the night before. She glanced up to see that the sign for the diner was still missing several bulbs. They were the same bulbs that she had noticed the very first time she had eaten there. *Things sure are slow to change in a sleepy little town like this one.* With a glance up she saw that the birds were sitting on the power lines having their early 'prayer meeting'.

Three days passed by, pretty much uneventfully. Jane drove down to town to get groceries and to pick up the mirror. Once she was back home again, Jane carried in the groceries she had bought at the store. After putting them away, she went back to the car, one last time. She took the mirror from the passenger seat of the car and carried it inside. She carefully placed it still wrapped up in the old quilt, down on the couch.

Jane walked back to the kitchen. She toasted herself a bagel and spread it with just a touch of cream cheese, just the way she liked it. *The days are passing by fairly quickly, at least,* Jane thinks as she munches on the toasty bagel. *They're passing quickly and more importantly, they're passing quietly, thank goodness. Maybe by this time next week, Jake will be back and things will return to normal.* Besides from the usual late night noises in the house and an occasional odd knock or squeak coming from somewhere in the attic, the days had flowed past easily. Of course, she still caught glimpses of movement out of the corner of her eye, along with her encounters that were just about every other day now, with little Minnie and Ruby. Somehow these things had become so commonplace that Jane had completely dismissed them from being 'not normal'. Jane knew without a doubt that her angels were around her constantly. Somehow, the idea of that had become even more comforting than ever before. She didn't mind her 'guests' at all.

Sometimes when the shadows fell long across the meadow, and the mountain seemed to sigh softly to itself, Jane thought she saw the silhouette of her father standing out on the porch. It was always when the light was just beginning to wane at the end of the day. Sometimes he appeared only fleetingly and sometimes the image was there for much longer than just a few seconds. He stood looking at the spot that he had loved for so many years. It caused Jane to feel a great flood of peace wash comfortingly over her. It was such a wonderful thought, to think that his spirit was still close by, watching over her and looking out for her. Maybe it was just wishful thinking on Jane's part; thinking it was actually him. But an occasional wisp of rising smoke could be seen near the shadow that the figure cast on the ground, just beyond the southeast corner of the front porch. The smoke appeared as if it were actually coming from someone smoking a pipe while standing on the porch.

Jane sometimes went to the bedroom window around dusk and waited. She was watching for the shadows of swirling smoke tendrils that rose and cast their shadows on the ground below. *If it's only my imagination, where's the harm in it?* She stood silently waiting, smiling in eager anticipation, hoping to smell the sweet aroma of cherry-vanilla tobacco floating on the air.

26

The Lord bless you and keep you; the Lord make his face to shine upon you, and be gracious unto you; the Lord lift up his countenance upon you, and give you peace.

~ NUMBER 6:24-26

WHEN JANE AWOKE the next morning, she remembered that she had left the mirror still wrapped up securely in the quilt, lying on the couch. She padded softly down the hall in the quiet, empty house and made her way to the front room. The morning was overcast, and the room was somewhat darkened and shadowed because of it. The lack of bright sun that normally filled the room made it appear rather too dark for Jane's liking. She walked over and clicked on the lamp. She brought the bundle over closer to the lamp, and she unfolded the quilt to reveal the mirror. It was truly beautiful, once again. It positively glowed in the lamp's light. The ornate design on the frame was exquisite and had to have been hand carved. It was quite old, but the wood was in remarkably good condition. There appeared to be very little real damage, despite an occasional small chip, here and there. The chips were small enough that with just an initial look, no one would have ever noticed them. The re-silvering of the mirror had been completed, flawlessly. It looked brand new. Jane was so pleased that she beamed ear to ear. *Grandma Sarah Ellender, if you could only see your beautiful mirror now. It is just as beautiful as it must have been on the day that Grandpa Sam gave it to you,* Jane whispered to the room with a voice filled with emotion. *This mirror has seen the years pass. What wonderful tales it could tell me, if it only could. Well, that was another 'Daddy' thought if there ever was one,* Jane thought as she smiled broadly. *I miss you, Dad. I guess some things will never change.*

Some losses in this life never leave you entirely, Jane heard the words of her grandmother echo from her memories. She held the precious mirror aloft and gingerly turned it around so that she could examine the back. She tugged on the wire that served as a hanger. She wanted to make sure that the wire was secure enough to hold the considerable weight of the mirror before she risked hanging it up on the wall. *What a wonderful, lovely addition to the room this will make. A treasured heirloom that will grace my wall for many years to come,* thought Jane. She carried the mirror around holding it up, trying to decide the best location for it. She settled on the entry, right by the front door. Everyone that came through the door couldn't help but see it. She would be able to check her reflection, easily, as she left the house. So, she hung it on the wall and stepped back a few steps to admire it. *It will positively glow in the light that comes in from the front windows. I absolutely love it, exactly where it is,* thought Jane with satisfaction.

Then, a sudden outpouring of grief for Sarah Ellender gripped Jane, catching her off guard. *The misery that poor sweet woman endured in her lifetime. This mirror was most likely the only thing besides her children that she had left in her older years. She didn't have much else left, I'm sure. Somehow she'd held onto this mirror, and she'd kept it with her, all those years after losing Samuel. She must have truly treasured it. Now, I will treasure it as well, always, and hang it proudly in my home to honor the love they once had for one another.* Jane walked over to the end table and picked up the journal she had been reading and opened it up to where she had absently marked her place with an old envelope.

She picked up the envelope and studied it intently. It was slightly yellowed and darkened with age. There was a name and address that she didn't recognize printed on it. The envelope was stamped with 'Cloudland Hotel' and there was a dated postmark with what appeared to be '1889', in fading ink. Jane sighed in amazement. She tucked it back into the pages of the journal for safekeeping. She was soon carried swiftly back in time. As she continued reading, she fell deeply back into the moments that had happened so long ago.

Tolbert decided that maybe he should go on ahead and finish chopping that last big log, before he went on over and fetched Ollie from her daddy's house. *That last log is already a'layin' out there in the snow by the chopping block, and there ain't no telling how long the snow's goin' to fall this time or how high it's goin' to pile up. Could last a couple a'days, and it could just blow in and stay for pert near a week, maybe even two. You just never can tell.* He'd seen it do that many times, and running out of firewood wouldn't be the thing to do, at all. *It just wouldn't do, not nary a bit, with Ollie getting to where she freezes nearly all the dang time, now. She never complains much about bein' cold, but I know her joints ache something fierce because of it. I've watched her rub her wrists from time to time. Ain't no need to have her a'being too cold. No good reason a'tall for it.*

He wanted her to be nice and cozy, sitting in her chair by the fire tonight. After deciding this, Tolbert trudged his way through the heavy snow. He went back over to the old stump and worked the axe loose from where it was stuck in the wood. The snow flew in thick flurries all around his head, and his breath blew out in plumes rising above him. He had always used the large stump that was out in the yard a small bit away from the house, as a chopping block for the smaller pieces. This last log was so large, that he quickly decided just to let it sit right there where it was. He would split it off into chunks, all the way around its circumference, first. By doing so, he would soon whittle it down to a more manageable size. He began to chop off outer sections that were about three to four inches in width, one chunk at a time. He made his way around the large log, working away at it, bit by bit.

Tolbert looked up at the sky and saw how dark it was becoming. *If'n the snow keeps up this pace it won't be long a'fore the road will be so covered over that it'll be near on to impossible to fetch Ollie home.* He began to hurry his pace, just as the snow began to blow sideways, with sheets of fast flying flurries. He turned up the collar of his worn jacket and the snow seemed to blow even harder. It filled his upturned collar, in just a few seconds, flat. As he walked around the log in the blinding snowfall, Tolbert didn't pay close enough attention to where he placed his footing. When he raised the axe to deliver the next hard blow to the log, the axe missed its mark and ricocheted off the outer edge of the log. The force of the blow sank the axe head deep into his foot, landing in the flesh between his second and third toe. The third toe was sliced off clean. A red hot searing pain shot upwards from his injured foot and radiated the heat of the intense agony all the way up his leg. He screamed out from the shock of it.

The blackbirds were startled out of the nearby trees they were roosting in, and flew skyward in a panic. The birds gathered and darkened the sky in an undulating black cloud of what seemed like thousands. Then, they suddenly flew off in the direction of the old home place. But Tolbert never even noticed.

Tolbert couldn't move his foot. The axe had sliced through the leather boot and then sliced through what little was left of the bones and sinew of his foot. Then, the blade had stuck itself solidly into the frozen ground. Tolbert felt the warmth of the blood as it spurted and quickly filled the ruined remains of his boot. The blood eventually seeped through and out of the slit in the sole beneath. His brain had a brief moment of clarity through the intense pain, and he knew that the axe had to come out, somehow. He was pinned to the ground and couldn't move.

Tolbert's mind reeled with the agony as he grasped the handle of the axe with his nearly numb hands. The slight movement of the axe head caused a jolt of unimaginable pain. He grunted with the exertion of trying to dislodge it. It seemed almost as if the blade has instantly welded itself into the ground. Tolbert swayed unsteadily on his feet. *I've got to get this here blade on up out of my foot before I pass clean out, or else I'm goin' to freeze to death right here in the yard.* No one at all had heard his tortured screams. He knew that no one was close enough to hear even on a clear day, but with the falling snow, the chances were even worse. He knew that the snow tends to act as an insulator and somehow it traps sound within it. *A muffled shout couldn't have been heard very far at all, not in all this.* The thoughts somehow form in Tolbert's brain, despite the intense torture of the agony that he feels.

Tolbert closed his eyes and prayed. He asked for God's help. He asked God to watch over his Ollie if this was the end for himself. "If you can see fit, dear Lord, please give me the strength to get myself up out'a this here mess I've done went and made." With a loud groan, partly from the exertion and partly from the pain, Tolbert grasped the handle of the axe and pulled with every bit of strength the injured man could muster. Fresh pain screamed and chugged like a locomotive straight up his leg from the injured foot. The axe blade slipped free, as if somehow of its own volition. The bloodied axe dropped away from Tolbert's hand as a spray of fresh blood squirted up from the slit in his leather boot. Just lifting the boot brought a fresh wave of agony, the likes of which Tolbert has never experienced in all his days. He dragged his foot along beside him while resting the weight of his heel on the snow. Behind him, the trail of blood quickly melted into the snow, and each drop's depression was quickly covered over by the fresh white flakes that are falling steadily from the darkened sky. Soon there would not be a trace of what had happened to poor Tolbert, visible in the pristine snowfall. He stares momentarily, as the blood that he leaves behind him sinks quickly away into the stark white snow's surface and out of sight.

Tolbert grasps the stair railing, and the steps before him appear to bend and warp crazily. *Dear Lord, don't let me pass right out.* His one good leg buckles, nearly causing him to fall. He steels himself and somehow makes it, step after agonizing step, closer to the landing. As he tries to lift the injured foot up from the last step and onto the porch, the sole of the boot catches on the edge of the wood. The searing pain that ensued causes poor Tolbert to faint. He passes out cold and crumples onto the porch, half in and half out. His head hits the floor squarely. The wind bats the screen door back and forth on him, as the snow blows in on his lifeless body.

As the minutes pass, the same owl perches on the tree limb close to the steps and peers down at the door as it swings back and forth in the wind, batting in the snow. The owl screams out into the snow-filled air, and its piercing scream rouses Tolbert back into a state of semi-consciousness. He struggles dazedly to his feet and drags the injured foot behind him as he makes his way inside the house. He leaves a grisly swath of blood behind. He never realizes that the owl's screech was what had awakened him. His brain was too clouded over by the intense pain. Once in the house he makes his way over to a kitchen chair and manages to sit down. After a few moments of rest, he bends down and clumsily wrenches the boot off of his bloodied foot.

Pain overcomes him once again, and he slumps over. The table was all that kept him from falling to the floor. When he comes back around and sees the full extent of the damage that had been done, he nearly faints, yet again. A wave of intense nausea washes over him. After bouts of pain followed by periods of blackouts, he manages to get his foot bandaged up, somewhat, with strips of clean sheets that he tore using his teeth. He had pulled the sheet down from a stack that Ollie had folded earlier in the morning and had left on the counter beside him, near the table. He remembered that she had hung the sheets out on the line early the previous morning. It didn't take very long at all until they had frozen, hard and stiff.

Tolbert laid his head down on the kitchen table and tried to regain some much-needed strength. He was exhausted from the terrifying ordeal and emotionally depleted. The pain had subsided back to a somewhat more tolerable level of excruciating. He had yelled out once again, from the searing sting of the whiskey that he had poured over the wound. He hallucinated that Ollie had already come back home. She had come to tell him that spider webs would help staunch the bleeding. "Ollie," Tolbert whispered in his pain-filled haze, "Ollie, sweetheart, come and help me." "Sweet Jesus, please help me. I don't rightly know what to do for myself." He knew for sure that his Ollie girl would know what to do. She would make the pain go away. *She knew most all of the old-timey remedies and for certain, all of the healing plants and herbs. She knew all those kinds of things, way better than most people did. She just knew, like her family had always known, generations before her.* She never forgot about any of the medicines that you could get from the land or how to use the herbs and roots. *Her family had always lived close to the land and Ollie just naturally knew these things.*

The white sheeting strips that he had wrapped around his foot were slowly stained a bright red, as the blood quickly saturated and seeped through his clumsy makeshift bandage. He knew that it wasn't the best, but it was the best he could do by himself. Tolbert watched in dazed and horrified fascination as the blood seeped through and dripped onto the floor below, forming a crimson congealed puddle.

Ollie saw that the blowing snowstorm was quickly getting worse. She watched, peering out the window, as the swirling snow fell harder and harder. Tolbert should have had plenty of time to get the wagon hitched up and come for her, by now. Something just had to be wrong, and she felt it down in the pit of her stomach. Sometimes,

Ollie had a way of knowing things and she had grown accustomed to it, over time. She couldn't hear Tolbert's screams, but she could feel them. She stared out into the distance. *Getting myself on home to see about Tolbert, is the only thing I should worry myself about, right now. Daddy's gone, and there's no changing that now. No matter how badly I wish it weren't so, there's nothing I can do now.* She felt that Tolbert could very well be in some sort of trouble. He may need her. So, she bowed her head, and said a quick prayer, asking again for her father's safe passage into heaven. Then Ollie did the only thing she knew to do. She left him there, just where she had found him. She pulled the blanket gently up over his head, to cover him. Then with one last forlorn look back, she turned and went to her father's room.

She layered on some of her father's heavier clothing that she found hanging in the closet. She made sure that very little of her bare skin would be left exposed to the frigid air. *I had better take care and not let myself get too cold or I'll welt up and start to itchin' like mad, just as sure as the world.* So, she put on his old work boots with several pairs of socks. She braced herself for the blast of cold air as she opened the door, and then carefully made her way off the icy porch. She stopped by the hedges, just beside the house and took one last look back at the bedroom window. *It's right beyond that very window, where my poor ol' father lies dead.*

Ollie turned and began making her way up the path, through the swirling snow, towards home. She tried to keep a steady pace, even though she struggled with every step. She was afraid to stop for fear that her feet would freeze. The boots were way too large, and they allowed snow to fall inside.

She could tell that the temperature was dropping fast, and she knew that the conditions up on the mountain can and do, change on a dime. It didn't matter much what season it was; the weather up here was always been unpredictable. Ollie knew this as well as anybody. Change was the one thing you could always safely predict when living on a mountain.

After trudging through the cold, blinding snow for what seemed like hours, she was able, just barely, to make out the outline of the house through the stark whiteness that was swirling before her. When she realized that she was close, she hurriedly made her way through the snow covered brambles and up the familiar path that led to the barn. She quickly scanned the yard and called out to Tolbert. She was thinking that he could be somewhere out here, lying in the snow if something had happened to him. Then she saw the mule hitched up to the wagon, and her heart fell. *Tolbert would have never left poor ol' Ginger hitched up like that, just standing out in this blizzard.*

Ollie half-ran the rest of the way, crossing over the yard, and guided the shivering old mule into the barn and unhitched the reins that were attached to her. She pushed hard and managed to roll the wagon back some. She rolled it just enough, so that she could close the barn doors and secure them from the fierce wind that was blowing them back and forth. With the mule put away good enough for now, she quickly made her way on up to the house, calling out for Tolbert as she went.

The wind seemed to snatch the sound of her voice immediately away from her, and she wondered if Tolbert could have heard her, at all. Up above Ollie, unseen in the swirling snow, sat the owl peering down on her. He was sitting silently on the tree branch, watching her with large dark eyes. Inside the house, with his head lying on the table, Tolbert thought he heard Ollie calling out for him from somewhere in his dreams. He murmured almost unintelligibly, *I'll be over there to fetch you, directly. Now, don't you go and worry your purty little self one little bit. I'm a'comin' right over to get ya', sweetheart. Just as fast as I can get there, I'm a'comin for ya', Ollie girl.*

27

So do not fear, for I am with you; do not be dismayed, for I am your God. I will strengthen you and help you; I will uphold you with my righteous right hand.

~ ISAIAH 41:10

Whether we think of, or speak to, God, whether we act or suffer for him, all is prayer when we have no other object than his love and the desire of pleasing him.

~ JOHN WESLEY

OLLIE NEARLY LOST it when she saw the porch. Panic-stricken, she tried to cry out but no sound came. The scream lodged itself down deep in her throat, and it stuck there. Blood was smeared and splattered just about everywhere. She raised her hand to her mouth and it trembled in horror of the scene that lay before her. But, even as bad as the porch was, the kitchen was even worse. Tolbert's bloodied boot was lying on the floor near him, and she saw how severely the leather had been cut. The mangled, bloody boot told the story. Ollie pieced it together in just a few short seconds. Her mind instantly calculated how much fresh bandage she would need to try and stop the bleeding. She had heard once that spider webs wadded up and poked down deep into a bad wound could help slow the bleeding, but she had never actually tried it, herself. *What am I thinking? Where in the world would I ever find spider webs in the middle of a snowstorm?* Shaking her head, she silently berated herself for even thinking such a fool thing. She screamed out in her head, *Think, Ollie! You have to think!* She took in a ragged breath and tried her best to focus.

A still voice spoke in her mind. *Just wrapping it up tight, often seems to be the best way. Pulling the edges of the wound together and binding it off tightly, would be the quickest option. Getting the blood to stop is the main thing right now. Just get the blood stopped.* She knew that the wound would need to be cleaned soon, maybe then she could sew it up. The risk of infection was high when an axe wound was not cleaned properly. *Lock-jaw could set in. But, but, I'm not going to even think about that. Lordy mercy, the pain that poor man has suffered.* Ollie felt weak in the knees from the very thought of what Tolbert must have endured.

She placed a hand gently on the side of Tolbert's head, and he opened his eyes and breathed, "Thank God you're here, and you're safe." His face was pallid and his eyes glittered from the pain. Ollie said, "Me? You're worried about me, and you've just about chopped off your foot?" Tears of anguish and compassion rolled freely down Ollie's face. She laid her hands on Tolbert. She placed one soothingly on his head and the other on his shoulder. Ollie bowed her head, and she prayed like she had never prayed before. When she had finished, she managed to get Tolbert into the bedroom and halfway up onto the bed. She had to lean on the bedstead and catch her breath after the struggle of moving him.

Ollie went around to the foot of the bed and reached for the loosened strand of sheeting that Tolbert had tried to bind around his foot. He hissed, "Now, don't you go and touch it!" Ollie recoiled.

"What in thunder do you mean, don't touch it?" Ollie exclaimed. "I have got to get that wound cleaned before it gets infected." Tolbert didn't want Ollie to see the full extent of the damage to his foot. He pushed her away with all the strength he had left in his body. *I just can't let her see the dumb fool thing that I've went and done to myself.* He was ashamed. Tolbert knew that his foot would never be right again, and he knew it without a shadow of a doubt. She deserved a man that could provide for her, and he was most likely going to be crippled from now on. He said, "You just go on and leave my foot alone, now, you hear me? I cleaned it. I poured it slam full whiskey and it's just as clean as it'll ever be." The shock from the manner in which he spoke to her caused Ollie to shrink back. He'd never, ever, spoken to her like that before, not in all their years together.

Ollie quickly decided that it had to be the pain talking, and she didn't say a word. She slowly ducked her head and walked out of the bedroom and into the kitchen. Standing just out of sight, Ollie wrung her hands as her tears silently spilled. She decided that she would unwrap and clean the wound to her satisfaction, just as soon as he went to sleep. *He's just suffering from the shock of it all, right now. Surely that's what it is.* Ollie took off her layered clothes that were quite wet from the melting snow and hung them up near the fire to dry. She put on dry clothes and dried her hair as best she could. After getting warmed up a little, she went to the kitchen with a mop and bucket and began the task of cleaning up the mess.

She slowly shook her head in amazement over the amount of blood he had lost, and how it was smeared nearly everywhere. She picked up the dripping boot and carried it out and set it on the porch by the door. She went back into the kitchen and after cleaning it all up she went out to the porch and did the same. Ollie boiled water over the fire and then set it aside, to allow it to cool. She gathered up some fresh, clean sheets and some cleaning rags. She tore the sheets into strips and then carried everything into the bedroom where Tolbert laid fitfully sleeping.

Ollie gently began to unwrap the foot, and Tolbert's eyes flew open wide. She began to talk low and soothingly. She said, "Tolbert, you are my husband, and I'm not going to let you die from infection. It's just not going to happen, not while I sit idly by and watch. You can't ask me to do such a thing; it just ain't right. You have to let me clean this up. I love you with all my heart, and I don't want to upset you. I know you are in a world of hurt right now. But you know that I've got to do this, and I've got to do this right now." Tolbert's raised his head to protest, and then he let his head fall heavily back onto the bed and didn't say another word.

Ollie took a deep breath and slowly and gingerly, she began to unwind the bloody strips of bandages. The gruesome sight and the size of the jagged gash caused Ollie to gasp out loud, but she bit down on her lip to quiet herself. The flap of still attached skin stuck up where the rest of the toe should have been, so Ollie naturally assumed the bloody, pulpy mess was his toe. *Thank you, dear Lord in Heaven. Thank you that his toes are all still there*, she breathed in prayer. She carefully washed the gash as much as she dared, lest she start it back up to bleeding again. She sprinkled it with calendula powder from the mountain marigolds she had gathered and dried last fall. Ollie knew that marigold powder had the ability to fight infection. She wrapped it up tightly and said a silent prayer. Ollie sat down on the edge of the bed in the dim room. The snow swirled outside the window, and her mind carefully went over each and every moment since she had awakened that morning. The morning's events swirled in such a cloud that it seemed almost like they had happened long ago. Her poor father lay dead in a cold house all by himself; her Tolbert lay here with his foot badly hurt, and a full blown blizzard was cutting off the rest of the world from them, on this ridge high up on the mountain. Ollie drew a shaky breath and slowly let it out. *God in heaven, help us.*

The snow kept swirling down. The drifts blew in and covered over the steps that led up to the porch of the house. Later, Ollie wrapped up warmly and carefully made her way down the snowy steps, to take care of Ginger and to milk the cow. They had vegetables stored down in the root cellar, and after clearing away the snow that had piled up against the door, Ollie went inside. She soon carried up a basket full of potatoes and turnips.

Ollie cooked the meal and brought it in to Tolbert. He refused to take even one bite. His sudden lack of appetite worried Ollie, considerably. The man never refused food. He hadn't, not even once, done so in all the years they'd been married. She looked down at the plate of untouched food and instantly thought of her father. He loved cooked turnips with cream, with a piping hot buttered biscuit. *Why, he loved them better than just about anybody she knew.* She looked down at the plate, and the tears fell from her swollen eyes, once again.

She walked back out to the porch, bent down and picked up the boot. The size of the gash in the leather was tremendous. She turned it over and saw the slit in the sole of the boot. Something rolled out of the boot and thudded softly onto the wooden plank floor. With the light mostly blocked out by the snowstorm, it was too dim for Ollie to see clearly, what it was. She bent down closer and reached out to pick it up. She instantly recoiled. Another silent scream of horror lodged in her throat. Ollie wrapped her arms around herself and rocked back and forth, shaking violently from the force of her tears. Tolbert's bloodied severed toe lay on the porch floor beneath her.

Jane's breath sucked in. *Oh, how horrible. How in the world did Ollie keep her wits about her enough to tend to Tolbert's injured foot, while her father's lying there dead and she has no one there to help bury him? How did she do it all alone, without losing her mind?* Jane closed her eyes as she thought, *Just how much can one person bear?*

Ollie crouched on the porch in the frigid air and cried. She sobbed until she felt a little better and then she began wiping the tears from her face. Feeling empty, she took a deep breath, stood up, and turned to go back into the kitchen. Suddenly, she heard a voice calling out from the yard. "Hello, Ollie?" "Ollie is that you, there?" *The Good Lord answers our prayers*, Ollie thought with relief and a slow exhale of breath. She couldn't believe her eyes.

It was Phil Carrigan and Ned Denton that lived in the next hollow over. They were both members of the nearby church that she and Tolbert attended. Ned opened the screen door, pushing the drifted snow away with the sweep of the door, and stamped the snow off of his boots onto the landing; Phil followed close behind him. Ned said, "Ollie, are you folks alright?" "We've been waiting on Tolbert to bring along that load of firewood that he promised, so we could deliver it on over to the Widow Holtsclaw. He never brought it this mornin', like he said he would." "We wondered if maybe you needed some help, so we came over to find out if something was the matter with the both of you." "Ollie, girl, now why are you takin' on so?" asked Phil intently. "We just thought we'd come on over here to make sure that you were alright." "Tolbert's a man that always does what he says he's going to." Ned and Phil nodded in agreement.

Ollie was overcome with tears of thanksgiving. *Once again, God has sent his angels to help me. His love never fails us.* She took a deep breath and through her tears, she told them about her father and what had happened to Tolbert. Within a few hours, there were better than twenty people there, ready to help bury her father and take care of everything else that needed to be done. Ollie was so relieved and thankful. Tolbert was in terrible pain, but his eyes shone with gratitude. He was thankful that their friends had come to help, just when they needed it so very badly.

Ollie hadn't had the heart to tell Tolbert about her father. So, she quietly went in and explained how it had been when she had found him. Tolbert grieved sorely along with his wife. He had grown to love the old man, just as if he was his own father. Ollie and Tolbert felt bad about not letting Billy know about it so he could at least come to the funeral, but neither one had any idea where he might be. The church members prepared her father's body for the funeral and after a few days, the weather had cleared enough that they were able to bury him. They laid him to rest right beside his beloved Calla, in the little cemetery that overlooks the valley down below.

Ollie felt some peace knowing that he was resting beside her mother and that they were together, once again. Not far from their parent's graves, laid the graves of little Ruby and Minnie. The service was brief but beautiful. Tolbert, of course, stayed at home, and she told him all about it afterward, while sitting on the bed beside him. "Thank the Lord that Ned Denton and Phil Carrigan came over when they did," said Ollie with heartfelt conviction. "God knew that we needed their help and that we needed it in the worst way." "Those men are Angels." Ollie bowed her head and thought prayerfully, *Precious Lord, my refuge and my strength.* Tolbert bowed his head and silently prayed his own prayer of thanksgiving while holding tightly to Ollie's hand.

28

*For the Lord himself will descend from heaven with a cry
of command, with the voice of an archangel, and with
the sound of the trumpet of God. And the dead in Christ
will rise first. Then we who are alive, who are left, will
be caught up together with them in the clouds to meet the
Lord in the air, and so we will always be with the Lord.
Therefore encourage one another with these words.*

~ 1 THESSALONIANS 4:16-18

*As long as I can, I will look at this world for both of us. As
long as I can I will laugh with the birds, I will sing with
the flowers, I will pray to the stars, for both of us.*

~ SASCHA

OLLIE WAS PERPLEXED. *I just don't understand it. I'm just worried something fierce, about that foot.* The color just didn't look
right and she had tried her best working remedies, one right after
the other on the wound. It just didn't seem to be healing up right.
The color of Tolbert's flesh was turning a darker and darker red.

The most troubling thing was that there was a small bubble forming underneath the skin, on the top of his foot. The sight of that kept Ollie from sleeping a wink that night. She had never seen a wound fester quite like this before, so she decided to send word over to the Bates' house and see what Trudy thought she should try as a remedy. James and Trudy had recently moved not very far up the mountain; just about a mile up the road. Trudy's father had passed, and they had come to help Trudy's mom with the farm. Trudy's mother one of the most knowledgeable of all the area's mountain healers. She was the best that Ollie had ever known, besides her own mother, of course. Ollie had exhausted all of the medicine know-how that she had herself, and most of the tried-and-true remedies that had been passed down to her, as well.

Nothing seemed to be working to bring the fever out of poor Tolbert's foot. He could hardly bear any weight on it, because the pain was just too intense. So, Ollie waved down little Bud McKinsey, a boy that happened to be passing by on the road, and asked if he would mind going over and asking Trudy Bates to come and have a look-see at Tolbert's foot. He was on his way to fish at a pond down below the farm. Little Bud was the grandson of Orbie and Sudie McKinsey that lived over on the North Carolina side of the Roan. Orbie and Sudie had themselves a large brood of children. All of their children had grown up, and soon enough had themselves a passel of their own children. Needless to say, Sudie and Orbie had been blessed with more than a gracious plenty of grandchildren. Ollie had lost count of just how many, some time back.

Little Bud seemed more than happy to fulfill Ollie's request. Ollie was grateful and wrapped up some biscuits for him to eat along the way. She stood watching after little Bud as he left. *He tore off from here like the woods was a'fire and his britches were a'catchin'*, Ollie chuckled nervously to herself, despite the knot of worry that she felt deep in her midsection. *God will help me find the medicine that Tolbert needs. He has always shown me the way, whenever I was in doubt.* The words from the book of Psalms, verse 143, came into Ollie's mind, and she spoke the words softly to herself, *Let the morning bring me word of your unfailing love, for I have put my trust in you. Show me the way that I should go, for to you I lift up my soul.*

Trudy and James Bates both came directly over to the house, the very next morning at first light. "I don't want to have to tell you this, Ollie," said Trudy in a tersely hushed tone with her head tucked. They were now all sitting at the kitchen table. They had all gone into the bedroom, just a few moments before, and talked with Tolbert while Ollie had changed his bandage. Tolbert had fallen back asleep just as Ollie had left the room, quietly closing the door behind her. Trudy's brow knit in obvious concern while her hands clasped and unclasped nervously in front of her. Ollie's eyes were steady on her dear friend. Trudy's dark hair and pretty good looks had always been admired by Ollie, as well as her honesty. Trudy continued, "Ollie, I've seen this before, and I'm afraid that it just ain't good--it ain't good at all." "James' good friend, you know the one that lived up over on Buck Mountain?" "Well, he got a terrible infection in his hand after a serious cut." James nodded his head somberly, in agreement with his wife. "The infection got so bad that the doctor had to be called in from Elizabethton," James said while shaking his head slowly. "By the time the doctor had come, the wound had puffed all up and bubbled, something awful like." "He had what the doctor called 'gangrene'."

Trudy reached out and took Ollie's hand gently and said, "Ollie, they had to cut off his arm to stop the infection from going any further." Ollie gasped, and her hand flew to her chest. Trudy quickly added, "Now, I ain't saying for sure that this is the same thing with Tolbert, but it sure seems like it could be." Ollie slowly pushed out her chair out from the table and stood up. Ollie had seen it once before, long ago, herself. She knew the signs, and she had suspected, down deep, what it was. She just hadn't been able to let herself think it. She couldn't have said it out loud, even.

Ollie couldn't help but think that it was all her fault. She should have insisted on cleaning the wound up better, no matter how much it hurt Tolbert. Now, he could lose his foot or maybe even his leg. She covered her face with her hands as her shoulders heaved. Trudy placed her hand gently on Ollie's shoulder, trying as best she could to comfort her. James told Ollie he was going to make sure she had plenty of firewood and that the animals were fed. He reached out and laid a comforting hand on Ollie's other shoulder as he got up and went out to help with the chores. James' help was a blessing, and Ollie was very grateful for it.

Ollie and Trudy stood at the table holding hands, and they prayed together. They prayed earnestly for a miracle of healing for Tolbert. In the days ahead, the swelling and redness soon turned into a sinister dark purple-colored mottling around the wound. The discoloration was slowly creeping up his foot to his ankle. Ollie walked into the bedroom and took yet another tray of untouched food back into the kitchen.

Ollie had made up her mind and she knew that it had to be done. She sat the tray of food sharply down onto the kitchen table. She took a deep breath and walked back into the bedroom where Tolbert lay. *You know that I don't have a choice. You're going to die if we don't take that foot off. You can't just lay here and expect me to watch you die. I love you with all my heart, Tolbert. I will love you no matter what. You know that how you look doesn't matter to me one bit. What does matter is that you are here and with me. I can't lose you, too, Tolbert. You have just got to understand that. I can't lose you, too.* Ollie's face went red, as it flushed with anger and pain. The anger soon dissolved into tears. *I just can't lose you, too. You are all that I have left in the world.* At the sight of Ollie's tears, Tolbert's eyes welled with tears of his own. He spoke almost in a whisper, *I love you, woman. You are everything to me. You have been the best wife a man could've ever had. Don't know why the good Lord saw fit to bless me so, with your sweet kind-hearted soul. But, I can never be any good to you with just one foot. I'd be just another burden you'd have to carry along in this life. I just couldn't live that'a way. Woman, now you know me, sometimes better than I even know myself. You know what that'd be like for me. Please understand. I can't let you cut my foot off, why it'd kill me just sure as the world. Being crippled would kill me deader than a bullet or any ol' blood poisonin' ever could.*

Ollie walked back into the kitchen and stared out the kitchen window, not seeing anything at all. She drew in a shaky breath and slowly exhaled as the tears flowed freely down her face. *How many more tears do I have yet to cry, in this life of mine? Dear Lord, show me the way. Show me what to do,* Ollie thought in desperation.

Each day in the weeks that followed, brought a fresh new hell for Ollie. She tended Tolbert as best she could and tried to make him comfortable. She used all the herbs and tonics that she could think of, to try and ease his suffering. But, there was only so much that could be done for him, at that point. When he finally succumbed to the intense pain, Ollie decided resolutely that the foot had to come off. She called Ned and Phil over to the house, and they agreed to help her with the grisly task. After they had removed the foot, Ollie sat in the chair beside the bed exhausted. She wept inconsolably. She knew that Tolbert's wishes were never to be a cripple, but she couldn't just let him die. How could she have just stood by and done nothing?

The days that followed were harder, still. The gangrene continued despite the amputation. It traveled further up his leg. Nothing could be done except to remove more of the leg. The doctor was summoned, as well as Phil and Ned. The lower leg and knee were removed, but the toxins had taken over, and there was nothing in their power to stop it from finishing its course. The stench of the poisoning became almost unbearable for Ollie. The other women that had offered help early on had finally stopped coming altogether. They fell away slowly, one by one. Ollie really couldn't blame them. It was a horrific thing to witness and even more horrific to have to smell it.

Ollie suffered on, in silence, trying any way that she could to soothe the man that she loved more than anything else on this earth. She watched as the horribly diseased flesh slowly drained the life right out of him. The only ones that stayed to try and help her were Ned and Phil, and, of course, Trudy and James. They came by regularly and did what they could to help make things easier on Ollie. Ollie thanked God daily for the steadfast and dear friends that she had been blessed with.

She sent word, once again, to the doctor over in town, as he was making his rounds. He had come quickly and looked in on poor Tolbert. As he walked out of the bedroom, he shook his head dejectedly. *Why that stubborn man refused your help, for so long, I will never understand. Losing a foot, even losing your whole leg, is a far cry better than losing your life. I just can't help him now, I'm sorry, Ollie, but I'm afraid that it's just too late*, the Dr. sighed resignedly. *Give him this laudanum once, every hour, on the hour. If it doesn't seem to help ease the pain, give him a dose on the half-hour.* Ollie gratefully took the medicine and tearfully shook the doctor's hand. The days to come were sheer torture for Tolbert, as well as for Ollie. After awhile, Ollie prayed fervently that a merciful death would come swiftly. Then she prayed for forgiveness for asking such a thing.

Tolbert's death finally came, but it didn't come easy. He suffered like no other that Ollie had ever seen in her whole life. It tore what was left of her heart, right out of her chest. Her hollowed out eyes haunted everyone that saw her, they couldn't bear to look at her. Her eyes told the horrid story of Tolbert's suffering in excruciating detail; with no words needed. The women of the community banded together after intense prayer, and came and took care of the preparations, as best they could. They brought in food, and quietly went about the house doing all the things that Ollie couldn't while she'd been faithfully tending to her husband. Ollie appreciated the help, but the smell of food in the house hung cloyingly. The aroma mixed with the lingering sickly sweet stench of decay was unbearably horrid. She wasn't sure she could actually still smell it or if it was just her imagination. She wasn't able to swallow down even a single bite, despite the urgings of the well-meaning ladies.

Ollie's living nightmare was finally over. They opened the windows of the house to let in fresh air, and Ollie forced herself to take a deep breath. It was her first in quite awhile. Ollie's chest was so heavy with grief that she felt like her lungs were filled with lead. As they began preparing Tolbert's body for burial, Ollie had allowed the women to take over without any discussion on her part. Ollie was exhausted, but she couldn't rest. Ollie had an even more pressing need at that moment; she needed to spend time in prayer. Ollie walked straight out of the house, weaving to and fro slightly on her weary legs and made her way slowly up the road. She was heading up to the small chapel nestled in the trees, just off the roadside. It was up just a short way from the house, in the bend of the road. Knowing when to seek God had always been easy for Ollie. Hard times and pain inspire many to seek God, even those that possess very little faith. But, Ollie had always sought Him, even during the brief times of her life when things were good. She prayed continuously and chose to seek Him often, but sometimes it was the finding Him, that was difficult. Ollie had quickly progressed through a full array of emotions, from utter desperation to red hot anger. Then her heartache and misery had taken her from complete devastation once again, to an amazing wash of relief. Her deep shame from the feeling of relief was what caused her to seek the chapel. She wanted to ask for forgiveness. She felt sure that relief like she felt just had to be sinful.

Ollie weakly pushed open the double wooden doors of the chapel and entered. The sun warmed wood beneath her hands felt rough and oddly comforting. The old chapel was crude and plain, but beautiful beyond description in its simplicity. The sunlight fell through the branches of the tall oak tree that stood towering over the chapel and peppered through the wavy glass panes of the chapel's windows. The dappled sunlight cast the patterns of the tree branches onto the worn, smooth floorboards below. When the wind blew through the branches, the patterned light danced all about on the floor, directly in front of the pew where Ollie sat. She watched the light as it danced before her with little expression on her gaunt, pale face. There was no reflection of the sparkling light in Ollie's darkened eyes.

The sun was still shining brightly down from the stunningly blue sky above, and her beloved Tolbert lay dead with a blackened stub of a limb. A stub was all that was left of the leg that she had hacked off, trying to save him. *No matter how he fought to stop me, I should've tried to save him, sooner. I have helped save people all my life with my remedies and herbs. I believe in my heart of hearts, that God put me here for that very purpose. Precious Lord and Father in Heaven, how could this have happened? How can the birds still sing outside the window when my world is gone?* Ollie prayed in earnest as she choked back a wracking sob. Ollie grew suddenly limp and slid off the pew, her head thudding on the wooden floor below. Ollie had fainted dead away, the pain was just too much to bear. It was some time later before one of the ladies thought to go and check on Ollie. They had figured that the poor thing needed some time to sort it all out and pray. When Ollie awoke, they were all gathered around her, their concerned faces looming out from the darkening shadows of the coming evening. Ollie flinched, then she suddenly remembered where she was, and she relaxed somewhat. Then the horrid memory of all that had happened came flooding back. Ollie covered her face with her hands and fresh tears flowed.

The Chapel

The men folk hoisted Tolbert's simple casket made of yellow pine up onto the horse-drawn wagon. Ollie followed along behind it, as they walked together to the cemetery. The smell of the newly cut pine wood was sweet and fresh. She remembered how much Tolbert loved to burn pine knots in the fireplace. *The pine knots would sizzle and pop when they were good and fresh. That sweet man dearly loved to smell new cut wood.* She saw his smiling face as he knelt to add more wood to the glowing fire. *My goodness how that man loved me. Love is such an amazing thing. You can never really know how wonderful the love of a good man can be, until you honestly have it for yourself. It's something that you have to feel; words can't tell the story of real love.* Ollie smiled wistfully as she remembered the love in Tolbert's eyes, as he looked up at her in the glow of that warm fire. She felt that she had been blessed more than most in this life, and she was grateful.

The townsfolk fell in behind Ollie silently, as they made their way down the road and up the rocky hillside toward the graveyard. Ollie waited, listening. She knew that they would sing as they walked, as was the custom. One lady began the song in a beautifully lilting voice. The lone voice mixed with the voices of all the other women and together, they lifted up the sweetest harmony that Ollie had ever heard. The sound carried itself along on the wind and down into the hollows that surrounded the road. Then all the men joined in the singing. Someone in the rear starting strumming a mandolin and then a ringing banjo joined as well. The beautiful music filled the cold air. It brought comfort to Ollie to hear the old familiar words once again.

> *"To the river of Jordan our Savior went one day, and we read that John the Baptist met Him there.*
> *And when John baptized Jesus in Jordan's rushing waters, the mighty power of God filled the air.*
> *I'm on my way to the river of Jordan, gonna wade right into the rushing waters.*
> *I'm going down to the river of Jordan, and let the cool waters cleanse my soul."*

They buried Tolbert up on the sunny knoll, that cold winter day. It was such a beautiful spot, overlooking the hollow down below. It wouldn't be too much longer before the snow melted away completely and once again, the mountain would feel the warmth of spring embrace it. She imagined the spot lush and green again, and that brought her comfort. Ollie stood with her head bowed low at the graveside. It was hard for any that had attended the funeral, to tell exactly what she was feeling. The truth was she hardly knew herself. She felt all hollowed out, on the inside, like an old rotten log that had been flushed with a hot fire. She felt numb clear down to the bone.

Despite the desperate emptiness that she felt, one thing in particular still caused her intense pain. Ollie still felt a vague sense of what she thought sure was that same feeling of relief. She was honestly relieved that he had gone on to heaven because he was no longer in such unspeakable pain. His suffering had been unbearable to witness. She felt guilty for feeling such relief, but she just couldn't help herself from feeling it. She still smelled the stench of the rotten flesh hanging sickeningly in her nostrils. *My poor, sweet Tolbert.* She knew she would smell that horrible smell for quite some time to come. Ollie shuddered as a single tear fell down her cheek.

29

"Though the mountains be shaken and the hills be removed, yet my unfailing love for you will not be shaken, nor my covenant of peace be removed," says the Lord, who has compassion on you.

~ ISAIAH 54:10

A sunbeam to warm you,
A moonbeam to charm you,
A sheltering angel, so nothing can harm you.

~ IRISH BLESSING

THE OLD WEATHERED oak tree stood tall in the cemetery. It had been there when they had buried her mother and sisters, and for many long years before that. It towered overhead proudly, standing sentry over all the graves. It was leaning slightly toward the valley below, with its gnarled limbs outstretched as if seeking to embrace those that had been laid to rest beneath it, down further in the hollow below. Ollie looked up at the old tree and imagined the steady flow of sorrow that it had witnessed in all of its years, overseeing burial after burial. She almost felt compassion for the twisted old tree. Ollie stood there in the cold wind alone as she studied on why God had seen fit to take away the only man she had ever loved. *Tolbert was the only man that ever loved me.* She stood alone and pondered why God hadn't just taken her instead. *Why have you left me here? Haven't I suffered enough for whatever sins that I have committed?* She wondered if there was a reason for it all. *Was there something that He has kept in mind all these years? Is there a reason for all my suffering? Why has my life been so hard?*

Then Ollie remembered that God himself had suffered. He had let his own son die, a selfless sacrifice for the salvation of all of mankind. He had allowed an innocent to die, to save us all. Ollie hung her head in shame. *Forgive me, Lord. Please forgive me.* She was truly thankful for all she had been given in this life and felt instant remorse for allowing herself to question God's plan.

Sudie Barnett, a tiny wisp of a girl that lived two hollow's over in a pitiful cabin, timidly approached Ollie as she stood by watching the men. They were beginning to fill in the earth over the grave. After the first shovel full had scattered out on top of the casket, Ollie suddenly realized that the little girl was standing right beside her. It startled Ollie and she flinched visibly. Sudie looked up at Ollie with eyes the color of the misty morning sky in October. She timidly reached out and touched Ollie's arm. Ollie managed a weak smile and bent down closer to her. Sudie sighed softly, and then she spoke in a small, trembling voice. *"Miss Ollie, I have to tell you something an' it's real important, honest." "Mr. Tolbert came over to th' house real early this mornin' and he told me somethin'. He came special to tell me that I was 'posed to say this to you and that I wasn't to forget it, no matter what."* Ollie blinked, suddenly frozen in place. She could scarcely breathe.

Little Sudie lowered her gaze and kept her eyes focused on the ground. It was obvious to Ollie that she didn't want to look directly at the casket, or down in the grave below. She raised her head bravely and looked back up at Ollie, beseechingly. Ollie, feeling an instant wave of compassion for the poor little girl, reached out and placed her hand on Sudie's thin shoulder. She was wearing a badly worn patched coat over her cotton dress. Ollie saw that it couldn't have kept her very warm, especially with the stiff wind that was rolling down the mountain. Ollie took off the shawl that was draped around her shoulders and wrapped it around the child. Sudie smiled wanly in gratitude. *"Mr. Tolbert told me t'be sure and tell you, not to stay all by yo'self in that ol' house, now. He said that it jest wouldn't be safe. He told me that you needed to move up on out of that ol' house, just as soon as you can."* Little Sudie Barnett stood there as shining tears welled up in her deep blue eyes and she whispered softly, *"Get out, Miss Ollie. Get out now. Jest as soon as you can."* Ollie was filled with a sense of dread that formed as a sickening lump deep down in the pit of her stomach, and all she could manage in reply was a shaky nod of her head. The child let her breath out slowly as if she felt immense relief. She then gave Ollie half a smile as she handed her the shawl, then turned quickly and ran down the hill. Ollie stood motionless by Tolbert's freshly dug grave. She watched Sudie run down into the hollow as her coat tail whipped out behind her in the strong cold wind. Sudie turned suddenly and disappeared into the dense tree line. She was gone from sight in an instant. Ollie's mind raced. There had to be some explanation. *There just has to be some way that this can make sense. That child wouldn't begin to know how to go about making up a story such as that. She's far too innocent.*

Ollie thought of Tolbert's passing. He had raised his arm and reached out to someone or something that he saw right before him. *He saw something, without a doubt. He'd looked straight ahead and almost smiled.* Ollie believed at that very moment, with all her heart, that her Tolbert had seen the face of God. *So, why in the world did that sweet little child believe that she had talked with him that very same morning?* Ollie puzzled for quite awhile over what the girl's message could have meant, and then she decided to simply let it go. She certainly had enough to worry about, right now. She had to think of things such as how to feed herself and how to somehow keep herself warm. She was suddenly alone and on her own, up on a very unforgiving mountain.

The days after the funeral were a blur for Ollie, but somehow she managed. A couple of women from the church took turns staying with her. They usually stayed for a few nights after the death, so that the widowed wife wouldn't have to be all alone. Ollie was grateful for all the help and kindness that they had shown her. Ollie's sadness had seemed to always keep people an arm's length away, and over the years most people just stopped going out of their way to be extra friendly. Ollie understood this without questioning it. *Sometimes folks just naturally steer themselves clear of those that are hurtin' real bad. They don't mean a thing by it; it's just the way people have of dealing with things that are hard to deal with. Especially when they don't know exactly what to do and they don't really know how to go about helping.* Ollie was very grateful for the few true friends that had stuck by her.

There were days when Ollie thought for sure that she had caught glimpses of shadows out of the corner of her eyes and some days it was nearly every time that poor girl turned around. She would sit and study Tolbert's chair where it sat empty, close to the fireplace. It was almost as if she thought she could bring him back, just by hoping it was so. It was sad. Even once she thought for sure that she had heard him calling out for her. She had run right out to the barn in a blinding thunderstorm because she had to 'just make sure' that Tolbert wasn't out there needing her for something. She knew that she wasn't actually hearing him call her, but her heart told her something else entirely. Ollie went out daily to check on Ginger and tend to the chickens and such. Some days she would hurry back inside and start to call out for Tolbert, simply forgetting that he just wasn't there. Ollie's tears would soon pour down like a hard rain. It was just about the saddest thing you ever did see. It's a wonder that woman had any tears left to cry. You know it's a mighty lonesome sound when you call out for somebody and you hear only the silence. It's enough to drive a person crazy, I tell you, now, it is.

The days passed by slowly for Ollie. With Tolbert gone, Ollie soon realized exactly how hard it was for a woman alone to make a life up on the mountain. She quickly decided that there was no way she could farm the land by herself. She plowed a small garden patch and planted it early in the spring. She thought she had planted plenty enough to see her through the winter, providing she stored everything she could in the cellar and canned all that she could. After all that hard work, the garden was slow to come up and then there was a late killing frost. She replanted, but there was no rain for weeks and all around the mountain, the gardens just dried right up. It was devastating, because most all of the folks in the area re-lied on their gardens for the food that would see them over the long winter.

Ollie suddenly found herself at the mercy of her neighbors. These same people often have barely enough food for themselves, let alone another mouth, as well. So, she reluctantly made the only sound de-cision that she knew to make. Ollie tearfully decided that she had to leave Happy Valley and head back to where she still had family. She could rely on her family, and she knew that without a doubt.

She waited until summer had come and the earth had warmed up some. The warmer weather would be more suitable for sleeping outside. *She packed what little personal belongings she could and hitched up ol' Ginger to the wagon. She loaded up only as much furniture as she dared onto the wagon.* She carried the rocking chair that Tolbert had so lovingly carved for her and put it on the wagon last. After gathering what wildflowers she could find from the parched meadow below, she lovingly placed them on all the graves in the tiny cemetery.

She stood in the yard beside the house and cried. She allowed herself to cry it all out, as best she could. There was no one close enough to hear her, so she released the pain that had been building up for days, in anticipation of this very moment. She took one last look back, at all of it. She looked at the home that Tolbert had built for them and the land that had been her home since she was just a babe. She tried to preserve the memory of exactly how it all looked because she knew she may never make it back again, to see it. She said a prayer for all her family that was gone and laid to rest in the ground that once belonged to her father, asking God to watch over them all.

Ned Denton and Phil Carrigan both had generously promised to tend the cemetery for her. Ollie was so touched by all the kindnesses they had both shown her, especially since losing her Tolbert. She had tearfully thanked them from the bottom of her heart, only to see that they both had tears in their eyes, as well. They were both wonderful men that loved their family dearly and their extended church family, as well. They had always been such good friends to her sweet Tolbert. They had all been there for each other, for nearly all their lives. James and Trudy had come over the day before and said their tearful goodbyes. The bond between all these friends had been a lasting bond. Leaving them and their sweet families behind nearly broke poor Ollie's heart all over again.

Ollie let her mind travel back to the day she had first met Tolbert. She remembered his shy ways and his first tender sweet kisses. She remembered working for Miss Hicks and helping with her washings and such. Then her mind quickly carried her back to the sound of a rushing creek, and she remembered once again, the horrible pale faces of little Minnie and Ruby. She stopped herself short and sternly thought, *You can't let yourself wallow around in self-pity for the rest of your life. You've got to get on with livin', somehow. It's God's will that I'm still here. Must be that God still has work for me to do.* Ollie sighed. *Well, it seems like I'm finally goin' to leave Happy Valley behind me. Where He has a will, He surely has a way.* She lifted up her head, looked up at the heavens and the beloved Bible verse Isaiah 51:6, came instantly to her mind. She smiled, feeling bolstered. Then she spoke it aloud, saying, *Lift up your eyes to the heavens, look at the earth beneath, the heavens will vanish like smoke, the earth will wear out like a garment, and its inhabitants die like flies, but my salvation will last forever, my righteousness will never fail.* Still wearing a triumphant but quivering smile on her lips, Ollie slowly turned and led the old mule up along the path to the familiar dirt road. *Come on Ginger, home's on up the road, just waiting for us.*

Not allowing herself to look back, not even once, Ollie struck out on the road heading straight for the beautiful rolling ridges of Roan Mountain. Weeks later, Ollie was still traveling along on the road toward the mountain. She was bone tired. Her clothes and hair were dusty and dirty. She was slowly trudging along, beside the wagon. Her muddied shoes were nearly worn out. She had taken strips of rags and tied them on her feet to keep what was left of the soles of her shoes from coming completely off. She thought that since the load was surely considerably lighter now, she might, just maybe, make it to the Roan before sundown. She had been forced to sell off her prized poster bed, but she knew she had to have a horse. That bed had been a gift from Tolbert, but somehow, she knew that he would've understood. Tolbert's amazing talent in wood carving had helped them through many tough spots and trading off the bed so quickly, had been yet another godsend for sure.

Ginger just hadn't been strong enough to pull the heavy wagon for very long. *The poor ol' thing, she was plumb give out.* When they had rounded that last bend in the road, the old mule had slid off the side of the ditch into the thick mud and the wagon had gotten stuck. Just when Ollie thought all was lost, God had provided for her, once again. A man had happened along that lived on the farm right across the field. He seemed happy to trade the horse he was leading for the bed and had even offered to take Ginger as well. Ollie feared that leaving Ginger behind was going to break her heart. Ollie thought contritely, *You know it seems strange, but after your heart's been torn in two, time and time again, having another heartache seems, strangely enough, not near as big.* Ollie instantly reconsidered as a lump formed in her throat. She thought, *Now, dad-blame it, you just went on ahead and let yourself get way too attached to that bony old mule. That's what ya' went and done, and you know it, just as sure as the world. You caused this mess for yourself,* Ollie lamented.

She had a strong tendency to 'mother' just about all the animals she had come in contact with through the years living on the farm. *You just went ahead and let that motherin' instinct get the better of you, that was what ya' went and done,* Ollie thought to herself with a heavy sigh. *Poor ol' Ginger, she was a sweetheart. Best mule that I ever did have the pleasure of knowing. Couldn't help but love her,* Ollie thought sadly. She wiped her tears and kept trudging along.

Ollie began singing hymns softly just to pass the time. She thought that maybe it would help take her mind off how scared she was. Her sweet voice rang out through the rolling countryside and over the pastureland. Surely, better days lay somewhere ahead for Ollie. Ollie knew she had made the best decision she could have; deciding to come back to the Roan. She felt that it had to be the right thing to do, heading back to the mountain that Calla, and Aunt Isabelle, both, had loved so dearly.

Ollie thought, *I am finally going back 'home' to the land that is surely filled with God's love and mercy. With God's help, hopefully, I can find a place where I can feel safe once again. Maybe, it will be a place where my heart will heal. Seems mighty strange to be coming home to a place that I've never seen, but then again, I've seen it in my dreams many, many times.* Ollie smiled. She steadily made her way up the dusty road, slowly passing by farms and fields.

The shadows began to stretch and lengthen, as they fell through the dense trees in the distance. The sun began its slow descent on the horizon as yet another day drew to a close. Ollie still walked slowly along. She thought, *I sure don't look forward to another miserable night lying in the wagon, listening to strange sounds that keep me awake.* Suddenly, she could see that the road forked up ahead.

Ollie dropped the reins she was holding and comfortingly patted the horse's neck. She whispered sympathetically to the horse, *Poor thing, I know that you've got to be just about as tired as I am. I think I might just call you Jolly Belle, you sweet thing, you.* The gentle horse had already won over Ollie's tender heart. Ollie turned her head and studied the road off in the distance and she could barely make out the lettering on a small weathered sign that pointed to the left. It was located at a fork in the road. Her words came out in a barely audible whisper; "Roan Mountain." *Praise the Lord!* A wide smile spread across her dirt-streaked face. She had finally made it. She was very near to her journey's end.

Ollie was dead tired, but her heart quickened in her chest. Tears of happiness threatened to fall, but she blinked them back. With newly-found strength, she climbed into the wagon quickly despite her sore legs, and she gathered up the reins and urged Jolly Belle onward. Within the hour, she was standing in front of the old Correll home place. It looked almost exactly the way her mother had described it to her, many long years before.

Isabelle came out onto the porch wiping her hands on her apron. She squinted into the bright glow of the setting sun, trying to see who it was out in the yard before her. She let out a cry of surprise and made her way as quickly as she could down the steps toward Ollie. The women embraced with their foreheads touching, while tears coursed down both of their faces. "Precious little Ollie, you've made it back home safely. You are here, safe and sound. Praise the Lord! God's love and mercy, lead you safely home!" Isabelle said in a coarse whisper as she choked back tears of joy. *God is so good!*

Welzia and Isabelle Correll Arrowood

30

Though care and trouble may be mine,
As down life's path I roam,
I'll heed them not while still I have
A world of love at home.

~ J.J. REYNOLD. 1844

Perhaps they are not the stars, but rather openings in
Heaven where the love of our lost ones pours through and
shines down upon us to let us know they are happy.

~ AUTHOR UNKNOWN

ISABELLE STEPPED BACK, pulling slightly away from Ollie. She intently studied her face. She noted the dark circles under Ollie's eyes and her bedraggled state. "You're coming right inside this house, this very minute. You're going to have something filling to eat, and then you are going to lie down and rest yourself a spell." Ollie smiled thankfully and offered up not a single word of protest. If she knew anything at all about the Correll women, she knew that they weren't easily dissuaded. There wasn't any use in trying to talk this lady out of what she thought was supposed to happen. You just did as you were told, and that was just about all there was to it.

Ollie was far too tired to think of anything but resting, so she allowed herself to be ushered inside the house. *I'm home, at last. Thank you, precious Lord, for seeing me safely back home, once again.* The smell of the kitchen was amazing. The stove had warmed the room up, almost to the point of being intolerable. Still, the smells coming from it had never smelled so good to Ollie in all of her life. The biscuits were steaming hot and wrapped up in a bread cloth. Isabelle had nestled them down into a wooden bowl that was sitting inside the warmer atop the old wood cook stove. There were chicken and dumplings bubbling in a huge pot.

Ollie had no idea of how hungry she truly was until that very moment. "Oh, sweet Aunt Isabelle, how I have missed you," Ollie said with intense emotion. Isabelle turned from busily rustling Ollie up a plate of food and smiled a tender smile at her. "You've been drug through a world of hurt, child. Your last letter nearly broke my heart. But, you are home now. I aim to see that you are taken real good care of, from here on out. Now, that's exactly what I aim to do."

Ollie sat down at the table and reluctantly allowed Isabelle to wait on her. The very first bite of the piping hot biscuit, slathered down in butter and covered with wonderful blackberry jam, took Ollie straight back to her childhood and her own mother's biscuits.

Ollie couldn't stop herself from becoming emotional. Tears welled up in her eyes and suddenly the sharp grief and intense pain of all that had happened came flooding out. Alarmed, Isabelle rushed over to her side and put her arm around Ollie's shoulders as she cried and said. "You just go on ahead, now child. You just go on ahead and let all of it right on out'a you. You have held it all inside, for far too long already." Overcome and bone-tired, Ollie did just that. She let it all come flowing out in a terrific torrent.

Isabelle had seen plenty of hurt in her life, but she knew that God's tender love would sustain them through this storm, just as He had all of the other ones. *Storms will blow and they come along often in a lifetime and that's just how it is. All a body can do is weather through them, as best as you can. This poor girl has seen more than her share, I declare she has,* Isabelle thought sadly. Isabelle had just turned 56 years old. Her age was beginning to show, and her hair had turned silver at her temples, but she still had the same twinkle in her eye that she had always had. Welzia was soon to be 58, come next February. Both considered themselves extremely blessed to have lived to see their family grow. Now the children were beginning to branch out and make families of their own. Life on the Roan had been good to them.

Welzia still regularly made the circuit preaching, and Isabelle tended to a few of the grandchildren now and then. They both loved the life they led. "Now, don't you go a'thinkin' about having to rush off and get yourself a house on your own, just yet. You'll not go and do any such thing. You'll stay right here with us, we got ourselves plenty of room, now that the kids have pert near all gone."

Isabelle told Ollie just a few days later, "You need to just stay put right here, where you are, for at least a good month or so, so you can rest yourself before you go off trying to get the 'little house' fixed up good enough to live in it." "Little house?" asked Ollie. "Yes. There's that little cabin that James Edward built out yonder, behind the house. It's yours; that is if you'll have it." "You're more'n welcome to it." Isabelle smiled broadly.

Ollie was overwhelmed and too happy to speak. Instead, she quickly walked over to Isabelle and hugged her. "Now, don't take on so, child. You'd be the one doing us the favor, by fixing it up. Otherwise, it'll soon go to rack and ruin." Isabelle said, "You'll be mighty surprised at how a coat of paint will work wonders for that little cabin."

Ollie smiled and shook her head in agreement. Isabelle and Welzia's cabin was behind the main house. Their eldest son, James

Edward, had built it in his teens. First James, and then Fielden had lived in it, when each had come of age. Neither had lived there for very long, before they found themselves a wife and got married. After they married, they moved out and built themselves their own houses. The little cabin was in need of some repair, but not a considerable amount. Just a couple of weeks' worth of work would have it back in tip-top order. The small cabin was close to the barn, behind the main house.

Isabelle felt that Ollie would feel more at home and more comfortable, in a place by herself. She would still be close enough to not feel alone when she needed companionship. Isabelle felt it was the perfect solution. Ollie didn't mind the thought of working on the cabin, at all. In fact, she welcomed the thought of hard work eagerly. It kept her mind from focusing on everything else. She soon had the cabin back in order, and they moved her in just over a week's time. Ollie loved the little cabin and was most appreciative of Isabelle's and Welzia's generosity.

Ollie soon began going out on the mountain and searching for special medicinal plants and herbs, just about every morning. She had always searched out and located the plants by their foliage when the weather was still warm. She knew that come fall, she could dig the roots and harvest the crop of valuable medicines that the mountain offered up for those that came to find them. She wanted to help bring in a little extra money for Isabelle. The herbs would certainly help pay her way. The ancient mountain's flora was diverse, and it offered many medicinal herbs and plants, many of which were not found elsewhere. These healing plants were in plentiful supply, pretty much all over the mountain. All a body needed to gather them was the knowledge of where to look to find them.

Ollie had been taught well and knew what to look for almost as well as her mother once had. She had gathered up quantities of squaw weed and wild cherry bark since she was just a young girl. Her mother had shown her how to identify the different plants, and how to determine which mushrooms were edible. She knew that the squaw weed was good for enriching the blood and strengthening the bowels. She also gathered a large amount of boneset. She used boneset quite often for aches and pains, and she also gathered up horehound for troublesome coughs. The 'sang' was best used on children that had diphtheria or on those that were croupy and coughing. For those with coughs that wouldn't go away easily, she always made a soothing salve. She'd often make a thick salve out of mutton tallow, mixed with turpentine and sulfur. Then she would advise them to coat their chests really well with the salves, especially at nighttime. She would even put some between their shoulder blades and on the bottom of their feet. The salves and concoctions that Ollie made sure smelled something awful, but they worked exceptionally well.

Ollie learned fast that 'sang' especially, could be turned into cash money very easily. It was always sought after, by the wealthier people as well as the regular folks, in the community. 'Sang', as Ollie and everyone else in the area called it, was wild ginseng root. If you were to break off a small piece carefully and replant a small 'leg' of the root after digging it up, the plant would replenish itself over time. Otherwise, digging up the entire root without replanting a portion, meant that eventually the ginseng would be gone. Ollie was careful not to deplete the mountain's ample supply, and she regularly replanted at each harvest. She gathered the ginseng by digging around it and carefully pulling up the root. Then, she hung it up in burlap sacks, high in the barn, to dry.

Ollie waited for the bulk of the 'sang' to dry out completely before she put the filled burlap sacks on the wagon and headed into town. Ollie started out early one morning with her wagon full. She drove the wagon over to the side of the road and set the brake securely then she tied a rope to the bridle, securing the horse. Ollie adjusted her hat and lightly brushed the dust from her dress. Ollie lifted her chin as she walked across the wooden walkway and strode confidently toward the store. It was her intention to try and look much more confident than she really felt. Ollie briefly glanced up and above the doorway, the shop's sign declared in bold black lettering: 'Shell's Mercantile'. She tried her best to recall all the things that Welzia had told her about doing business in town. Ollie knew full well that it wasn't considered to be a woman's place to do business such as this, especially a woman that was unaccompanied by a man. She felt that it was indeed an old-fashioned manner of thinking, one that surely needed to be changed. She knew that she had every right to do her business here. *Why, she had just as much right as any man had.* Ollie had decided quickly that she was more than capable of attending to her own business and declined Welzia's well-meaning offers to accompany her to town. She was quite confident that she could handle any business transaction with just as much savvy as any man she had ever known. She was on a mission to prove just that, once and for all.

Ollie stiffened her spine and lengthened her neck, drawing herself up as tall and straight as possible. She took a deep breath and placed a demure smile of satisfaction on her face. The smile belied her true state of mind, as butterflies commenced a frenzied flight in her midsection. She pushed open the door and strode briskly over to the counter. The shopkeeper had his back turned to the counter. He spoke without turning his head, back over his shoulder. "Be right with you, now." He continued rummaging through the shelf, evidently searching for something in particular, but not seeming to find it. As the seconds ticked slowly away, all of the confidence leaked right out of poor Ollie like a rapidly deflating balloon. *What in thunder was I thinking, coming up here to do business by myself? I don't have the slightest idea in the world of what I need to say to this man. This is something that men take care of, not some woman that hasn't even been to a real mercantile in nigh over fifteen years, maybe even more!* The storekeeper slowly turned around, and their eyes met. "Well, what can I help you with today, ma'am?" He said the words with softly smiling eyes.

Ollie's mind went totally blank. The man was handsome and tall. His dark eyes were friendly and attentive. He towered over Ollie and looked down at her with obvious interest. She felt a sudden flame of heat as her cheeks began to glow from the embarrassment of his intense stare. She stammered at first then quickly drew her wits about her and spoke in a clear voice. She recited nearly word for word what she had rehearsed over and over, as she had hitched the horse to the wagon. "I, I have excellent ginseng root for sale. It's good quality root, and it has been dried right well and proper. I aim to get not a penny less than the fair price that I'm asking for it." The shop keeper's eyebrows rose as he continued to look Ollie over with interest. He sniffed and reached over to the side of the counter to adjust several of the items on display. Ollie's brow knit with consternation, taking his manner as an indication that he was trying to dismiss her. "I have quality ginseng for a reasonable price, but, if you, my good sir, are not interested, I will gladly take my business elsewhere." He looked up at Ollie with widened eyes and said, "Now, jest hold on there, Miss. No sense flyin' off the handle and gettin' your fur all riled up, over nothin' at all." "I'm not interested in your 'sang,' alright, even if your price is reasonable." Ollie tensed and her lips set in a hard line. "I'm just not interested; that's the thing. But look, if you're aiming to sell it, why, take it right on up to the Cloudland Hotel." "They've just opened it up, and it's a mighty fine place. People are saying that they are buying local produce, even lots of them wild mushrooms, and some 'sang,' too, I'd imagine."

Ollie's hard-set lips softened and spread into a wide smile in the blink of an eye. Ollie had heard people talking about the new Cloudland Hotel and how the rich were flocking up the mountain to stay there. She'd even seen the wagons pass on the road, herself. The hotel was being advertised as a health retreat destination with abundant clean mountain air. 'Come find Abundant Health and Relaxation, Up Among the Clouds' is what Ollie had read on the paper poster hanging in town. Ollie thought, *Well, land sakes, how come I didn't I think of that, myself?* The delicacy of wild, locally harvested mushrooms would be highly desired by rich out-of-towners.

Those rich highfalutin folks would soon be flooding up the mountain, by the dozens. Ollie's sharp mind quickly calculated the number of people that would surely come up the mountain on the train, just to eat in the hotel's fancy dining rooms. Ollie smiled broadly. "Why, I thank you kindly, sir. Have yourself a wonderful, blessed morning." The shopkeeper nodded his head with an approving smile and turned back to his work.

Ollie emerged from the store just a few moments later with a tow-headed young boy wearing an apron following closely behind her. She had hired the boy to drive the wagon up the rugged mountain road and to assist her in delivering her goods. Once they had made their way up the mountain to the hotel, Ollie was instantly struck by the impressive structure. There were people milling about everywhere. She could barely take her eyes off the place as she stepped down from the wagon. She asked the boy to tend to the horse and the wagon, and she walked over to the main entrance.

Ollie walked inside the hotel entrance and saw the largest rock fireplace that she had ever seen. The entrance itself was impressive, but the hotel was much more so. Ollie was quite taken by the posh and beautiful lobby. She walked to the front desk and asked for assistance, and she was soon directed by a stylish young man, to bring her goods around to a back entrance. She talked with several men before striking a deal with the assistant to the owner of the hotel, himself. She went back out to the wagon and gave quick instructions to the hired boy. The boy then hoisted the burlap sacks, one by one, up off the wagon. He somehow managed, after shouldering the heavy bags with quite some difficulty. Ollie walked behind the wagon and paused briefly. She then quickly cast a furtive glance all around her. When she was satisfied that no one was watching, Ollie raised her fists and shook them about in the air, happily. Ollie was absolutely elated that she had made her very first successful business transaction, all on her own. She had also gotten the full price she had asked. The man hadn't even batted an eye at the price that she had quoted. Not only that, but they wanted her to regularly supply the hotel with ginseng and mushrooms. She felt empowered and very happy with herself, very happy indeed.

The man that she had just done business with had introduced himself as Charles Gouge. He had also seemed to be interested in more than just Ollie's mushrooms or ginseng. Ollie allowed herself a small smile remembering the exchange in detail. She made trips twice a week up to the Cloudland to peddle the mushrooms and the herbs that she had gathered. She and Charles Gouge got to know one another pretty well as the months wore on.

31

Turn your face to the sun and the shadows fall behind you.

~ MAORI PROVERB

Forgiveness is the fragrance that the violet sheds on the heel that has crushed it.

~ MARK TWAIN

OLLIE STAYED ON with Isabelle and Welzia, contentedly living in the cozy little cabin. Every evening she would walk out onto the grassy balds and watch the beautiful sunset as the mountain took on an amazing peachy glow. She understood fully why her people had settled here. She knew in her heart that she was home. She continued gathering mushrooms, various herbs, and of course, the 'sang'. She sold them periodically to bring in extra money, in exchange for her board. It was a welcome boost to Welzia and Isabelle's meager income. Not only did she sell her sang and mushrooms, but she also regularly used her healing herbs to help those who were sick and in need. Her medicinal knowledge and doctoring abilities became widely known in a short time, and people traveled many hard miles from distant communities, to get her advice and help. Ollie was always more than happy to oblige.

Charles Gouge was known about town for quite more than just being a manager at the Cloudland Hotel. According to many, he had a serious drinking problem that he had struggled with for many years. Because of Ollie's honest interest in trying to help people, she casually mentioned to Charles that it was thought that 'sang' also helped some people want to drink liquor less. She offered to try and help him with his struggle, one day while she was up at the hotel, delivering her mushrooms. Ollie could tell just by looking at his complexion, that he had a penchant for the bottle. She had a keen eye, and she could often tell what was ailing a body with just a look.

He reluctantly agreed to try it, and it turned out that it truly helped him. He was clean and sober for quite a few months. After a few more months had passed, he asked Ollie if she would like to attend a church social that was planned for later that month. She happily surprised even herself, when she accepted his invitation. Soon, the day arrived, and Charles rode up to the house in a fancy carriage to get Ollie. Welzia had never seen a carriage like this one, at least not up close. He stared at the carriage from a distance, but he didn't approach it.

Welzia stood out on the front porch as Isabelle was cooking supper inside. He was just plain leery of the likes of Charles Gouge and felt that he had plenty enough reason to feel the way that he did. Rumors had been milling all around town that he had killed his first wife in a drunken rage. Everyone felt sure that he had done it, but he had never been brought to task for it. The local constable had determined that she had hit her head on the hearth and that it was completely accidental, but according to the talk around town, it was no accident. Accident or not, the truth of the matter was that his wife was dead. But, it had been observed by many in town that he never seemed to show much grief over her loss. Quite honestly, he hadn't even shown an ounce of grief. His actions were just not what you would expect from a grieving widower. He went right on back to work, the very next day after the funeral, just as if nothing had ever happened. His actions just didn't sit well with most of the towns-people. *That sure started the tongues that wag to commence to waggin', and in the worst way. Where's there's smoke, there's more than likely fire,* Welzia thought as he watched Charles's fancy wagon roll up to the little house and pull to a stop, in front. *Better not start playin' with fire, now Ollie girl. Playing with fire can get you burned real bad. I may not be able to stop it, but I'm sure goin' to try.* Welzia had grown quite fond of his niece by marriage. He felt protective of her and he wanted no more hurt to come to her. *Ollie had surely been through enough heart-ache already.* He couldn't just stand by and watch someone hurt her. He was a man of God, and he knew that sometimes you just can't barge right in and interfere in another's life. But this, now this was something altogether different. This was something that he couldn't just take lightly or easily dismiss. Ollie could very well be in danger. He decided to pray earnestly about it and that he would have to tell her about his misgivings concerning Charles. He couldn't live with himself if he didn't, and something bad happened. Welzia knew that they'd have to talk, and talk soon.

Even to her own amazement, Ollie was happy. She felt almost like a queen around Charles. He went out of his way to do special things for her. Everyone in town watched from a distance, most with their own unspoken doubts and suspicions. No one dared to speak to Ollie about the whispering that was going on behind her back. Everyone had grown to love her and depend on her, especial-ly for the medicinal herbs that she gathered and her knowledge of healing that she so eagerly shared. Sometimes she offered her help, never expecting a thing in return. When Ollie saw that there was a genuine need and that they had very little with which to pay her, she brought the medicine to the sick anyway. It was just the right thing to do, as far as Ollie was concerned. When a neighbor lady came down with a croupy cough that lingered on for quite awhile,

Ollie made her tea out of mountain mint, and she soon felt better, in almost no time at all.

Ollie seemed to have finally found a place where she could be truly happy, in the small community of the Roan. She had always felt that she should put her knowledge of medicinal plants to good use, helping those around her. This ability made her feel needed and connected to the community. The knowledge she possessed was simply amazing to many of the folks in the area, and word of it spread quickly over into neighboring towns, as well.

Ollie especially loved to gather wild mushrooms and had become an expert on how to identify them. She could easily distinguish the edible ones from the poisonous ones. She tried to share this knowledge often, and she taught others how to tell them apart, as well. She hoped to prevent the children, or anyone else for that matter, from eating the wrong ones. She knew that any wild food that could supplement the diet of those that had very little, would be of great benefit. She seemed to just naturally draw the area's children around her, almost like a magnet. The children loved being around Ollie. Many mornings Ollie would step outside the cabin, and find them sitting quietly out on the porch, waiting for her to guide them on a happy romp through the woods to find mushrooms, pokeweed, and such. On some mornings when it was cool enough, Ollie would let the children lead Jolly Belle along with them on their excursions. The horse was so gentle and dearly loved being around the children. Jolly Belle seemed to flourish with all the extra attention that they gave her.

One morning, after an exceptionally invigorating trip into the woods with the neighboring children, Ollie came back into the house with a basketful of fresh ramps. She set the basket down on the edge of the table with a light laugh of delight. Ollie adored spending time with the children and absolutely relished each moment. Isabelle was busy kneading bread in a huge wooden bowl that Welzia had carved out for her many years before. With her hands coated in flour,

Isabelle looked up at Ollie and quietly said, "We need to talk a bit betwixt us, Ollie."

Ollie's questioning eyes lifted to meet Isabelle's gaze, immediately. She could hear in Isabelle's voice that something was amiss. Ollie's eyes narrowed. Isabelle drew in a long breath and said, "You know that we want only the best for you. You've become like a daughter to Welzia and me, and you've certainly become very special to our little Pat and Esther. Why, all the kids have gotten close to you. We all love you dearly, child." Ollie smiled. "Yes, and you all are very special to me. You've all welcomed me with open arms, and I'm very touched and grateful for it," said Ollie. "You have shared your home and made me feel as if I truly belong here."

Isabelle slowly wiped her hands on her apron with her head bowed low and said. "What I need to say isn't something that'll come easy-like. You're a full grown woman. You're fully capable of making your own decisions in life. Welzia wanted to talk with you himself, but I decided that it would be best, coming from me. I know you seem to have your heart set on that man. But, Charles Gouge has some demons hidin' in his past. Demons that he's still a'dealin' with, to this day. People just don't trust him, and there's good enough reason not to. Welzia feels that you oughtn't to go around with him anymore. Charles is just bad seed. I tell you, girl, now that man surely is. I just know it, down in my bones, and so does Welzia. We've both got a terrible bad feeling about this; had it straight from the start. We both love you, Ollie girl. You've done already went and gone through some mighty powerful hurt in your short years, and we surely want to protect you from having any more hurt heaped on you."

Ollie stood with her hand still resting lightly on the handle of the basket as it sat on the table. She looked at Isabelle with her dark brows knit together in distress, as she carefully thought over her words. Ollie drew in a deep breath and then she said gently but with determination, "I appreciate you concerning yourself so with me, but I know full well what I'm a'doing." "Charles Gouge is good to me, and my heart is set on marrying up with him, come August."

"I'm tired of being alone, Isabelle. Who knows? If I marry Charles, maybe the good Lord will see fit to allow me a baby of my own." "I have waited so long, Isabelle." Tears began to fall from the pain that she felt. "Can't you both just find it in your heart, to be happy for me?" Isabelle cast her eyes down at the floured apron that she wore, and she sighed heavily. "I want to try and focus on what tomorrow holds for me and not just keep looking back on yesterday," Ollie said. "There's just too much pain in the past to look back, anymore." "Whatever happened with Charles, also happened in the past." "He's a changed man, wanting to make a fresh start." "I want to look forward to my future - our future, together," Ollie turned and left the kitchen and went out the front door. She hurried down the porch steps and out into the yard.

Ollie had known about Charles' first wife, for quite awhile now. She had heard the whispers, but she didn't believe any of it. He had explained to her what had happened. The poor woman had fallen and hit her head. It was unfortunate, but it had been an accident, and that was all it was. Ollie trusted Charles completely. He had no part in his first wife's untimely death. Ollie had made her decision to marry him. She knew in her heart that she would make this marriage work. Life was finally going to give her a chance at a fresh start.

Ollie and Charles married in the town hall with the Justice of the Peace performing the simple ceremony. It was short and perfunctory, but Ollie was happy. She simply glowed. Not many were in attendance, but that didn't matter that much to Ollie. She moved what little she had out of Isabelle's and Welzia's cabin and into Charles' fine house across town. She now had fine china and silver settings, the likes of which Ollie had never even seen before. It was all almost too good to be true. The first month or so of being Mrs. Gouge was wonderfully exciting. There were fancy dinners to attend up at the Cloudland Hotel, important people to meet, and fancy new dresses were made just for her. She delighted in the fact that she had beautiful things for the very first time in her life. Ollie was actually happy.

But, soon Charles seemed to lose interest and she was left alone in the large house, more and more often. Life for Ollie was very different from the life that she had experienced before, and she began to long for the peaceful morning walks along the beautiful rolling mountain ridges that she so loved. She began going over to visit with Isabelle in the afternoons and the children soon began to meet with her again, taking the walks over the mountain, just as they had before.

Charles didn't exactly cotton to the idea of her going over to see Welzia and Isabelle. He knew that Welzia suspected him of murdering his first wife, and he knew full well how Welzia and Isabelle, both, felt about his and Ollie's relationship. He was afraid that Welzia would soon alter Ollie's way of thinking, and so he forbade her from taking the wagon over to see them. Ollie complied with his wishes, not wanting to cause him any further upset. She knew that any marriage, especially one that had only just started, took an ample amount of give and take. But complying with Charles' wishes didn't stop her visits to see Isabelle, altogether. Ollie simply walked over to their house and didn't take the wagon. As soon as Charles became wise to what she was doing, Ollie saw a different side of the man that she thought she knew so well. His kind demeanor disappeared. Soon his soft words gave way to mean and vicious ones, and it terrified Ollie.

Reeking of some foul smelling perfume and with liquor on his breath, he came home late one night after a long night of carousing. Charles flew into a sudden blind rage and hit Ollie about the head, mercilessly. She was shocked into immediate silence. He went into a tirade, telling her how it was all her fault. Later, Ollie became profusely apologetic, believing that it truly was something that *she* had brought upon herself. She hadn't listened to his wishes, after all, and had intentionally done the opposite. Charles mumbled his own apology to Ollie first thing the next morning and promised her that it would never happen again. Ollie in her naivety and eagerness to appease him, believed him without question. But, the beatings didn't stop. If anything, they grew worse over time. Ollie was beaten so badly once, that Charles became alarmed after seeing the difficulty she was having trying to walk, the next morning. He had summoned the doctor from over in Bakersville, using the excuse that Ollie had taken a tumble down a flight of stairs.

Life became a series of terrifying moments that were usually followed by many days of intense pain for Ollie. She endured this torture of periodic beatings for three long years. She had just about given up that Charles would ever change and love her, once again. He had her convinced that everything bad that had happened during their marriage was her fault. Ollie was immensely relieved when she found out that he had been quietly slipping off to court the young Widow Martin that lived just across town. At least, she thought, the beatings would be somewhat fewer if he was otherwise entertained. Ollie rambled around like a ghost in her own house. She was afraid of doing anything that might stir up Charles' drunken rampages, so she kept quiet and safely out of his sight as much as she could. *Out of sight, out of mind*, Ollie often thought to herself.

Charles had taken a shine to quite a few of the pretty single women in town, as well as a few that lived in nearby townships. Ollie meekly endured his many indiscretions. She didn't care what he did, so long as he left her alone. It was his sin, not hers, and she could endure it. But, it was painful to Ollie when he would parade through town escorting his latest fling on his arm, for all to see. The embarrassment was often overwhelming. Welzia and Isabelle worried themselves sick over the predicament that poor Ollie was in, but there was little they could do about the matter, besides pray. And pray they surely did. Poor Ollie became thin as a rail over time, mostly from all the constant worrying. The sunken, haunted eyes and constant bruises told Isabelle everything that she needed to know. Ollie tried her best to hide the bruises, but Isabelle knew that all the excuses in the world couldn't hide the hurt that she saw in her dark eyes. She asked Ollie to come back home and move back into the little cabin. Ollie had told her time and time again, that she had said her vows before God and that she wouldn't break her sacred promise. She couldn't ever see herself leaving Charles, no matter what he did to her. That sort of thing just wasn't right in Ollie's heart. So she stayed with the cruel man and endured the pain. Over time, the beatings worsened dramatically.

The only ray of sunshine in Ollie's life was Charles' eldest daughter from his first marriage, Jenny. Jenny was a beautiful, sweet spirited soul and Ollie had grown to love her dearly. Jenny had married her childhood sweetheart, Robert, and they had built a house over in Mitchell County, near Buladean right along Big Rock Creek. Jenny had soon been blessed with twin daughters that were born back in March of that year. She brought the girls over to visit Ollie, regularly. Jenny and Ollie had taken a true shine to one another, right from the very start. The two women had soon grown to care genuinely for one another.

Ollie positively doted on those two twin baby girls, just as if they were her very own grandchildren. Charles continued with his shameless carousing and running around with unsavory women. Practically the whole town knew the shenanigans he was up to, by now. Everyone knew, but not one said so much as a word to Ollie. They all just stood by, silently watching and waiting. Everyone felt sure that it would all come to some sordid ending, eventually. Often these things do, but they could only speculate on what kind of ending it might be.

32

when a rose stands alone,
thriving where no others thrive,
a rare bouquet of one
still strong, still alive....
and I smile...

~ HAZELMARIE "MATTIE" ELLIOTT

As a ring of gold in a swine's snout,
So is a beautiful woman who lacks discretion.

~ PROVERBS 11:22

THE YOUNG WIDOW Martin was a very stylish woman that lived over on the other side of town. She shared her time between her sprawling house in town and her other large estate up near Elizabethton. She had been born the only daughter to a wealthy tobacco farmer from Virginia. She was considered by most, to be the most highly sought after socialite in the area. She had looks, friends, influence, and plenty of money to boot. She had always known a lavish lifestyle. Hers was a very different life from the one that Ollie knew. *The fact was those two women were nearly as different as night and day.* Ollie secretly watched her from a distance, each and every time she'd happened to see her while she was in town. Ollie tried not to stare, but the impulse was often too strong to resist. She was totally fascinated by the mysterious woman who had seemingly, won over the heart of her husband. Ollie knew she could never compete with an exciting beauty like Selena Martin. *Why, just one pair of her fancy shoes costs more than every piece of clothing that I own, combined*, thought Ollie. Ollie felt woefully inadequate whenever she compared herself to the likes of Selena. Even her name was elegant and beautiful.

Selena's golden hair was always perfectly styled and cascaded down in curls. She looked like a picture, perfect in every way. Just why Selena Martin had decided to spend her time entertaining a fairly common man like Charles Gouge, Ollie was sure she'd never know. Ollie just couldn't understand it, no matter how hard she tried. Selena had a lot more money and stature within the community than Charles Gouge had ever had. She had traveled all over the world and done it in such a fashion that Ollie couldn't even have imagined. *Yes, Selena Martin had it all. And now she had Ollie's husband, as well.*

Ollie continued to make her trips out onto the meadows and up the beautiful rolling hills of Roan Mountain, whenever she could manage to slip away for awhile, unnoticed. With Charles spending so much time away from home, it became less and less difficult. Ollie still loved to gather the berries, wild mushrooms, and various greens and prepare herself a feast from the bounty of the land. She was a simple soul, and would always remain simple. Nothing would ever change that. The mountain was *in* Ollie, just as surely as she was part of the mountain. She loved the beautiful Roan, dearly. She had grown to fully understand why Isabelle had felt so compelled to make her way back home.

Charles came home quite earlier than Ollie expected, on a warm Sunday afternoon. He had been in town just about all weekend. He went straight to his bedchamber without speaking so much as a single word to Ollie. She usually waited for him to come in and then she cooked him his supper. She didn't know whether to go up and check on him or not. She was afraid it might somehow set him off and spark his unpredictable anger, so she decided against it and went on to her bed, as well. She just assumed that he didn't feel well. The evening wore on slowly. Ollie read from her Bible by the light of the oil lamp, just as she did every night, and she prayed earnestly that Charles would recover quickly from whatever malady it was that afflicted him.

A few hours later, Ollie reached over and blew out the flame of the kerosene lamp that sat beside her on the nightstand and nestled herself down in the bed covers. She soon drifted off into a fitful sleep. She awoke to a sudden, loud clanging noise that rang out in the house. Ollie thought, *I'm sure he was out all weekend with that horrible woman, again. He's been cavorting all around town, and now he has taken sick.*

Later, the sound of violent retching followed by another loud banging noise slowly registered with Ollie, still somewhat groggy from sleep. She quickly sat up on the bed and flung the covers back. She hastily relit the lamp and hurried down the hall with it, toward Charles' bedroom. Ollie cried out when she saw him. He was lying curled on his side on the floor, just inside the doorway of his bedroom. He had dropped his candlestick, and the melted wax was spreading in a pool on the floor. Ollie grabbed it up and quickly extinguished the flame of the candle. It appeared to Ollie that Charles had collapsed while trying to come out into the hallway. He laid there with limbs askew and his face was a ghostly pale white. He opened his eyes and tried to reach out toward Ollie, and then his arm sank weakly back to the floor.

Ollie shook with terror at the very sight of him. Charles looked like a man possessed. His eyes were sunken, and they darted frantically every which way. He just didn't act right; not like himself at all. Ollie tried to help him sit up, but he flailed his arms around wildly, striking her about the head and shoulders. Ollie finally gave up and ran for help. Her yelling finally awakened Mrs. Stillwell, the neighbor lady that lived just across the street. Mrs. Stillwell woke up her sons and together they managed to get Charles back up into the bed. He still wasn't acting normal. Ollie nervously stood beside his bed wringing her hands. She didn't know what to do or what to think.

Mrs. Stillwell backed quietly away from the bed where Charles laid, writhing in pain, and motioned for Ollie to follow her out into the hall. Ollie quickly complied. "Now, I tell you what, Mrs. Gouge, it's looking like to me that he's done gone and et himself something bad. Probably some poison mushroom or somethin' or other. My brother's boy et them poison mushrooms and the poor thing went the very same way. I hate it worse'n anythin', to have to tell you this a'way, so blunt-like, but Charles more than likely ain't even goin' to make it through the night. He's too far gone to come back out of this, now. I've seen it before, child, and this just ain't no good, at all. Poison mushrooms'll kill you deader than a doornail, in hardly no time."

Ollie's mind reeled. The words that the lady had spoken began to sink slowly into her brain. *Poison mushrooms? Where in the world would Charles have gotten poisonous mushrooms?* She knew that there were plenty of them around, but surely Charles hadn't really eaten them. Her heart fell. Ollie dropped to her knees instantly. She fervently prayed that God would spare Charles and allow him to live. She knew from the tales she had heard, just how horrible a death could be from such a poisoning. She knew that symptoms usually manifest themselves in less than twenty-four hours, sometimes even less. Her mind quickly calculated the time frame. *He had to have eaten them while he was with that vile woman in town. If they were together, then there's a chance that she ate them as well.* Ollie quickly sent one of Mrs. Stillwell's sons over to check on Miss Selena Martin. She didn't even pause to take into account what time of night it was. The boy looked at her a bit bewildered, but he ran off in the direction of town lickety-split without asking any questions. The look on Ollie's face had told him that it wasn't the time to be asking any questions, it was the time to do just as he was told. So he did exactly that, and Ollie was thankful.

It turned out that Miss Selena Martin was fine. She was quite better than fine, actually. She wasn't home to answer the Stillwell boy's knock, but he asked around and soon found her. She was over at the church, praying all by herself in the middle of the night. The Stillwell boy had seen the lights on in the church and had walked over to ask those standing along the street outside if they knew where he could find Miss Martin. They had all looked at him with raised eyebrows and one of them had pointed over to the church. She was down in the front of the sanctuary, kneeling, and she looked positively wild. She had been drinking heavily, and she had beaten on the doors of the church until nearly the whole town had been awakened. She had wanted inside to pray and had raised such a ruckus that there was just no denying her request, despite the late hour.

Selena Martin owned quite a bit of the town, as well as a large parcel of land on the outskirts. Most of the people living close by were somehow supported by her money, or at least connected to it in one way or another. So, the fact that the church was opened up for her, in the wee hours of the morning, was not all that surprising. No one had even asked her any questions. Seeing that she was pretty intoxicated but otherwise okay, the Stillwell boy had quietly slipped out of the church and made his way back to tell Ollie.

Ollie breathed a sigh of relief at the news but was perplexed at just how Charles had gotten the mushrooms that had poisoned him. Charles' condition only worsened as the night wore on. Then, he suddenly appeared to be quite better. He sat up in bed and acted as if he was going to be alright. Ollie could hardly take a full breath because she knew what lay ahead for Charles. Sadly, there was very little that she or anyone else could do for him now. She told him that he was surely better, and she reassured him that he would be back to his old self, in no time at all. But, Ollie quietly waited for what she knew was coming. Sick dread filled her, but she could only try and make him as comfortable as she could.

Ollie knew that once the toxin from the poisonous mushroom enters your system, the damage begins. Eventually, you do begin to feel somewhat better, but the body's reaction belies what is happening deep inside you. In actuality, the kidneys are preparing to shut down, as the body prepares itself for death.

Jane sucked in her breath sharply as she read what Ollie had written. *Poisonous mushrooms? What a horrible way to die.* She laid the pages in her lap and rubbed her grainy eyes. She slowly shook her head from side to side as she pondered on what poor Ollie must have been thinking while such a thing was happening. She shuddered involuntarily.

Reluctantly, Jane decided that it was high time for her to go on to bed. She was just plain tuckered out. She didn't want to stop reading, but she was having a hard time keeping her eyes open. Moments later, she crawled up onto the bed, nestled in, and pulled the old worn quilt up over her shoulder and sighed in contentment. She turned over on her side and almost instantly, she fell fast asleep.

33

In God's care and in His keeping
I now place myself ere sleeping;
And, as stars and moon shine brightly,
Spirit loved ones guard me nightly.

~ GERTRUDE BUCKINGHAM

JANE BEGAN TO dream and suddenly, she found herself standing in the middle of a street. She slowly turned and looked at the storefronts bordering either side of the dusty street. *This has to be some kind of small town, just like you would see in an old movie*, thought Jane. She saw up ahead that a man was walking down the street directly toward her. She squinted in the brilliant sunshine, trying to make out his face. *Don't I know him? He seems familiar to me somehow*, Jane thought. The sound of hammering suddenly rang out in the street. Off to the right of where Jane stood, there appeared two men that were busily hammering away at a wooden structure. The sound of the hammering echoed so loudly in Jane's ears that she put her hands up, covering them.

There were people standing together, talking in hushed tones in front of the largest storefront that bordered the street. One portly man in an old style of dress suit pulled out his pocket watch from his vest pocket. Jane saw that the watch was hanging from a gold chain that glinted in the sunshine. He glanced down at it and then quickly tucked the watch back into his pocket. The man squinted and looked up at the sun. He didn't seem to see Jane standing right before him. He turned and commented to a slender older fellow that was sweeping the wooden walkway, *It certainly won't be much longer now, Jesse. They'll have him swinging high before you know it.* The man tossed his head nonchalantly in the direction of the crowd of people nearby. *Seems particularly odd to me, that the womenfolk wouldn't dream of coming to watch a cock fight, but Lord'a mercy, how they'll come right out and line up in the streets, to see a man a'swinging'*, said the portly man with the watch. The well-dressed man chortled heartily at his own comment, as the slight man sweeping the sidewalk just paused briefly and looked on, seemingly ambivalent.

Jane turned away to look again at the wooden structure the men were busily building. She could see now that they were building gallows. There was going to be a hanging, right here in this old town. Jane's stomach tightened and ground into a tight knot. Beads of sweat formed on her upper lip. She turned and peered down the dusty street, and the tall, dark man was still walking steadily toward her. He walked slowly and seemingly with purpose, never saying a word. When he was standing directly in front of Jane, just a few feet away, he took off his hat and lightly beat the dust off it, onto his pants leg. She noticed that he had a large revolver strapped to his waist. The holster slung low about his hips and there were leather straps fastened around his thigh, holding the holster securely in place. The gun's metallic finish glinted in the bright sunlight. "Morning ma'am," the dark man spoke in a low, gravelly voice. The words twanged with a definite southern drawl. Jane was sure that he had spoken the words aloud, but somehow he had spoken them without moving his lips. Jane was instantly confused. She knew that she had heard him speak, just as plain as day. He nodded his head curtly at her. He seemed to be tired and maybe even a little sad, but he didn't seem threatening to Jane. She didn't fear this man, but she wasn't sure exactly why. Jane allowed herself to relax a little. *Just where am I, anyway?* Jane asked the man. *Well, let me jest start right off by a'sayin' that I'm Deputy Marshall Smith.* Jane's eyes widened, and she blinked in amazement. *Ok, I, I get it now,* Jane chuckled, *I've got to be dreaming. This whole town is just a dream, and so is this man; even the bright sunlight. It's all just a dream. There are no gallows. There'll be no hanging, or anything else for that matter. None of this is real. None of it is happening. It's just because I always dream in 'Technicolor'. That's exactly why this seems so crazy and real. The Deputy that I dreamt up sure is a handsome man. There is something about his eyes that reminds me of someone. He reminds me of someone that I used to know,* Jane thought to herself as she allowed herself a tentative, trembling smile. *Oh well, I might as well enjoy myself while I'm here, in this here ol' law abiding town. Wonder where 'Miss Kitty' is hanging out these days?* Jane giggled nervously. Somehow, it almost felt too real to be just a dream.

The realization slowly sunk in, that she could actually feel the warmth of the sunshine beaming down on her neck and shoulders. Deputy Smith stood not much more than a couple of steps in front of her. His steely gaze was intense, as he studied her carefully. He didn't even blink, never taking his eyes off of her. Then, he suddenly cast his gaze down at the dusty street and almost self-consciously, kicked a small pebble with the toe of his boot. He tightened the muscles in his jaw and tilted his head off to the side as if he was sizing Jane up. Jane wasn't sure what he was thinking or what to think of him, and it made her nervous. *So, uh, Deputy Marshall Smith, could you please tell me why it is that I'm here?* Jane surely remembered who Deputy Smith was. He was the man that had brought David in for the murder of the soldier. This Deputy was one of the reasons, certainly, that her second great-grandfather, David, was hung for a murder that he didn't commit. He most definitely played a big part in it. Jane felt a wave of instant dislike for the man that stood before her, and he seemed to sense her feelings.

Deputy Smith bristled physically, and his nostrils flared slight-ly as he said, *Yes ma'am, that's why you are here. I came to explain to you exactly what happened way back then. Sometimes, things don't always pan out the way that they oughta'.* He studied the ground between them intently and then looked back up at Jane. *What I got to say to you now, girl, just ain't somethin' that'll come easy. I've gone through that whole ordeal, from the very beginning of it, clear to the end. I've gone over it in my mind, more'n a thousand times. Don't rightly know what it was that I could've done any differently about it all. Your great grandpa confessed to the killing, and rightly so, I had to arrest him. It was my sworn duty to uphold the law. There just wasn't no other way for me to handle it, not as far as I could see. We didn't have enough evidence otherwise. The soldier was in the wrong, and there was never a doubt about that. It was just one of those things when all the wrong things somehow came together at the wrong time. But, I know for sure, that it just ain't right for an innocent man to hang. It didn't set well with a lot of the townsfolk; not just me. People are mostly good-hearted, and they knew it was wrong. Those that should've didn't step forward and do what was right. I have mulled it over in my mind all these years. Just don't know what it was that I could have done any different.*

That young David sure loved that great grandma of yours. They had a true bond between them; that's for sure. For him to confess without a sec-ond's thought and sacrifice himself for her, why, they had a love to last for all ages. There's not a doubt in my mind, about that. Deputy Smith sadly shook his head.

Jane could clearly see the pain on his face as he mentally traveled back to that moment in time. She could almost see it all, through the misty memories that still lingered in the depths of his steel blue eyes. She somehow knew that he had never found a love of that magnitude for himself. He had searched for it, but he'd never found what David and Nancy had. They had the real bond of true love, if only for a short while. Suddenly, she felt deep, intense sorrow for the man that stood before her.

I just needed to come and get this on off my chest, if I could. I needed to tell you that I know in my heart that David was free of any guilt. He put that noose around his own neck, just sure as the world. He was to blame just as much as I was, or anyone else was. He wasn't the only one that suffered from that wrongdoing. You probably don't even know the full tale of the story. But I figure you got as much right to know, as anyone. Your Grandma Nancy had a terrible time bearing the weight of her sins. She was so ashamed. She wasn't the one that had done any evil, she was just trying to protect herself and her baby, but sometimes folks just don't always see things for what they really are. She carried that weight like a chain of lead, wound all around her.

Her little girls were too little to remember much about how it was in the beginning, and I reckon that was a blessing, itself. She somehow got the notion that it was God's punishment on her for letting that savage man have his way with her. Like it was something that she had done wrong, even though she had done ever'thin' she could, to try and stop it. That's what tore her up the most. That was Nancy's torment; the feeling that God had punished her for her sins against Him. She had no other option than to shoot that soldier and I know that to be a fact. He would have killed her afterwards, just to keep her quiet.

After they had hung David, I checked in on Nancy from time to time, and tried to help her out as much as I could. I felt responsible for her in a way, I guess. I brought her food and helped as best I could, over the years. I loved her, after a time. But she wouldn't let herself love again. Guess she just didn't love me. She still pined for David and that was just how it was. I wished I could have changed her mind, but I couldn't. When the girls, Isabelle and Mary Calla, had grow'd up big enough to help their momma, I didn't come around so much anymore. Guess the good Lord knew what was best, giving her two strong daughters to help her when she needed it the most. Your great grandmother was a strong woman, but surely ever'body has a limit. She was a woman that held fast to her deep faith in the Lord above. She accepted the pain and endured it because she knew that killing's wrong. Atonement had to be made for the taking of a life. She also had a heart as big as the mountain for those two beautiful daughters. You should be mighty proud of the stock that you come from Miss. Jane looked intently at the man as a tear rolled down her cheek. *Guess I've done said what I come to say.*

Deputy Smith put his hat back on his head and adjusted it slightly. He nodded his head and with sadness in his eyes he turned away to leave. He had taken two steps away from her, and Jane somehow found her voice and said, *Deputy Smith, I, I want to thank you for telling me this. Thank you for telling me all of it. I knew Nancy was a strong woman, but I didn't know everything that she went through. Now, I think that I understand it all much better. Thank you for that. I'm very grateful to you. And so very grateful that you tried to help her.* Deputy Marshall Smith stopped, glanced down at his boots, and then turned back to her and nodded once more. Jane could feel his deep remorse like a wave washing over her. The man before her was a good man; a man of integrity and compassion. He was still hurting over what had happened on his watch, even after all these years having passed. Jane watched him walk away and slowly he disappeared into the mist while tears of compassion fell steadily down her face.

Jane awoke, wiped the tears from her cheek with the back of her hand and then sat up. She remembered everything. *Dreaming in amazing Technicolor once again*, she thought absently. She got up from the bed and went to get a glass of milk. It was still dark outside. She stood at the kitchen window, sipped her milk, and looked out over the darkened ridge. Stars twinkled up in the nighttime sky. The glow of the moon lit up the yard and the rolling hills beyond. She heard the low and sweetly familiar sound of the wind blowing through the pines, singing as it came down off the Roan and she wondered about it all. *Why had two people that had loved each other so completely, not been allowed to spend their time here on earth, together? What purpose had there been in all the sorrow and pain that they had been forced to endure?* Jane just couldn't understand it. But, she knew that we are not to question. She felt better just knowing that others, even way back then, had known that David was innocent. She breathed deeply, closed her eyes and said a silent prayer. It was a prayer for peace for both David and Nancy.

Later that week, Jane decided that she needed to talk with her aunts, Hilda, and Ann. Maybe they knew more that they hadn't told her about Ollie. She felt a sudden pressing need to get back to Gastonia. She quickly packed a 'just in case' overnight bag and tossed it into the trunk of her little red car. The drive down the mountain passed by uneventfully, and she felt sure that coming back had been a good idea. She turned her car down Laurel Lane and soon pulled into the driveway and parked. Hilda's house looked just about the same as it always had. It was homey and inviting. *Sometimes things do stay the same, and it sure helps at times like these, to know that.* The feeling of pressing need seemed to get suddenly stronger and stronger, and she could hardly wait to close the car door behind her, as she hurried up the walk to her aunt's home.

There was a huge basket of pink petunias smiling up at her from beside the front door. The welcoming sweet scent wafted up to her and stopped her in her tracks. Petunias were one of her Grandmother Maude's, favorites. Every summer, as you would come through the front yard to her grandmother's house, you were greeted by the smell of the petunia's sweet perfume wafting on the breeze. Their brightly colored blossoms had always brought a smile to Jane's face. She stood looking down at the basket of flowers, taking a pleasant stroll deep down memory lane for just a few wonderful seconds.

Then, suddenly, the front door opened, and there stood Aunt Ann. *Mercy, Jane. Girl, you just about scared the mush, plumb outta me!* Ann exclaimed with her hand covering her heart. *Oh, gosh I'm sorry!* Jane said excitedly. *I was lost deep in thought, thinking about these sweet petunias.* Ann smiled and said, *Petunias take me exactly to where they must take you, sweetheart. So good to see you, sweetie!* Ann hugged Jane tightly and led her quickly inside the door.

Ann said, *Hilda Fay, come on in here and see who has come to visit.* Ann reached out and deftly snagged Jane's bag from her hand and placed it quickly on the bed in the guest room right off the den. Ann looked back and intently studied Jane's face. *What is that look you had, just now, Janie girl?* Ann asked with raised eyebrows. *You can't hide that something's weighing on that mind of yours. Never could, even when she was just a tiny thing, could she, Hilda?* Hilda came from the kitchen wiping her hands on a towel. The smell of something wonderful baking was coming in from the kitchen. Jane felt better instantly. It smelled just like 'home'.

Hilda and Ann both could make just about the best tasting cornbread that Jane had ever had. *If that is cornbread that I smell baking, maybe that was the pressing need I felt to get back here to Gastonia as quickly as possible,* Jane chuckled at her thoughts. Hilda walked straight over to Jane and hugged her tightly. As she hugged her, she whispered in her ear, *Now, you just go on and tell me all about it, don't you dare leave out a single word, sweetheart.* Jane inhaled quickly. She pulled away from Hilda, startled. She looked deep into her eyes. Hilda only smiled and offered up no explanation at all to Jane. *It's as if she already knows what I am going to tell her,* Jane thought.

Hilda started in right away, fussing over Jane, just as she usually did. Jane smiled. *Now, you have to be hungry. You're one lucky girl because you're just in time for some piping hot cornbread and a delicious bowl of chili. Ann's been cooking up her special chili all morning, and I just got finished baking up a cake of cornbread. It's cooling on the stove right now, even as we speak. Let's just go on in and eat ourselves a bite, before we do anything else. I even baked us a good ol' pound cake.* Hilda looked at Jane with a glance that spoke volumes to Jane. Jane breathed a small sigh of relief. She was so glad that Hilda somehow, already understood. She felt that she needed a few moments to collect her thoughts. She welcomed the thought of some warm and delicious cornbread, and that was for sure.

Hilda and Steve

34

"Blessed are those who mourn, for they will be comforted."

~ MATTHEW 5:4

"The Lord is close to the brokenhearted and saves those who are crushed in spirit."

~ PSALM 34:18

Let your tears come. Let them water your soul.

~ EILEEN MAYHEW

WHEN THEY HAD finished, they cleared away the dishes and tidied up the kitchen. Then, Hilda cleared the table off completely. She carefully wiped the table before spreading a clean tablecloth over it. Hilda went to the bedroom and got a large hat box off the shelf in the closet and brought it back over to the table. The box was brightly covered with a pretty butterfly print. She also had a smaller wooden box. She sat the hat box down in the center of the table and with a flourish she leaned over and opened the lid.

Ann smiled broadly and said, *We both wanted to surprise you. Hilda Fay finally found Mom and Dad's box of old family photographs. We knew that we should show them to you as soon as we could and make sure that names have been written on all of the pictures. Some are so old that we're not even sure of just who they all are, ourselves.*

Jane was thrilled. Her face lit up with her first glimpse inside the huge box full of old tintypes and antique photos. The pictures were stacked in the box, along with old letters, certificates, and diaries and such. *What a true treasure trove this is.* Jane knew that she would finally be able to attach faces to the names that she had learned from reading the journals. She could finally begin to truly connect with her ancestors. She hadn't yet told Ann and Hilda about the newest find that the old house had offered up to her. Jane figured that now was just as good a time as any. *I need to tell you both, some exciting news. I finally got up enough nerve to venture up in the attic among the spider webs,* Jane said. Ann and Hilda's expressions showed how surprised they both were to hear that. Ann said, smiling all the while, *Well, did you find more up there in the rafters, than what you had bargained for, girlie?* Both Ann and Hilda looked at one another, and a knowing glance passed between them. The strange look lingered in their eyes.

The weighted glance that passed between the two sisters went completely unnoticed by Jane. She was too caught up in the moment of telling them about her find. She told them about all the spider webs, and how she was hesitant to even climb the ladder, at first. Jane told them that after finding the small niche in the wall and seeing the journals that had been hidden away there, how much she loved the attic now. Hilda and Ann sat quietly, with their eyes locked intently on Jane. They listened as her story began to unfold. The rocking chair was something that Hilda especially, remembered well. *Oh, yes, that beautiful old rocking chair with all that intricate carving, I remember that chair from a long time back. Pretty sure that grandma rocked both of us, when we were just babies, in that old rocker. That was Ollie's chair; I do believe. My, what a beautiful chair it was,* Hilda said, her eyes misted over as she traveled back in her memory. *Tolbert carved that chair so beautifully. It was a gift to Ollie, many years ago. That's the story that I've always heard. I always wondered what had ever happened to it. Surely, you are planning on bringing it down and polishing it up and putting it to good use, aren't you now, Jane?* Hilda asked. Hilda clucked her tongue lightly and said shaking her head, *Such a waste. Just horrible to let that beautiful chair just sit up there in the dusty attic, for all these years.*

Jane didn't know what to say when Hilda finished speaking. She needed some time to think that one over. She now knew all about the heartache that the chair had held for poor Ollie, all those long years. Somehow, using it just didn't seem like the right thing to do. She knew for certain that not right now, it didn't. Something kept her from telling everything that she had experienced with the chair, but she wasn't quite sure why.

Jane thought that changing the subject was the best way to go at the moment. She wanted to know what pictures they had found and how they had happened to find them. Jane turned to Ann, who had fallen suddenly quiet. She had walked over and sat down in the chair over by the window. Curious, Jane walked over and sat down by Ann. *Ann, can you tell me anything more about these old pictures?* Jane asked. *Sure, darling. I'll be more than happy to tell you all I know. But sadly enough, it's not all that much,* Ann lamented. *I do have one thing to tell you. Well, quite a few years ago, I brought back an old cedar chest that was in that upstairs back bedroom. Do you remember it, sweetheart?* Jane nodded and said, *I think I do. You're talking about the cedar chest that was up in the old house originally? Yes,* Ann said quietly. *It was in the house, the one in that back bedroom. There was a lot of stuff piled up on it when I first saw it, right after that last reunion we had there, if I recall correctly.* Ann spoke quietly and just a tad slower than she normally did. This sudden change in her manner caused instant concern in Jane. Jane leaned in slightly and said, *Ann, sweetheart, is something the matter? Is there something else I should know?* Ann said, *No, darlin'. There just seems to be something in the back of my mind that keeps troubling me about that cedar chest. Can't for the life of me figure out what it might be. Don't you go worrying yourself not one little bit over me, now. You know I'll be just fine.* Ann smiled at Jane, but the uneasy feeling that Jane had, didn't dissipate as it should have with Ann's reassurance.

We had just cleaned up after the big meal, at that last reunion up at the old home place. Then, your Daddy and I went upstairs, just to make certain that all the windows were closed up tight, Ann spoke with her eyes trailing off into the distance as she remembered it all in vivid detail. Jane tried to remember being in the house, at the last reunion they had there, but she was sure she had been mostly outside talking to her cousins under the shade tree. They had all had such a good time, talking and laughing together. They weren't able to be all together very often, so that time was a special treat.

Jane traveled back into her own memories for just a brief moment, and she saw Sonya laughing with her brother Chris, as they were sitting out under the old tree, out in the backyard. Sonya had such a wonderfully light and musical laugh. It was a laugh that was instantly contagious. She always had such an easy and beautiful way about her. It was her gentle spirit that put everyone around her at ease. Jane's cousin, Sonya, was just as beautiful on the inside as she was on the outside. Sonya had been diagnosed with leukemia while she was pregnant with her third child. Sadly, she passed away at barely 38 years old, when the baby was only a few months old. She and her husband had just started their family, and then in an instant; the whole world came crashing down, right on top of them. Sonya was Aunt Ann's only daughter.

Jane's head dropped, and she closed her eyes momentarily, remembering the devastating pain of losing her sweet cousin. Reaching out, Jane laid her hand on Aunt Ann's hand and squeezed lightly. *All of this reminiscing has to be extremely hard on Ann,* Jane thought. *She's remembering back to that last time that we were all together. Worse yet, I am causing her to have to remember it all, in detail,* Jane thought painfully. Jane waited patiently for Ann to speak, once again. With raw emotion evident in her quavering voice, Ann began. *It's hard for me to talk about this, but I do so want to tell you, especially so that you can remember all the things that your Dad said to me. Maybe he could sense what lay ahead, or maybe it was just some strange fluke, but he told me that day to be sure not to take even a single second for granted. He said that life comes fast, and we need to cherish the small moments because the small moments are going to be what matters most, one day. He said that all of those small moments of happiness make up the whole of your life and your sweet daddy was so right,* Ann said as a tear formed in her eye and slid down her cheek.

Please don't cry, Ann. You'll have Hilda and me both, blubbering away in no time at all, Jane said, trying her best to raise Ann's spirits. Ann smiled slightly and pushed Jane's hand off, playfully. Ann said, *Sugar, none of us can afford to miss one single, solitary blubber-fest. Not even one. They are each precious, and each one is so needed. They help us to heal, sweetheart. Remembering is painful, but forgetting is even worse. I want to remember every moment, and I want my precious Sonya to be remembered, too. I want her life to have mattered.* Jane smiled through her tears and nodded in agreement. When she looked over at Aunt Hilda, she was nodding, too. Tears were flowing from all their eyes. *Well, that is more than enough squalling and taking on for any one day, I suppose,* Ann said bravely. *Mercy me,* Ann said as she drew in a deep breath and let it out slowly. Ann said, *Your Dad always had a special way of saying the exact thing that I needed to hear the most. I have thought back on that day many times and wondered if he may have known what was going to happen. Maybe he did, maybe he didn't. Who honestly knows? Guess we'll just have to wait and ask him later on,* Ann said with conviction and a wavering smile. She slowly nodded her head, as she stared off, seemingly lost in reverie.

Can I get you a glass of water or some tea, Ann? Jane asked with concern. *No, I'm fine, sweetheart. I have my little squalling and 'leaking session' just about every day, but I do try my very best to keep it down to just twice a day, or so. You know, just for good measure.* Ann chuckled and took a deep breath. She reached over and lightly patted Jane's hand

and then she sighed as she determinedly wiped a tear as it trickled down her cheek. Ann's lips trembled slightly as she began to speak.

Sonya Williams Dismuke

Your Dad was the first one to spot that old chest, and then we uncovered it the rest of the way, together. You know me, I do have a special affinity for antiques, and that chest was an absolute beauty. My goodness, but it sure was. That chest was so heavy. My lands, was it ever. But your sweet Daddy just kept on insisting that I take it home with me, that very day. So, I did. Your cousins, Chris, and Darin, both came upstairs to help us. All of us together somehow managed to get it down the stairs, still in one piece.

When we got it back to Gastonia, Hilda and I cleaned it up and went through the stuff that had been stored in it. We never even lifted the lid, until when we were back here at the house. We never once looked inside that chest to see what was there. Probably should have; we could have made it considerably lighter. But having all that old stuff inside, tucked away unseen for all those years, just made it all the more special to me, you know? It was a real, honest-to-goodness time capsule; a treasure chest. I wanted to examine each piece and take my good time doing it, you know?

Jane flashed a sideways grin at Ann, and Ann instantly knew what she meant by it. If anyone knew about that sort of thing, these three ladies sure did. *Miss Sentimental, way on past the third degree. Boy howdy, that's me,* Jane smiled when she thought. *And that's us, as well. I'm surely a kindred soul to these two sweet ladies.*

Ann continued on with her story. *Afterward, we cleaned the chest up and started looking at it. Then we decided that we needed to clean the bottom of it, as well. It had cobwebs between the feet, you know. There were just gobs of them hanging down from underneath it. So, we emptied it all out and gently laid the chest over on its side.* Hilda interjected and said, *Yes, that's when we both first saw it.* Ann's eyes widened, and Jane's eyes unconsciously mirrored her aunt's. *It was a hidden drawer. A secret compartment, just tucked up underneath that old chest, just as pretty as you please,* Ann said in an excited quick flow of words. *It had a strange sliding mechanism, and it took us a few minutes or so, to figure out how to get the darn thing open,* Hilda chuckled. *We'd never seen anything quite like it before. It had a strange design etched into the wood as well. We weren't quite sure what to make of it. Maybe the design could have been some way of distinguishing your furniture, a way of marking it or something. We aren't sure what it symbolizes, but it surely must mean something.*

Jane clasped her hands together in her excitement. She didn't even realize that she was mimicking her father's favorite gesture exactly. Both Ann and Hilda smiled knowingly at Jane when they saw the familiar gesture. Jane never noticed she was way too engrossed in the moment. *Good grief. You surely had to have almost fainted dead away when you saw that compartment!* Jane said giggling. *Weren't you excited?* Ann said, *Honey, 'excited' ain't even the word for what we were feeling at that particular moment. Hilda started squealing, and she began to take on so, that I seriously began to worry about her.* Ann grinned widely. *Me? Squealing? Aw, come on, now Ann*, Hilda said as she shook her head and laughed. *Jane, your Aunt Ann, right there? Why she hollered out so loud, that I was afraid the neighbors were going to think she was being killed or something even worse.* All three giggled. Then Ann said, *Well, let's just say, that we were both way 'over the moon' that day. It's just not every day that you happen upon your very own treasure chest. Especially not a treasure hiding right out in plain sight, tucked in the back room of your family's old home place*, Ann said with smiling confidence.

Jane couldn't hold her excitement any longer, and she blurted out, *Tell me what you found!* Both Ann and Hilda laughed and looked at each other. *You couldn't be any more like the both of us if you tried, Janie*, Ann said shaking her head back and forth. Hilda smiled and gestured toward the smaller wooden box sitting beside the hatbox, *It's all, right here. We both want you to have it.* Jane's expression told them both all they needed to know. She hadn't really taken much notice of the carved wooden box until now. On the lid was carved the same strange insignia that had been carved onto the hidden compartment underneath the chest. Jane picked it up and opened it. Inside were bundles of faded birth certificates, death certificates, handwritten letters from long ago, along with two tiny boxes.

Inside the first box was a pair of delicate, dangling amethyst earrings. The amethyst stones appeared to be set in gold. They were ornately beautiful. Inside the other box was an exquisite gold ring. Set into the mounting was a stunning rectangular amethyst stone. The band was encrusted with emerald and opal stones. Hilda said, *We both are pretty sure that these once belonged to Ollie. We want you to have them.* Jane covered her mouth with her hand. *Back in the Victorian days, they believed that your guardian angel lived in the amethyst stone, and it became very popular to wear them. If any of us has a true guardian angel that they can call their very own, why it's definitely you sweetheart,* Ann said with a smile. *Well, it seems that I have quite a few guardian angels, looking over my shoulder these days,* Jane thought to herself. Jane was thrilled with the beautiful old jewelry. She couldn't wait to wear it, so she put the ring on right away. When she slipped it on her finger, both Hilda and Ann looked at one another with matching raised eyebrows. The ring slid on effortlessly, and it fit her finger perfectly. Jane admired the beautiful ring in amazement.

Ann said, *Come on, we'll get us a bite of that buttermilk pound cake before it gets stone cold. We can talk more about all of this, as we sip our coffee and eat our cake.* Hilda and Jane both nodded in agreement with that idea. Hilda said excitely, *I'll go get the dill pickles.*

Ann and Jane immediately shot a glance at one another. They both knew that Hilda dearly loved to eat the sourest dill pickles that she could find with her pound cake. Jane solemnly shook her head, then she grinned, and Ann nodded briefly with a wide grin of her own. Ann puckered her mouth comically and pointed in the direction of the kitchen. Jane giggled. Then Ann turned to follow Hilda into the kitchen. Jane watched both of her sweet Aunts through the doorway of the kitchen. *I know that Ann is trying her best to put on a brave front. I sure admire her strength. She's an amazing woman. We all miss Sonya dearly. Both of them have lost precious children. Poor Aunt Hilda has lost four out of her five children. Imagine how that must feel. There can't be many things that hurt more on this earth, than the heartache of losing your children. Losing the child that you lovingly bring into the world would be almost an unbearable pain. You have such high hopes for their lives and the promise of all the years yet to come. You try your best to protect them, to shelter them, and above all, you love them completely and unconditionally. Then, illness or an accident just happens. Suddenly, there is nothing at all you can do to help them or save them. All you can do is let them go. You simply have to put your trust in the Lord, place them over into His loving care, and you let go. You rely on your faith, on God's words, and you trust that God's love will shelter and protect them.* Jane couldn't imagine any pain that would be any worse than losing your baby. It doesn't matter what age that 'baby' happens to be. *Both of these women are truly amazing.*

Jane's mind went straight back to Ollie. *I would imagine that never getting to hold your baby after all those years of torment hurts tremendously, too.* She thought of that beautiful rocking chair sitting up in the attic, back up on the Roan. Jane sent up a silent prayer for all the would-be mothers that had broken hearts and idle rocking chairs of their own.

The rocking chair began to rock slowly back and forth once again, up in the shadowy attic of the house sitting high up on the mountain. The chair kept up a slow and steady rhythm as it rocked all by itself beside the window. The sunlight streamed brightly into the attic, illuminating the small flecks of dust that floated gently in the shaft of light. The floorboards creaked beneath the weight of the chair as if someone was actually sitting there, slowly rocking back and forth.

An owl landed on the tree branch right outside the window that overlooked the Roan. A light breeze ruffled the feathers along the top of the owl's wings. The owl sat staring out into the distance, motionless. It looked out over the mountain and then turned its head back, seeming to peer into the window. The owl suddenly screeched, and the sound echoed down into the valley below. The sound rolled even further still, down into the grassy meadows. But no human ears were there to hear it. There wasn't another living soul around for miles, in any given direction.

35

In childhood, we press our nose to the pane, looking out. In memories of childhood, we press our nose to the pane, looking in.

~ ROBERT BRAULT

Gratitude is an attitude that hooks us up to our source of supply. And the more grateful you are, the closer you become to your maker, to the architect of the universe, to the spiritual core of your being. It's a phenomenal lesson.

~ BOB PROCTOR

AFTER EATING ANOTHER warm slice of the best tasting buttermilk pound cake ever, Jane reluctantly decided that she should probably be making her way back up the mountain. She wanted to get back home before nightfall, and she knew that if she left now, she'd arrive right around dusk. She had learned quite a bit listening once again, to Aunt Ann and Aunt Hilda. She had learned stories about the family that she hadn't ever heard before. She was again amazed at all that her aunts knew and could still vividly remember from days long past. *Next time, I'm going to bring my tape recorder along, and that way I won't miss anything that they happen to remember.* Ann and Hilda both were sad to see Jane go, and she invited them to come up and stay with her, for as long as they liked. Hilda said, *You just get yourself good and ready now, Jane. We're going to surprise you and come up and stay for a month of Sundays!* Jane said with a wide smile, *Nothing in this world would make me any happier.*

Jane turned the key and started the engine of her little car. She smiled and waved to Hilda and Ann through the windshield. They were standing on the porch beside one another, with their arms intertwined about each other's waist, waving back at Jane. Jane silently breathed a prayer asking God to watch over each of them, while she was away from them. They were both very precious to her. She smiled as she turned and glanced up at the rearview mirror. She reached for the gearshift and shifted the car into reverse. Jane stopped in mid-motion as her hand rose to adjust the mirror.

Jane's hand fell slowly back to her lap. Her eyes were magnetically locked on the image reflecting back at her. There, in the tiny back seat of her car were two little smiling girls with braided pigtails sitting side by side, holding hands. Minnie and Ruby were smiling back up at her, swinging their legs beneath them nonchalantly. Jane quickly sucked in her breath and turned and looked forward, hurriedly. *No, they didn't just hop in the car and come along with me for the trip. My mind just has to be playing tricks on me again. It just has to be.* One quick glance back again, and Jane sees nothing but the empty seats behind her. She blows out a long breath through her pursed lips. *I'm going to have to make myself a long overdue appointment. Boy-howdy, I'm really going to need to see someone and talk about all this.* She closes her eyes and giggles to mask her nervousness. Once again, she slowly turns and glances back over her shoulder once more. She quickly determines that, yes; she is completely alone in the car. Satisfied, she backs her car out of the driveway and starts up the road. She drives on out of town and toward the mountain. She sighs as she thinks, *Going back, once again. I'm always eager to get back to my beautiful old mountain. Yes, back to that wonderful old mountain that I call home.*

Ann watched Jane finally back out of the driveway, and she thinks, *There's something curiously strange about that girl, just can't put my finger directly on what it is.* She ponders over it, as she reaches out and parts the curtain on the front window so that she can watch Jane's car leave. She keeps her eyes on the glow of the tail lights as the car travels further down the road and completely out sight. Hilda silently watched Ann from across the room, and then she says sympathetically, *Now, you know that girl can certainly take care of herself. She's got more than enough Arrowood in her, to see her through whatever life heaps on her. You know that, just as surely as I do.* Ann said, *Well, I've been thinking hard on it. Maybe the time has come to tell her everything. She'll need to know since she's staying up in that house all alone until she marries Jake. We're going to have to tell her everything sooner or later, you know.* Hilda moved closer to her and placed a hand comfortingly on Ann's shoulder, *Now, just isn't the right time. You know it isn't, same as I do. She can take care of herself just fine. That girl's tough. We'll tell her soon enough. I agree she needs to know, but maybe we should wait a bit. These things often have a way of working themselves out if they are left as they are. You should know that's true.* Ann turns and looks at Hilda and says, *Sometimes, when things 'work themselves out' it's not always for the best.*

Ann sighs softly, smiles at Hilda and then nods her head thoughtfully. *Maybe she's right,* Ann thinks. *Jane can surely take care of herself. But what other secrets does that creaky old house hold in store for her? She seems to love living there. Maybe she can find peace there. Maybe she's the one that's meant to be there. Maybe the restless spirits of those that came before want her there. Who knows, maybe she'll raise yet another generation of our family up there on the beautiful old Roan and continue the line. Imagine that, yet another generation of us, up among the whispering trees that line those ridges. Another generation to learn her secrets as she whispers to her own*, Ann's smile widens and positively radiates with her thoughts. Tears slowly fill her eyes and blur her vision.

Later, after tidying up the rest of the dishes, Hilda and Ann sit quietly in the den. The lamp's glow illuminates the room in warm tones. Full evening slowly began to settle over the house on Laurel Lane. The last rosy colored rays of the sunset slowly fade in the sky. The stars began to twinkle on, overhead, one by one, until many are visible in the blanket of deep purple that quickly covers the night-time sky. Ann's thoughts slip back to a simpler time in her life. She turns and looks out the window as the street lights slowly flicker on. The lights come on all at once these days, but in her mind, she sees back to a time when the street was lit only by the glow of the moon. The faint sound of crickets chirping reaches her ears. She looks out and sees the hazy scene from years gone by, once again.

Two small boys are scampering out by the dirt road in the dwindling daylight. *Those two are both up to no good, and I'm just about certain of it.* Ann chuckles to herself. She is a little girl with freckles sprinkled across her high cheekbones, once again. Little Stevie and his cousin Ott Long, are tying something up, all along a length of rope. *No telling what this mess right here is all about*, Ann thinks as she shakes her head with feigned dismay. *Those two are up to something or other, nearly all the time. They better just wait till I tell Momma all about this. Yes sirree, they'll be sorry that they didn't let me play with them. Just 'cause I'm a girl don't mean that I can't play same as them.*

Ann dips her chin and keeps her eyes trained on the shadowy figures. The two boys quickly separate, and one runs across the street in the dimming light like a streak. He lies down in the ditch, staying down low and out of sight. Ott carefully peers up over the ditch, and soon he sees headlights coming up Laurel Lane, still some distance away. Steve runs to the other side of the dirt road and flings himself into the side ditch as well. Both keep hunkered down. They lie low and wait for the car to approach. It slowly comes down the road with a cloud of dust rising up from behind the tires. The dim light of dusk scantly illuminates the billowing dust so that it looks almost like real smoke. Slowly the car comes closer to where the boys lie in wait. Steve calls out to Ott in a hoarse whisper, *You just wait for my signal!* Ott gives a 'thumbs up', back to Steve. The car approaches and both boys are quivering with excitement. Neither has done anything quite this exciting before. When they both realize that the moment has come, they instinctively know that there is no turning back now. Both of their hearts thump wildly in their chests. Steve jumps up and yanks hard on the end of the rope that he holds in his hands. Ott pulls his end of the rope taut at the same time.

The cornstalks that they had tied to the rope spring up and stand tall, strung out all across the road. The action causes the rope to sway wildly, and the stalks sway as well, along the length of the rope. The car suddenly slams on the brakes. The tires squeal in protest on the hard packed dirt road. The tires slide and the car skids slightly sideways. Steve suddenly sees a quick flash, as the falling moonlight briefly illuminates the car's door. He sees a large emblem on the door. Both boys realize what the marking on the car door is, at just about the same time. *Good grief, I've stopped a police car!* thought Steve. His panic quickly escalates. Both boys chunk their end of the rope down into the grass, instantly, and each one high-tails it away, running off as fast as they can in opposite directions. Neither one stopped running for quite some time. Out of breath, panting and still shaking, Steve waited in the shadowy tree line far on the other side of Laurel Lane for Ott to finally double back and find him. Later, they somberly vowed that they'd "never do that dumb thing again." "Boy-howdy. Not ever again." Each of them spat on their stubby fingers before intertwining and locking them together, tightly. They pinky swore to never do it again, and they didn't.

Ann had seen it all, as it was happening. Later, Ann had realized just how frightened Steve was, and she decided to keep all that 'mess' that they had been up to, to herself. She stayed quiet and never did tell on them. So, their Momma, Maude, never knew a thing about it.

Ann chuckled lightly. She shook her head at the memory, still as crisp in her mind as if it were only just yesterday. It slowly dawns on her, that she didn't ever tell a single soul about how Steve and Ott had nearly wrecked the Sheriff, himself. She never breathed a word of it, to another living soul. Ann smiles as she reminisces, and a tear falls silently down her cheek. *I miss my brother so much*, Ann thinks solemnly. *Steve was a wonderful brother and I loved him dearly.*

Time has quickly passed and the years have somehow flown on past all of us, Ann reflects. A mist lightly settles over her eyes as she remembers. Ann thinks of how truly thankful she is, for the sweet memories of her family. *What a treasure and what a blessing to have been born into this precious family. There just wasn't always a lot of extra anything to go around back then, but each and every one of us sure had love a'plenty. We shared what little we had in possessions, but we always had plenty enough love and then some. How very blessed we truly all were. God was good to us.*

Ann steps away from the window and then glances back, once again. She wistfully lingers over one last look. But, the shadows that dance just outside the window are only from the lights of passing cars. There are no mischievous little boys diving into the ditches to hide from headlights, out there tonight. *Time has surely moved on*, Ann thinks to herself, silently. A tentative smile plays across her face and steadily turns into a radiant and whole-hearted grin. A single tear rolls over her smiling cheek. She turns and reaches down and clicks off the lamp.

36

*Pay attention to your dreams – God's angels often speak
directly to our hearts when we are asleep.*

~ EILEEN ELIAS FREEMAN

*God's Word never said we were not to grieve our losses.
It says we are not to grieve as those who have no hope.
Big Difference.*

~ BETH MOORE

A FEW DAYS LATER, Jane drives her car up the country road, winding back and forth taking each hairpin turn carefully. She remembered that she doesn't much like driving herself through the mountains, especially when the view is this lovely. She can't enjoy the beautiful view and still keep her eyes safely on the road.

The sign up ahead reads 'Happy Valley'. She drives until she reaches the old family cemetery. The small car turns up and doubles back, as it slowly crawls up the steep incline of the dirt road. The fence surrounding the cemetery is still standing. But, the gate sags sadly underneath its own weight. She wonders again, how many times her family attended a funeral up here on this very knoll. The tree still stands, after all these years. It is a towering sentinel guarding the loved ones buried beneath its sheltering branches. It was the very tree that Ollie had stood under when she buried her Tolbert. The branches are twisted and knotted; time has taken its toll on the old tree. But as Jane looks up at it, she thinks with all her heart, that it's truly beautiful. Sometimes, even gnarled and weathered tree branches can be a thing of beauty.

Jane stops and leans on the open door of her car as she ponders the past and wonders just as Ollie did, what the old tree has stood witness to, down through all these passing years. She reaches back into the car and gets the bundle of fresh flowers that she brought along with her. The rest of the way up the drive, Jane walks purposefully. She opens the gate and hangs the loose latch back on the gate, behind her. As she approaches the graves, she sees familiar names and reads each aloud. There, near her great grandparents is a grave that has an unfamiliar name etched into it. The stone is covered over with a thick overgrowth of lichen and moss. There are several different types of moss clinging to the stone and obscuring the writing.

She glances at the other stones and sees they are free of any moss or staining. *Strange that this one stone is the only one that looks this way.* She looks around and quickly finds a tiny branch to use and she tries to gently remove some of the thick moss, so that she can better read the name and dates. Jane squats down in front of the gravestone and reaches out to try and remove more of the moss with her hand, and she suddenly stops. She recoils backward. Something inside tells her to leave the moss alone. She just instinctively knows that she shouldn't disturb this grave. She reaches around and grabs her camera strap that's slung over her shoulder. She cups the camera in her hand and peers through the viewfinder, snapping several pictures. She figures she can enhance the image on her computer and the name, dates, and inscription should be easier to ascertain, even through all that moss that's covering it. After walking through and taking pictures of all the graves, Jane takes one last look around. Just why she felt so compelled to come to the cemetery today, she doesn't know. But she knew that feeling wasn't something that was going just to go away on its own. So, she just decided to come.

As she drove, she imagined poor Ollie trudging along with ol' Ginger pulling the wagon, making her way home to the Roan. Jane pulled off the road several times to take pictures of the breathtaking views that the drive back offered her. She stopped in at the diner for a quick bite before she drove the rest of the way back up to the house. Later, she downloaded the pictures from her camera onto her laptop. She quickly glanced through the first ten or so, smiling in satisfaction. She had gotten quite a few beautiful shots of the mountainside. She was bone-tired, and she decided to call it a night. She closed the laptop and got herself a small glass of milk and a couple of cookies. She finished her snack and cleaned up the cookie crumbs and rinsed out the glass. She turned off the lights and went on to bed.

Jane fell into a deep sleep, almost immediately after she had closed her eyes. Soon she found herself in a totally unfamiliar, stark bedroom. It was decidedly the bedroom of an older house. It had red embossed wallpaper on the walls. The only furniture was a small poster bed sitting in the middle of the room. The bed appeared to be lit from above by a dimly shining light. There on the bed slowly arose a figure whose silhouette cast a shadow on the wall behind it. It appeared to be the figure of a young girl. The girl's hair was tousled about her head wildly, and her dress was torn and ragged. She turned her head and slowly looked at Jane. She pressed her first two fingers up against her lips as if to shush Jane. Then she slowly shook her head at Jane. Jane had an instant understanding that she meant 'don't say anything at all'.

Without warning, Jane awoke with a start. She was disoriented at first, but soon realized that she was back in her bedroom, once again. She took a deep breath and rubbed her hands over her temples. As she became fully awake, she realized that it had only been a dream.

She wondered what it could have meant. Later, after she had fallen back asleep and the night progressed, she returned once again, to the dream of the same bedroom with the embossed red wallpaper. She watched the scene replay itself, once again.

As soon as she had awakened in the bright light of morning, Jane couldn't wait to take another look at the photos that she had made on her trip to Happy Valley. She sat down at the desk and opened up her laptop. She took a sip and then sat her steaming cup of coffee on the desk. She clicked on the photos saved in the folder and intently studied them, one after another. She read aloud each name inscribed on the gravestones, searching for something that stood out. Maybe, something would shed some light on the peculiar dream. She just had a feeling that somehow, the answer had to be in these pictures.

Each picture displayed on the computer screen in front of her, as she clicked through them all, one by one. Then suddenly the picture that flashed across her screen stood out starkly different from the rest. It was very oddly lit. It was overexposed and appeared almost to be a reverse image. It looked strangely unlike any of the other pictures, despite the fact that they were taken under the same conditions and at the same time. The settings on her camera hadn't been altered either. Jane's eyes widened, as she finally figured out just what the image was, flickering back at her from the brightly lit computer screen in the early morning's light.

It was the moss-covered gravestone; the stone that appeared to be so different from all of the others. The other pictures that she had taken were normally exposed. This was the only picture that turned out so oddly. Jane peered closely at the screen, and she could plainly see a red spider perched on the stone. Its spindly legs hugged the moss and they appeared to be an even deeper shade of red than the spider's body. Jane was positive that the large spider hadn't been there when she had taken the picture. *If it had been there, I would have surely seen it. There's no doubt about that*, Jane shook her head as she thought. *I know that I must have my own brand of special radar or something when it comes to any sort of creepy crawler. I know I'd have seen that huge red spider right there in front of my face. It was only inches away. That's just plain weird. And it's super creepy, too.* Jane shivered involuntarily. *What would have caused the background of the photo to overexpose and white out like that?* Jane was truly perplexed. *None of the other shots taken at nearly the exact same time had turned out anything like that. In fact, she'd never taken a picture that had turned out quite like that one.* She had taken thousands of pictures with that very same camera with no overexposures, ever. *And it's digital, so it can't be defective film.* Jane didn't understand it and she surely didn't like it. All the hair on the back of her neck stood up. Jane shuddered. What in the world could it mean? *Red spiders and red embossed wallpaper?*

Jane can't seem to get the thought out of her mind. She walks into the great room and clicks on the lamp. She plops herself down on the couch and tucks a thick cushion behind her back. She has decided that she needs to read more from the old journals. She soon found herself immersed, once again, in the lives of her family that lived many years ago.

The gavel repeatedly struck the wooden desk with resounding thuds that echoed throughout the room. Sound traveled well with the sparse furniture, wooden floor, and high ceilings of the courtroom. The aging judge peered out with a brooding pucker on his lips as he stared out across the crowded room. His eyebrows were wild and bushy, sticking out above his wire-rimmed glasses. He called out for silence and by the tone of his voice, he meant business. The clamor of chattering about the room died down swiftly. The judge nodded curtly with satisfaction, although his puckered lip scowl remained affixed to his face. All eyes turned toward the portly judge, and everyone waited expectantly.

Ollie tried to calm herself by slowing her breathing, as perspiration beaded and slowly trickled down the center of her back. Her dress was nearly soaked, but there was nothing that she could do about it.

Her thoughts were clamoring against one another in a tumbled heap, each desperately vying for her attention. Ollie dimly realized that she was nearing a state of total panic. The preceding week had been a flood of nightmarish moments, one right after another, and there seemed to be no end in sight. Ollie could feel the palpable contempt of the people in the courtroom. It was brutally obvious that they had already tried and convicted her long ago, in the circles of idle chatter in this town. *She's nothing but a 'murdering, no good she-devil'. She killed that poor man in a fit of jealousy, pure and simple. He should have had more sense than to marry up with a woman such as her. He should have stayed clear of her and now he has surely paid the price. You can't care for a woman that's nothing but pure evil.*

The people in the town that owed the very lives of their children and loved ones to Ollie had even turned their backs on her. She had tended the sick with selfless compassion and sometimes she had even jeopardized her own health to do so, but all that was completely and conveniently forgotten. She was totally on her own as she stood before her accusers. She only knew of two souls that truly believed her; her sweet Welzia and Isabelle. Ollie forced herself to slowly raise her head and look about the room. She searched the crowd of angry faces that loomed before her, and she flinched as she felt the white-hot burn of their hate reflected back at her, chillingly evident in their cold stares. She saw Welzia and Isabelle and quickly lowered her gaze. Isabelle's face was gaunt and ashen. Welzia looked at her with sad eyes; a look of quiet grief and consternation. Ollie quickly said a prayer asking God to look out for both of them, during this difficult time. The stress on both of them had been terrific and they had to deal with all the gossip, as well.

Ollie never asked for anything from either of them. She knew that the chances of her being acquitted of Charles' murder were pretty slim, indeed. She had accepted it and decided that maybe it was all for the best. She couldn't prove her innocence, and most people had already made up their minds, anyway. Small towns are like that, sometimes. She didn't blame the people in the town. She held no malice in her heart for anyone. If it were time for her to go and meet her maker, she was ready. *Life here in this ol' world, hasn't always been the best for me. Maybe God will show me His sweet love and mercy, and take me on home, to be with the others that have already crossed over. I reckon I'm just about as ready as I'll ever be,* Ollie sighed with resignation. *If you're ready for me, Lord, here I am.* Ollie hung her head but no tears came. She had no more tears left.

37

---

*Life is thickly sown with thorns, and I know no
other remedy than to pass quickly through them.
The longer we dwell on our misfortunes, the
greater is their power to harm us.*

~ *VOLTAIRE*

The soul would have no rainbow had the eyes no tears.

~ *JOHN VANCE CHENEY*

*To the lamp of love: may it burn brightest in the darkest
hours and never flicker in the winds of trial.*

~ *AUTHOR UNKNOWN*

THE JUDGE QUICKLY called the crowded courtroom to order and
the noise level dropped dramatically as they all took their seats.
Ollie took another furtive look behind her and quickly scanned over
the faces of the crowd. Her eyes suddenly came to rest on the face
of her husband's lover. Staring back at her was the beautiful Miss

Selena Martin. Ollie's gaze locked with Selena's. Ollie wondered what she might be thinking, as she studied Selena's face. She was trying to get an inkling of what might be going through the woman's mind. Selena offered up no telling display of emotion, whatsoever. Totally perplexed, Ollie turned back to face the judge as the trial commenced.

The minutes that passed inside the courtroom on that eventful day seemed to flutter right on past Ollie as she sat in a near dream-like state. Her brain refused to fully comprehend what was happening. Everything had happened so fast. Just about all that Ollie knew, and all that was her world, as she knew it, had simply ceased to be. When the jail door had clanged shut behind her, she had entered a mental state of anguish so deep that she wasn't able to think with much clarity, at all. She had sat on the dingy cot in that cold, dismal cell while her mind went completely blank.

Many mistook her conduct as a clear indication of her guilt. The town was catapulted into an uproar of disparity over Charles' death. Many felt that Ollie had been very fortunate to have had a man like Charles take her in, give her a beautiful house, furnished with beautiful things and provide her anything she wanted, as well. The very idea that she had killed him, after he had shown her nothing but generosity was just unthinkable. On the other hand, some felt that given his immoral acts; that he got exactly what he deserved. The tongues that usually wagged went quickly to it, especially when the news of the poison mushrooms hit the gossip circles in addition to everything else. Nothing quite this juicy had ever happened in this tiny mountain town.

Ollie didn't care that everyone was talking about it, what she cared about was that Charles was gone. Her heart didn't want to believe that she still loved him, after all he had done to her, but she did. She truly did. Ollie's pure heart only allowed her to see the good in people. Welzia tried to come see Ollie, but they wouldn't allow it. Isabelle was mentally exhausted from praying as hard as she knew how to, without ceasing. She had prayed around the clock. She had at first refused to believe that Ollie would even stand trial for such an impossibly heinous act, but indeed, she was.

Ollie was on trial for the malicious murder of her husband, and her life hung precariously in the balance. Many believed that there was very little hope that Ollie would ever see the light of day again. Ollie herself, was convinced that all hope was lost. The defense tried to defend Ollie dutifully, but the prosecution brought a hard case against her. All the damning evidence that they could gather was brought forth against Ollie. The prosecution finally rested, and the jury sat staring at the woman that they all believed had cold hearted-ly murdered her own husband. *She was nothing but a monster, to almost every person in that courtroom. They were positive that she had murdered him by feeding the poor man those deadly mushrooms.* She couldn't deny the fact that she did know just about all there was to know, about mushrooms and herbs. She knew more than anyone else around, about such things. That knowledge proved to be the 'final nail in the coffin'. It was the nail that closed the coffin that seemed surely meant for poor Ollie.

The moment had come. There was complete silence. Ollie was asked to stand, and she stood up, slowly. She swayed slightly from side to side. She felt faint and deathly sick to her stomach. Her mind reeled as she tried desperately to take in every detail of what was happening around her. The judge's face loomed before her as grainy darkness crept in around the perimeter of her field of sight. Ollie crumpled to the floor, as if in slow motion. The clamor of excited chatter bubbled up and swelled in the crowded courtroom, and the judge banged the gavel fiercely on the desk, as he tried desperately to regain control of the crowd. Lying prone on the hard wooden floor, poor Ollie was out cold. The doctor was summoned, and he pushed his way through the crowded courtroom. He knelt down by her side. After they had managed to bring Ollie back around and she was able to sit in the chair, the lawyer motioned to the judge that they were ready to go ahead with the proceedings.

Ollie's face was as white as a sheet and perspiration beaded noticeably on her forehead and upper lip. She stared straight ahead with a dazed expression on her face. While Ollie had fainted dead away and lay motionless on the floor, there had been only three faces that held true concern and no contempt for her in the crowd. Two of the faces were Welzia and Isabelle's, and the third was Miss Selena Martin. When the Judge began to speak again, suddenly a female voice rang out strong and sure from the crowd of onlookers assembled in the courtroom. "Your Honor," said Selena Martin as she stood up. Then, in a strong but slightly trembling voice she said, "You all must let that poor woman go. She didn't kill Charles Gouge." Then she paused and added, "I did it."

There was sudden silence that fell over the courtroom like a shroud. For at least five whole seconds, not one sound could be heard. The silence seemed to buzz with an electricity, all its own. Everyone was positively stunned. Then suddenly, the silence was broken by a clamor of gasps and a few high pitched screeches. Miss Selena Martin moved to the center aisle while every eye in the crowded courtroom locked intently on her. She walked confidently straight up to the judge. With her head held high, she said in a clear voice that rang out theatrically, "I fed him those dang ol' mushrooms. I gave him those same mushrooms that he loved so much. I fed him what I thought were the same ones, anyway. He was always going on about how delicious they were when Ollie fixed them for him, so I thought I would just gather some up for him, as well. I saw them growing right out there, all around in almost a circle, right out on the front lawn, so I gathered up about a dozen or so of them." There was a collective gasp of astonishment that came up from the crowd. She had gathered up the deadly mushrooms from a so-called 'fairy ring' and offered them up to her lover, apparently completely unaware of the danger.

The realization of what had actually happened to Charles Gouge seared like a white bolt of lightning through everyone's mind, leaving a scorched trail behind it. The hushed silence seemed to suck the very air out of the room. The lawyers gaped at one another across the room with comically raised eyebrows and slack mouths. The look on the judges' face, told it all. He was totally blindsided by the scene that was playing out right in front of him. Ollie slowly turned to stare at Selena, and as she closely studied her, she slowly shook her head back in forth in disbelief. Ollie finally began to understand the full implications of Selena's words, and she felt her legs go limp as they buckled beneath her once again. Somehow, she luckily managed to plop herself down soundly in the chair that sat slightly behind her.

Charles had been served up the ominous 'white angel of death' by the very woman that he had been having an affair with. He had eaten, not one, but probably several, of one of the deadliest mushrooms of all. There was very little chance, if there had been any, that anyone could have saved him after eating those. *What excruciating pain, he must have endured in the agonizing last hours of his life.* Ollie hung her head and wept inconsolably. Thinking simply, that she didn't understand, her lawyer reached toward her and grasped her shoulder excitedly. He tried to convey to her that she was now a free woman, but Ollie paid no attention to him. She only kept crying.

The judge finally appeared to recover somewhat from the shock. He gathered his wits about him and proceeded to bang the gavel on the desk with more force than he had ever used in all the years he had sat on the bench. Not one soul could hear it through the cacophony of noise that erupted within that small Carter County, Tennessee courtroom. No one could quite believe this unforeseen turn of events.

Isabelle hung her head where she stood amidst the shouting crowd around her, and wept right along with Ollie. But Isabelle's tears weren't tears of sadness; they were tears of joy and thanksgiving.

God had performed a miracle that day, and her deepest prayers had been answered. Welzia put his arm around the woman that he so loved and drew Isabelle close to his chest, as a tear coursed down his cheek, as well. God was watching over them all, once again.

Ollie was a free woman. *God has saved me.* It began to sink slowly in, at last. She stood and turned to search the crowd for the face of her beloved Aunt Isabelle. She felt the sting of tears once again, as a shaft of sunlight suddenly fell through the high window of the courtroom and warmed her face. The clouds parted and brilliant sunshine flooded the room. With her face upturned to the sun, Ollie breathed in deeply, drawing in the first real breath she had taken into her constricted lungs, in weeks. It was the blessed breath of freedom. She prayed silently that she'd never have to spend another single night behind a locked door, ever again. She smiled at Isabelle and Welzia, as they both shed tears of joy.

Then suddenly, Ollie felt an agonizing pain seize her body. It seared through her midsection like a hot flame, and she couldn't keep herself from crying out. Doubled over in pain, she stared down in astonishment, as bright red blood coursed down her legs, drenching her stockings. It flowed onto the floor and pooled at her feet. Ollie slowly raised her eyes once again, to look at Isabelle. Isabelle had a look of absolute horror on her colorless face. Complete darkness descended on Ollie, and the courtroom faded to black.

Ollie had lost the tiny spark of life that she had held within her womb. She hadn't even known that she was carrying a child. The precious baby that she so desperately wanted her whole life, was lost in an instant.

She never even got to experience the joy of knowing that a tiny life had begun inside of her, Jane thinks silently. She quickly turns the page and sees that the story continues with Ollie back home, at the cabin. Jane shuffles the pages of the journal frantically but finds nothing that indicates what happened right after Ollie's tragic loss of the unborn child. *Maybe some things are just too painful to write about*, Jane thinks. Saddened and somewhat perplexed, she reads on.

Ollie walks out onto the small porch of her little house and leans lightly against the railing. The sun is shining brightly, and the leaves on the trees are beginning to fall. Ollie replays the events of the past summer over once again, in her mind. So much has happened, and so much pain has been endured. She wistfully sighs as she rubs her hand over the small swell of her belly. "I know God has a plan for me, and I shouldn't question his ways." "I am thankful for God's faithfulness." Ollie looks over at the small delicate red rose that is blooming on the rose bush that she planted beside the porch steps of the tiny cabin. *If my baby wasn't meant to be, then it just wasn't meant to be. Life isn't always a bed of roses, but God always gives us a few perfect roses, at least, along the way. God is good.*

Isabelle comes to the edge of the porch up at the big house and sees Ollie standing in the sunshine and smiles with a hint of sadness. Isabelle bows her head and prays earnestly, *Please, dear precious Father, show me the way to help Ollie get on past all this wickedness that has happened to her. Help her to be able to mend, body and spirit, after losing her baby. I pray for Charles's soul as well, Father. Send your angels of mercy, to watch over Ollie in the hard days that most certainly lay ahead, Lord. In your precious name, I pray.*

Isabelle placed her hands solidly on the railing and leaned forward slightly to be able to see Ollie's house better. Isabelle called out to Ollie, *Come on up here, Ollie dear, and eat a bite with us.* Ollie took another lingering look out at the rolling ridges and the trees that towered overhead, swaying in the light breeze. She longed to take a long walk out on the beautiful flats and along the balds where the red lilies bloomed. She always found such wonderful solitude and peace when she was up on the Roan. She could lose herself along those windswept ridges, and she longed to do so, once again. She sighed, turned, and made her way up to the house to join Isabelle for lunch. Welzia opened the door for Ollie and gently held her arm as she stepped inside. Ollie smiled and said, *You needn't make such a fuss over me, Uncle Welzia. I am nearly back to my old self now. I don't feel near as weak as I did last week.* Welzia nodded soberly and went to help Isabelle at the table.

Isabelle watched Ollie closely and then turned to put the plates on the table, seemingly satisfied that Ollie was indeed doing alright. They sat down to a table filled with good food. Isabelle was always a mighty fine cook, and this meal was no exception to that fact. They each ate the meal with very little conversation; each lost in their private thoughts. *A lot had happened in a short time, and people sometimes seem to have their own way of mulling it over and then trying to move on past it. Lots of love and lots of prayer can pretty much see you through whatever happens in this life, and they all knew that much, for sure.*

Over time, Ollie slowly came back around to being her old self. She began taking the neighboring children on afternoon excursions again, into the woods and up along the rolling ridges of the Roan. She began to smile again, and then eventually, she began to laugh again as well. She knew that life was not going to stop because Charles was gone and she had lost her baby girl, so Ollie decided just to try and keep on living. She chose to take it just one step and one day at a time. *That's about all that any of us can do, I guess.*

One early Saturday morning the children had all gathered up, and they were patiently waiting for Ollie out on the porch. She came out and greeted them with a smile. She had her basket for the ginseng tucked under her arm. She made her way past the chattering group of sweet-faced children, and she glanced up and saw that a buggy was parked up on the drive by the big house. She held up her hand over her eyes to shield them from the bright morning sun, and she saw who was standing by the buggy. Ollie cried out in sheer delight and dropped the basket. She immediately took off in a full run straight toward the buggy.

Standing beside the buggy was Charles' beautiful daughter, Jenny, with her twin daughters, Judy Leigh, and Sadie Leigh. Ollie gathered them into her arms and hugged them tightly, as her face beamed with pure joy. Jenny and her girls had soon realized that they needed Ollie as much as she needed them. After Jenny had gotten through the painful time of grieving for her father, she realized that Ollie was the only grandmother that her girls had ever known and that they all loved her dearly.

So, they were held fast by a bond of love. It was a bond that lasted for the duration of Ollie's lifetime. She was the grandmother to those two girls and to the three more children that came along later, just as surely as if they were her own flesh and blood. Jenny soon asked Ollie to come live with them, as a part of their family. She and Robert had a large house with plenty of room, up on the mountain, just on the other side of the Roan. Ollie readily accepted the offer and never has a woman positively glowed with happiness, quite like Ollie did. *There was a definite glow about her that no one could have missed.*

She doted on those precious girls, and they truly adored Ollie. She taught them the old ways that had been taught to her as a child. She showed them how to heal sickness with certain brews and concoctions made with specific plants and herbs that were readily found up on the beautiful rolling ridges of the Roan. They learned quickly, and they learned exceptionally well, as they sat in the tall grasses that sway in the breeze, high on the Roan.

They all were eager to learn, especially little Sadie Leigh, who was the spitting image of her second great-grandmother on her father's side of the family. *Robert's grandmother was the one and the same, ol' Lady Schnitzler. And yes, little Miss Sadie Leigh did seem to have a 'special way' about her. She had a way of somehow knowing things that most ordinary folks just don't. She knew things long before they happened, and she knew things never told to her about the family, generations back before her time.* Ollie noticed this gift in Sadie Leigh right away, but chose to let it be something that her mother, Jenny, would discover on her own. *Some things are just better left to sort themselves out. Sometimes you just need to let things happen as they are supposed to happen.* Ollie finally found the true peace in life that had escaped her for so many long years. *She sat for countless hours and rocked those little girls in the beautiful rocking chair that Tolbert had so lovingly made for her. She missed Tolbert every single day, for the rest of her life. You don't ever get over a love that runs that deep between two true hearts. But, she learned that being truly thankful for what you have been given in this life, will carry you through a world of hurt.*

She loved all her grandchildren, unconditionally. She rocked them each and every one, in turn, as they came into the world. She rocked them in the beautiful large bedroom that was given to her, by the family. She had decorated the room in her favorite color. The beautiful embossed red wallpaper on the walls brought a smile to Ollie's face each and every morning when she opened her eyes. The woman that life had dealt blow after blow upon, had finally found her own true love and mercy. She managed to bestow far more love on others than she had ever received for herself. *Which, as we all know, is a true measure of a life well lived.*

38

If there ever comes a day when we can't be together, keep
me in your heart. I'll stay there forever.

~ A.A. MILNE

A sunbeam to warm you,
A moonbeam to charm you,
A sheltering angel, so nothing can harm you.

~ IRISH BLESSING

JANE WAITED ANXIOUSLY by the front window in the old house
that overlooked the beautiful view of the rolling Roan. She
watched as the last rays of golden hued sunlight greeted the mountain
ridges as only a Roan sunset can. She marveled at the way the light
transformed the mountain into such a wonder of amazing beauty,
yet again. Every evening's sky was displayed on a newly painted can-
vas, so every day at sunset, there was an entirely different show. *God's*
very own miracle that displays itself each and every evening, in a wondrous
show of color and a dazzling display of light, Jane smiled to herself with
the thought. Jake was coming back home finally, and he was due to

be there just any minute. She held her breath in excitement, as she heard the crunch of tires on the gravel drive. She bolted to the door, crossing the room in scant seconds. Her feet didn't even touch the steps, as she raced off the porch and down the walk toward the truck. She skidded to a stop and then stood breathlessly still and watched.

Jake drove the truck into the drive and parked, killing the engine. The door opened, and he jumped out and raced toward Jane. They fell into each other's open arms. Embracing each other tightly, Jake whispered in Jane's ear, *Never again, lady.* Jane needed no explanation of that statement. She understood completely and was in total agreement. She nodded her head, too emotional for words and pulled the man she dearly loved, even closer to her.

Exactly one month later, Jane stood in the bedroom looking at her reflection in the old oval mirror that once belonged to her second great grandmother, Sarah Ellender. The shadows played lightly on the wall as the sun began its slow descent in the distant western sky, and the rolling clouds began to take on that rosy-peach glow that she loved so well. She couldn't help but get a little teary-eyed as a lump slowly formed in her throat. She reminded herself, *Well, it's perfectly natural. I am an Arrowood, after all. We cry over just about every darn thing. We don't even need any ol' excuse.*

The day had finally arrived. The preparations had all been made. The invitations had been sent, and her precious husband-to-be was waiting for her just outside, under the huge old tree that had once sheltered Sarah Ellender's wedding party, so long ago. The cake was set up in a white tent that was festooned with heavenly scented flowers and decorated with tons of ferns. Even the barn had been decked out in lace, ribbons, and bows.

The band had been set up to provide the music for dancing, and bales of hay were positioned out in the yard as benches for the attendees to sit upon. Jane had always thought that she would have a traditional church wedding, and initial plans had been made for them to exchange their vows in the tiny chapel just over the mountain.

But, at nearly the very last minute, those plans had quickly changed. It had suddenly occurred to Jane exactly what she wanted. This was the way that she was supposed to get married.

It just seemed perfectly right, to have the wedding right here, under the same old tree where so many weddings had been held, down through the years. She felt in her heart that this was the way it was supposed to be. She wanted to stand right where Sarah Ellender had stood when she had married. She felt that somehow, she would know and give her blessings to this happy union. In her heart of hearts, she knew she had made the right choice. Jane had never been happier. The only way it could have been any better, whatsoever, was if her Dad could have been here to walk her down the aisle. This time, she was sure she had finally found the right man.

Jane whispered, *Dad, I hope you are going to be here with me. I so want to believe that you are.* She picked up the bouquet and admired the lovely bundle of pristine, white flowers. Jane's precious friend, Ruth Benoy, had arranged her bouquet, as an amazing gift. She smiled when she thought of sweet Ruth and the love that she had poured into the making of the beautifully delicate bouquet. Jane leaned in and sniffed the exquisite fragrance wafting up from the flowers that she held in her hand. Ruth had added an assortment of beautiful white lilies mingled into the bouquet, and Jane remembered something about them that her Dad had always told her. Jane sighed as his words echoed in her mind from her memory of years ago. *White lilies came into being from Eve's tears, the tears that fell as she was leaving the Garden of Eden.* Jane was so glad that Ruth and her husband Richard would be with her on this special day.

Nestled in the bouquet, among the white lilies, were exquisite white teacup roses. Jane knew that they were symbolic of pure love, unity, and new beginnings. She had also asked Ruth specifically, for tiny white 'Lily of the Valley' blossoms to be added to the bouquet. They were another favorite of her precious grandmother, Maude. They symbolize the sentiment 'you have made my life complete'.

Jane smiled as she remembered her precious grandmother, Maude. Her heart was full, and she was so unbelievably happy.

Her thoughts turned once again to the love of her life; her precious husband-to-be, Jake. *I feel as though all those dear souls that mean so much to me are each here in spirit, if not in body. They each bring something special that adds so much to this unbelievable day. I am so very blessed. Blessed beyond measure,* Jane thinks to herself. The music outside starts to play, and Jane turns to take one last look at her reflection in the beautiful oval mirror. She is astonished to see that it isn't her own reflection, but Sarah Ellender's, looking back at her. Sarah Ellender is holding her own wedding bouquet and wearing her wedding dress. Jane smiled, and Sarah Ellender smiled back at her. She was young and beautiful again. She stood smiling broadly, with her blonde flowing hair cascading about her shoulders. She raised her hand and beckoned Jane just as she had done the first time Jane had seen her in the mirror. Only this time, Jane was not frightened. She felt the love that bonded them together, a deep bond of family that warmed her heart. Not even the passage of time could separate them. Jane knew at last, that she surely had Sarah's blessing.

She smiled and whispered, *Thank you, sweet, great grandmother, I'm glad you approve, and I'm so glad that you are still here with me. Wouldn't Dad be so happy if he were here, as well?* Jane watched as the image in the mirror slowly transformed and melded itself back into her own reflection. She was ready to be married, and it was actually going to happen this time. *Once and for all, here comes my very own, 'happy ever after'.* She glanced back in the mirror one last time, and she lifted the hem of her beautiful white dress and saw in the mirror's reflection the shiny slippers that once belonged to her precious grandmother, Maude. They were embedded with rhinestones and quite impossibly 'over-the-top' and outlandish. Jane thought, *Oh, grandma, they are absolutely perfect.*

Jane turned and walked confidently outside, ready to start her new life. Jake waited for her, standing beside Minister Bob McCully.

They both were so handsome, waiting there under the shade of the massive old tree. Reverend McCully had been so gracious to drive up to perform the ceremony, and Jane felt very blessed to have him there. She couldn't think of anyone that she'd rather had to perform the service. *Everything's absolutely perfect.*

Jake's wide, broad shoulders were prominent in the tuxedo that fit him perfectly. Even as handsome as he was, Jane was struck again, at the way that he looked at her. She could see the love beaming from his handsome face, and she was simply amazed at how much love she felt for this sweet man. How lucky she was, to finally be marrying a man that loved her every bit as much as she loved him. Surely, he was sent straight to her by her angels. Jane smiled, and Jake beamed a broad smile of his own, right back at her. She slowly walked toward him, until she stood beside him.

There were happy murmurings coming up from the crowd of people that surrounded the couple. They could all feel the strong love between them. Minister Bob McCully stood before the couple smiling and signaled for all to rise. There was a slight clamor of noise as the crowd rose to their feet. Jane looked over to her side and blinked in astonishment. She saw her Dad. *Oh, Daddy!* Jane thought with unrestrained joy. He was standing right there, shimmering in an iridescent halo of light. Bright rays of illuminating light shone all around him. She could barely breathe when she realized that it was truly him. She marveled at the way that the light danced in the space around him. He was so very handsome in his tuxedo. She bit down on her lower lip to keep from crying.

Standing right beside him, in equally dazzling bright light, was Sarah Ellender. She was young and beautiful once again, dressed for her own wedding day, so long ago. Sarah Ellender reached out and took Steve's hand, the hand of her own great-grandson. Tears of joy spilled unchecked from Jane's eyes. They had both come to support her on this beautiful day and give her their blessings. They turned and smiled at Jane, and she smiled back, slowly shaking her head, marveling in the moment. Then from around the side of the tree, Jane caught sight of movement. Suddenly, there appeared two small smiling faces. It was Ollie's two little sisters, Minnie, and Ruby. They had ribbons and flowers tucked into their braided hair and they wore gowns of white.

As they came around the tree and into full sight, Jane saw that holding fast to Ruby's hand, was Ollie. Ollie was young again, just as she was when she had lost Minnie and Ruby. Ollie's dark tresses were bound at the nape of her neck in a bun. There were a few tendrils of dark curls that fell about, framing her face. Her dark eyes flashed with happiness. They laughed merrily and ran off together through the swaying grass, still holding hands. Jane sighed in relief and happiness. Dressed in their finest attire, Jane suddenly spied Isabelle and Welzia, as they stood off to the left. They were smiling broadly at Jane while holding tightly to each other's hands. Jane was amazed and so happy. Out in the field of swaying grass, Ollie looked back and nodded her head, smiling at Jane. Jane understood exactly what Ollie was trying to convey without a word ever being spoken aloud. Jane nodded her head in understanding.

She could feel that all of the loved ones in her lifetime, as well as all those that had gone on before her, were now standing close by her. She knew that they as well, could feel the bond of love that survives forever, no matter the passage of time. Days, years, or even centuries, cannot stop love. The love of the thousands of ancestors that had come before her, was drifting on the breeze that floated high above, atop the Roan.

Looking handsome in his white robe, Minister Bob McCully took a few steps closer to Jane and Jake. It was evident to Jane, that no one else had seen her father or Sarah Ellender or any of the others. Jane was the only one that could see them. *Maybe I'm dreaming in Technicolor once again*, Jane thought with a smile.

Jane turned her attention back to Minister McCully, with tears in her eyes. Then in a clear voice, he said, "Who gives this woman to be married to this man?" In answer to the Minister's question, Ann and Hilda both stepped forward. They stood beside Jane. They spoke in unison as they said, *We both do. We stand in for our brother, Steve Lewis.* Jane's eyes radiated her deep love as she turned toward them and kissed them each on the cheek. She handed her bouquet to Patti and then reached down and took both of her Aunt's hands in hers. Patti smiled at her with tears streaming down her beautiful face. Jane thought, *Patti has never looked more beautiful than she does right now, at this very moment. My precious friend.* Patti's husband, Bryan, looking very elegant in his tuxedo, stepped forward. Bryan looked over at Jane and smiled as he moved to stand beside Jake as his best man. He reached out and poked Jane in the side and grinned mischievously. *This couple understands exactly the happiness that a good marriage can bring. Having them both here, standing beside us, means so much.* Jane smiled radiantly at both of them.

Minister McCully said, *I will read now, a passage from the Holy Bible. First Corinthians chapter 13, verse 1 through 3. If I speak in the tongues of men and of angels but have not love, I am only a resounding gong or a clanging cymbal. If I have the gift of prophecy and can fathom all mysteries and all knowledge, and if I have a faith that can move mountains, but have not love, I am nothing. If I give all I possess to the poor and surrender my body to the flames, but have not love, I gain nothing.*

Aunt Ann leaned in close to Jane and whispered quietly in her ear, *Now don't you think for a minute that I'm going to let this moment pass without 'dancing a jig' for your sweet Daddy. You know he promised that he'd dance for you at your wedding, but he's busy dancing on streets of gold, right now.* Jane smiled at Ann and turned back to her right, where she saw her father, Steve, still standing. She winked at him, and he grinned and winked back. She gasped in absolute delight when she saw her father begin to dance a jig, all the while, bathed in the bright white iridescent light. She laughed again when she turned back to face Ann and saw that she had daintily lifted the hem of her dress and had begun dancing her own jig as well, right there on the grass. Jane put her hand over her mouth and giggled. Jane whispered, "Yah-Ta-Hay", through tears of happiness.

Ann finished her dancing, and she waved a tiny wave with a kiss before she turned in a flourish and made her way to her seat on the first row of hay bales alongside Hilda. Jane hadn't thought of that old Navaho expression in years, but her dad had used 'Yah-ta-hay' in most of his comings and goings. He had always said it with one of his lop-sided smiles. His lopsided smiles had always made her laugh, and she had always loved them the most.

When she looked back to where she had seen her dad dancing, she now saw nothing, at all. Her smile faded slightly, then it quickly reappeared, as she realized the full extent of the gift that she had just been given. Her precious Dad *was* there for her wedding day, after all. And he got to dance the jig for her that he had promised, since she was nothing more than a 'tadpole'. *What more could a girl ask for, anyway? Why, nothing much at all, girlie.* Jane smiled broadly.

The months after the wedding were nothing but a blissful blur of happiness. Jane was so unbelievably happy. She had a smile plastered on her face that even lye soap couldn't have washed away. She had never known what 'happily married' had really meant, until now. She was intent on soaking up and savoring every single beautiful moment of it.

Jake was working on a new construction over in Elizabethton and Jane had gotten up early to see him off that morning. The day dawned clear and beautiful. Jane had washed the sheets and decided to hang them out on the clothesline in the bright sunshine because they always smell so wonderful after they've been air-dried out on the line. She loved to lie down on fresh sheets after a full day. She relished the scent of pure sunshine wafting up from her pillow. She bent down to grab the edge of the sheet from the basket, to hang it up on the line, and she caught movement out of the corner of her eye, once again.

She thought for certain that she had seen a woman sitting in the tall grass alongside two small girls. She had appeared to be reading something to them. Jane made her way closer over to the edge of the meadow for a better look. The woman was a dark haired beauty with laughing eyes. Jane's eyes widened when she realized just who it was. It was an older Ollie, reading to her granddaughters as they enjoyed the beautiful sunshine-drenched meadow underneath the ridges of the beautiful Roan. Jane waved, and Ollie smiled up at her and in that very instant, they were all simply gone. Jane searched the meadow but didn't see them anywhere.

She walked over to the small graveyard that lay up the path, just beyond the edge of the yard. She stopped and picked a handful of blue cornflowers that were blooming along the path and made her way over to her second great-grandpa's grave. She laid half of the handful of flowers down on David's grave and then she placed the remainder of the delicate tiny blue flowers on the small grave right beside his. It was marked with a tiny pink marble lamb.

Jane had found the tip of the lamb sticking up out of the earth one day, as she was clearing away the weeds. She had dug it out of the soft ground and scrubbed the moss off of it. When it was pristine and glowing once again, she had lovingly placed it back on the grave where it had been placed so many years ago. Ollie's little girl had been buried right here in this beautiful place. Sadly, she had never lived long enough to draw her first breath, but her tiny earthly body now rests here near the beautiful Roan. Her body lies beside that of her grandfather and her loving mother, Ollie. But, her free spirit runs through the tall grass and romps and plays on the beautiful high mountain ridges of Heaven.

39

A bell is no bell 'til you ring it,
A song is no song 'til you sing it,
And love in your heart
Wasn't put there to stay-
Love isn't love
'Til you give it away.

~ OSCAR HAMMERSTEIN

The mountains are calling and I must go.

~ JOHN MUIR

JANE WALKED ALMOST every day that she could, out on the ridges of the Roan. The mountain called out to her, and she felt the inexplicable urge to go. It was just as simple as that. She loved walking the path that led along the balds and along the meandering trails. It held surprises for her at every turn. The Roan was constantly showing Jane a new jewel to marvel over, and Jane was thrilled to discover each and every one. She walked this morning up along Carver's Gap and slowly she made her way to where the Cloudland Hotel once stood, in all its glory. She stood and stared at the spot, mesmerized. So little was left, that it was hard to believe that something as grand as the Cloudland, had ever existed at the location. She wandered through the dancing grasses a short distance away and decided to sit there for awhile.

Jake wouldn't be home from the worksite over in Elizabethton for at least three hours or more. She adored the time that she spent on the Roan and allowing herself the time to take in its beauty had never been considered a waste to Jane. It fed and nurtured her soul. She always felt soothed here and being out on this mountain had always made her feel closer to God. She thought about her ancestors and how they too, had truly loved this place. It *was* in her blood, and she would never leave it. Even if one day she moved away, it would always be a part of her. There would always be a piece of it, tucked deep within her heart. In truth, she couldn't see herself ever living anywhere else.

She glanced back over her shoulder, sensing that someone was there and when she turned her head, the sight before her caused her to gasp in astonishment. She saw the Cloudland Hotel standing proudly before her on the ridge. The hotel was regal and resplendent, just as it had been on its opening day so many years ago. There were people walking to and fro, out on the lawn in front of the hotel. There was bustling activity as patrons went in and out of the hotel, and others milled about on the porches. They were dressed beautifully, just as they had dressed in days of old. The ladies were carrying pretty ornate parasols and wearing fancy dresses and matching hats. They were beautiful in their finery. It was an amazing sight to see, and Jane tried her best to take in all that she saw before her. She slowly stood up, reaching down to feel the grass that waved and danced all around her, nearly hip high. She wanted to touch it to be certain that she was awake and that this was really happening. She laughed lightly when she reached down seeking something tangible, and she felt the tips of the grass in her hand, warmed by the sun. *It's real, just as real as this grass beneath me. I can hear their laughter.*

Rolling wagons brought in supplies and vacationers alike, up the mountain. Many patrons rocked in rocking chairs that lined the large stately porches. There were a lot of different sounds that filled the air and billowed in the breeze that blew placidly over the ridge. Jane could hear the distinct sound of the horse's whinnies. The sound of chatter and people's happy laughter carried easily on the wind, over to where Jane stood watching it all, in rapt attention. *What must it have been like to have stayed at the beautiful grand old hotel?* Jane would have loved to have known, firsthand. The Cloudland had been well known by those seeking relief from the oppressive heat of the lower elevations and also for the healing properties of the cool and pure air of the mountain. It had been advertised as a 'health getaway' for those needing a relaxing health retreat that rests among the 'clouds'. That was where it got its name. It was the hotel 'up in the land of the clouds'.

Jane marveled that this was where the music had came from, that beautiful music that she had heard on so many still nights. *It's that very same music that I sometimes hear, wafting down through the pines near my house. On some nights, the old Cloudland dance floor is in full swing still, even after all these years.*

Letter from the Cloudland Hotel, dated March 1893, postmarked Burbank, Tennessee.

Jane imagined what the locals must have thought about such a lavish hotel being built nearby such humble log cabin homes. They had to have been amazed by the grandeur of it. *Goodness, I'm still amazed at it,* Jane thought with a smile. *I must be looking at a mirage of some sort, but I don't ever want it to end. It's an unimaginable glimpse into the past.* The shimmering hotel before her started to waver slightly and glimmer in the sunlight, and then it slowly faded away completely. Just as suddenly as it had appeared, it vanished from sight. Jane blinked and softly shook her head. *Well, mercy me, girlie. You're dreaming in Technicolor once again, this time while you're still wide awake. Whatever will your poor husband think of this?*

She laughed out loud and said, *Well, maybe it's better if I just keep this to myself. Maybe I shouldn't even try to dissect this. Some things are truly better, left as they are. Simply consider it as yet another gift this mountain has offered up for you, girlie because surely that's what it was - a gift.* She took once last look at the swaying grass where the old hotel had once stood. There wasn't much left that indicated anything had ever been there. *Did I really see what I think I saw?* Jane slowly turned and made her way back toward home. She stopped and took one last look over her shoulder. *The Roan never forgets,* Jane breathed softly to herself, shaking her head. *I guess she really and truly, never does.*

Jane started making dinner as soon as she got back to the house. She loved cooking for Jake. He was so appreciative of just about everything that she did for him. She loved watching him eat. *Boy howdy, does that man ever love to eat. His appetite is something else.* She loved to cook and bake and he loved to eat. They were simply meant for one another, and she was positive of it. She rolled the dough out thin for an apple pie crust. The apples were from the tree that stood at the edge of the yard, not far from the house. It was an old tree, but it still produced the best tasting apples that Jane had ever tasted. Jake would be so surprised. He had no idea that she could make a mean apple pie. They were almost as good as her grandma's fried apple pies, but only almost. *Nothing was as wonderful as Maudie's fried apple pies,* Jane thought with a sigh.

She finished cooking and had everything just about ready. She had the pie in the oven, baking. Its aroma filled the house and smelled heavenly. She washed her hands and toweled them dry at the sink while looking at Isabelle's apron hanging up on the wooden peg beside the cabinet. She thought about the beautiful jewelry that Aunt Ann and Aunt Hilda had given her. It was amazing that those treasured pieces had really once belonged to Ollie. They had to have been gifts from Charles early on in their marriage.

Jane made her way into the bedroom to get the ring. She wanted to wear it tonight, at dinner. This was going to be an extra special night for them both, complete with freshly baked apple pie to go along with a sumptuous home-cooked meal. Jane smiled to herself as walked past the oval mirror and she suddenly caught a flash of movement. Startled at first, she looked back, and there in the mirror was the face of a man with a dark complexion and dark wavy hair. It was a face that she didn't recognize. He was smiling at Jane and didn't appear to be threatening. Jane walked over closer to the mirror, to take a better look. She knew from experience that she most likely wouldn't see him anywhere else in the room. He would most likely only appear in the mirror, just as most of the other images had, before. As she drew nearer, the image faded away completely.

Jane wondered just who he may have been. She had never seen the image of this man in Sarah Ellender's mirror. *Who in the world was that, anyway?* Jane was perplexed. She quickly mulled it over in her mind. She turned back to face the mirror and stood peering into it for a few moments longer, but she saw nothing but her own reflection. She walked over, fished the ring out from the old velvet lined jewelry box sitting on the corner of the dresser, and slipped it on her finger. She held out her hand and admired the beautiful ring. *It's amazing that it fits so perfectly. Something this beautiful deserves to be worn with something nicer than worn out jeans.*

Soon, Jake was home, and dinner was piping hot and ready on the table. Jane had taken extra pains to make the meal truly special for her new husband. She had set out the fine china and silver, and had even arranged a vase of beautiful fresh flowers that she had picked that very morning. The overall effect was quite stunning. The effort she had taken to make the meal special was not lost on Jake. He was quite impressed and told Jane so. They took their time, and both enjoyed the delicious meal. Jake was especially impressed with the wonderful flaky crust of Jane's apple pie.

After dinner was over and the kitchen was tidied up, they snuggled up together to watch a movie. The white moonlight fell in through the window, and it soon caught Jake's eye. He took Jane by the hand and led her out onto the front porch that was bathed in white. The light of the strong moonlight illuminated the night beautifully. Jake pulled Jane into his arms and held her close as they stood looking out over the ridges of the Roan. Jake whispered words of love into Jane's ear. She had no doubts that she had married herself the perfect man. He knew she was perfect for him.

She was so thankful that he had appeared right when she had needed him the most. The timing had been spot-on. God had sent many angels into her life, and somehow he had seen fit to send her yet another one. *He had sent her the perfect man and one that was hopelessly romantic to boot*, Jane smiled with the thought. *How lucky can one girl get?* They walked back inside to watch the rest of the movie. A few moments later, they both heard a strange noise. They quietly listened and determined that the noise had to be coming from the bedroom. They walked slowly, hand in hand, back toward the bedroom together. Jake leaned down and picked up a large piece of firewood from the basket sitting on the hearth, as he passed by it. Jane's eyes grew wide when she looked over and saw the stick of wood in his hand. They walked into the bedroom, and the shrill unearthly sound echoed through the room, once again. It was the unmistakable piercing screech of an owl, and it came from right outside the bedroom window.

The hair on the back of Jane's neck stood up on end. She took a sudden intake of breath. Jake turned and looked at her. He suddenly burst out laughing. Jake said, *You, Missy, have been reading those spooky stories in those journals way, way, too much. You should see the look of complete horror on your face! You're nearly as white as a sheet. Come on now, sweetheart, it's only a little bitty owl. There's nothing out there that's going to get you, I promise you that, darlin'. I won't let it.* Jake handed her the stick of firewood and Jane slowly began to smile. Jake picked her up by the waist and twirled her around before setting her lightly back down. *You, my lady, are something else, but I do so love you,* he said with a genuine smile. Jake leaned down and softly kissed her, and she reached up and kissed him back.

Jane sheepishly grinned up at him and she gave him the best 'Elvis' snarled lip that she could manage. She looked so comical that Jake couldn't help but laugh. He shook his head at her with his own lopsided grin and a long sigh, as if to say, 'I give up'.

They turn and walked hand in hand back out to the living room, and soon they had settled in comfortably on the couch, once again, to watch the rest of the movie. Jane's mind was not particularly focused on the movie playing in front of her. She knew in her heart that her angels *were* real. Sometimes, they were even a bit too real, to suit her. But, they were hers, and she accepted that. She had owned up to that fact many long months ago. She had angels all around her, keeping watch. She was blessed. She had been blessed beyond her wildest dreams to have been given a chance to honestly know the ancestors that had come before her. She knew this, with certainty. The fact that the journals and letters had apparently been left for her to find, made her feel truly special. She was grateful for this gift and determined that she would make the angels that walked alongside her, proud of her. She came from a long line of determined, God-fearing people. They were good-hearted people as well. They were people that loved one another without fail. She would do her very best to continue along on the very same path. She would follow along in the footsteps of those strong hearted folks that had come before her. God had watched over them, down through all of the generations that had come and gone. Jane felt certain that He would continue to watch over her and her house, as well. She silently sent up a prayer, *Thank you, precious Lord. I am so thankful that I have been allowed to know from where, and from whom, I come. Finding the past has somehow given me a precious glimpse into exactly who I am. I am Sarah Ellender's great granddaughter, and I am so very proud of it.* Jane raised her head and thought, *God has been so good to me.*

Back in the bedroom, there slowly appeared a misty reflection of a woman's ghostly pale face in the old mirror. A smile slowly spreads on the woman's face as she peers out from the mirror as it hangs on the bedroom wall. The woman in the mirror intently watches the couple through the bedroom doorway. Jake and Jane notice nothing as they sit on the couch in the other room. Suddenly, Jane intuitively feels something, and she turns away from the TV, and she lifts her gaze and peers into the darkness beyond the open bedroom door. It's an unsettling uneasiness that she just can't seem to shake.

Jake had recently moved the old mirror to the bedroom, thinking that it would look great on the wall, by the dresser. Jane, as of yet, hadn't been able to bring herself to mention anything about the mirror to Jake. *How could she tell him that she had seen faces looking back at her from that mirror? How could she say that she had seen faces that weren't her own? How does something like that come up in casual, everyday conversation?* She didn't want him to think he had married himself a lunatic, especially not right off the bat. *I just can't, especially not this early on in our marriage.* So, she had simply kept silent when he had moved Sarah Ellender's old oval mirror to the bedroom wall. *Besides, you can't criticize a man when he tries to help decorate. I mean, can you really, now?* Jane thought with a grin. She wanted him to feel that this was truly his home now. So, she had just watched and never said a word.

Over in the darkened corner of the bedroom, right by the window, sits the ornately carved rocking chair that once belonged to Ollie. Jake had brought the old rocking chair down from the attic, just a few weeks back. He had seen it right away when he had gone up to install the new steps to the attic entrance. He had been delighted when he saw it, thinking it would be perfect for the bedroom. He thought that maybe, one day, Jane would rock their baby boy, in that very same old rocker.

Jane had kept silent once again, and she'd not said a single word about the rocker to Jake. But, she had crossed her fingers and breathed a silent prayer as he had moved it down from the attic to the bedroom. Jane's thoughts wandered every time she looked over at that rocker. *I don't really feel all that apprehensive about the rocker. Well, not exactly anyway.* But, she did feel something that she didn't quite understand. Sometimes strange feelings just came to Jane; ones that she just couldn't explain.

Jane got up from the couch and walked past Jake. He looked up and smiled and watched her curiously. Jane turned back and blew him a kiss. She tossed her head lightly in the direction of the porch, and Jake nodded.

Jane stepped back out onto the porch, and her eyes take in the amazing view that she still can't quite believe that she has, right outside her door. The stars twinkled up above in the nighttime sky.

I don't know what tomorrow holds in store for us, Jane thought. *I haven't got the first clue. But, I do know that this beautiful home of mine is filled with my very own angels. I am so thankful to be here and thankful to be so very blessed.* Jane wraps her arms around herself and smiles contentedly.

Back in the house, sitting on the newly carpeted floor of the bedroom, the rocker starts to slowly move back and forth. The movement of the chair was as if someone was actually sitting in it, but no one was there. It rocked slow and steadily, never making even the slightest sound in the darkened room. The latch on the old trunk clicked as it opened in the empty room. The moonlight coming through the window glinted as it fell on the old gun.

Outside the window, in the darkness, the moonlight softly illuminated the outline of an owl. It sat on the branch over the window, perfectly motionless. Suddenly, it turned its head and peered down into the window. The owl appeared to be searching for someone or something.

Rhododendron blooming high atop the Roan

Up on the high ridges of the Roan, the wind blows musically through the pine trees just as it has done for countless centuries. The music from a forgotten era floats down from somewhere above the tops of the pine trees that line the shadowy ridge. Sarah Ellender sighs from time to time, as she looks down from the ancient rocky ledge where she sits. She sits here almost every evening, now. The light breeze gently lifts and blows her long blonde hair softly out behind her. Her tanned legs dangle beneath her. She loves the way the moonlight caresses the dappled ridges and the way that it sparkles across the grasses that dance down in the meadows below. Sarah Ellender loves this old timeless mountain that she calls her own, and she will never leave it.

She listens to the old familiar music, as it floats along in the wind that blows through the trees and down across the grassy balds. The rhododendron flowers bask in the moonlight, as the magenta blossoms are kissed with glistening dew. Sarah Ellender smiles a wistful, knowing smile. The Roan remembers, no matter how many years have come and gone. A slender dark haired man appears and sits down on the rock ledge beside Sarah Ellender. She turns and smiles up at him. He smiles back and together they look out over the misty ridges of the mountain that they love.

This old mountain draws in those that love her and holds them close. It always has. The years may roll on by and time may pass, but her children remain a part of this old mountain. They may float along in the gentle breeze that caresses your face as it rolls down over the meadow. Or they may be just a sparkle of light in the pristine snow that falls softly down, along the icy ridge deep in wintertime. They may nod their heads among the scented Gray's lilies that adorn the summer's grassy fields. They may even soar above, on the wings of a bird in flight, high above the Roan, but they are there. You can be certain of that.

The Roan never forgets. ♣

Poem by:
Hilda Arrowood Morgan Olive 05/17/2016 ♣

Oh, the memories and tales from the beautiful old Roan, some from our friends and a few of our own.

Just think how many times that they have been told. I'm losing some of them, for heaven's sake, I'm getting old.

My ancestors were tough as nails, as you can see. I came from mighty good stock, what happened to me?

Imagine having to grow all your own food, if you could, you couldn't keep warm without chopping that wood.

No time to get bored from sunrise to sunset, no, not much free time for your friends, I would bet.

Our ancestors dug themselves a living out from the ground. No taking off every day and going to town.

No that corner store back then didn't even exist - you didn't have to waste any time making out a list.

Our ancestor's hands were calloused and rough. Raising beans and potatoes up there had to be tough.

A lot of the men left home at times, to preach, leaving the women at home with the children to teach.

Some of them turned out pretty good, if you're asking me. My sweet Daddy was the best there ever could be.

He always told us that his mother was a Cherokee squaw - yes we're part Indian, both me and my paw.

I hear the mountains call me, the Roan often speaks my name, being in the mountains seems to take away my pain

♣

I pray that I will someday be able to leave the pain of the past behind me. It has weighed heavy on my soul. I think of all the dreams
that never were to be. Sonya was my one and only daughter. I feel
as though I could have had a dozen daughters and lost them all, and
still the pain wouldn't have been near as bad as losing my Sonya. I
know in my heart, that when I reach Heaven's door, her sweet face
will be the first one that I see.

B. Ann Arrowood Williams - 6-01-2016 ♣

Made in the USA
Columbia, SC
09 February 2022

54967097R00198